EDUCATION, POLITICS, AND PUBLIC LIFE

Series Editors:
Henry A. Giroux, McMaster University
Susan Searls Giroux, McMaster University

Within the last three decades, education as a political, moral, and ideological practice has become central to rethinking not only the role of public and higher education, but also the emergence of pedagogical sites outside of the schools—which include but are not limited to the Internet, television, film, magazines, and the media of print culture. Education as both a form of schooling and public pedagogy reaches into every aspect of political, economic, and social life. What is particularly important in this highly interdisciplinary and politically nuanced view of education are a number of issues that now connect learning to social change, the operations of democratic public life, and the formation of critically engaged individual and social agents. At the center of this series will be questions regarding what young people, adults, academics, artists, and cultural workers need to know to be able to live in an inclusive and just democracy and what it would mean to develop institutional capacities to reintroduce politics and public commitment into everyday life. Books in this series aim to play a vital role in rethinking the entire project of the related themes of politics, democratic struggles, and critical education within the global public sphere.

SERIES EDITORS:

HENRY A. GIROUX holds the Global TV Network Chair in English and Cultural Studies at McMaster University in Canada. He is on the editorial and advisory boards of numerous national and international scholarly journals. Professor Giroux was selected as a Kappa Delta Pi Laureate in 1998 and was the recipient of a Getty Research Institute Visiting Scholar Award in 1999. He was the recipient of the Hooker Distinguished Professor Award for 2001. He received an Honorary Doctorate of Letters from Memorial University of Newfoundland in 2005. His most recent books include *Take Back Higher Education* (co-authored with Susan Searls Giroux, 2006); *America on the Edge* (2006); *Beyond the Spectacle of Terrorism* (2006); *Stormy Weather: Katrina and the Politics of Disposability* (2006); *The University in Chains: Confronting the Military-Industrial-Academic Complex* (2007); and *Against the Terror of Neoliberalism: Politics Beyond the Age of Greed* (2008).

SUSAN SEARLS GIROUX is Associate Professor of English and Cultural Studies at McMaster University. Her most recent books include *The Theory Toolbox* (co-authored with Jeff Nealon, 2004) and *Take Back Higher Education* (co-authored with Henry A. Giroux, 2006), and *Between*

Race and Reason: Violence, Intellectual Responsibility, and the University to Come (2010). Professor Giroux is also the Managing Editor of *The Review of Education, Pedagogy, and Cultural Studies.*

Conflicts in Curriculum Theory

Challenging Hegemonic Epistemologies

João M. Paraskeva

Foreword by
Donaldo Macedo

CONFLICTS IN CURRICULUM THEORY
Copyright © João M. Paraskeva, 2011.

First published in 2011 by
PALGRAVE MACMILLAN®
in the United States—a division of St. Martin's Press LLC,
175 Fifth Avenue, New York, NY 10010.

Where this book is distributed in the UK, Europe and the rest of the world,
this is by Palgrave Macmillan, a division of Macmillan Publishers Limited,
registered in England, company number 785998, of Houndmills,
Basingstoke, Hampshire RG21 6XS.

Palgrave Macmillan is the global academic imprint of the above companies
and has companies and representatives throughout the world.

Palgrave® and Macmillan® are registered trademarks in the United States,
the United Kingdom, Europe and other countries.

ISBN: 978–0–230–11275–9

Library of Congress Cataloging-in-Publication Data

Paraskeva, João M.
    Conflicts in curriculum theory : challenging hegemonic epistemologies /
João M. Paraskeva.
        p. cm.—(Education, politics, and public life)
    ISBN-13: 978–0–230–11275–9
    ISBN-10: 0–230–11275–7
        1. Education—Curricula—Philosophy. 2. Education—Philosophy.
    3. Critical pedagogy. 4. Knowledge, Theory of. I. Title.

LB1570.P256 2011
375'.001—dc22   2011000536

A catalogue record of the book is available from the British Library.

Design by Newgen Imaging Systems (P) Ltd., Chennai, India.

First edition: July 2011

10 9 8 7 6 5 4 3 2 1

Printed in the United States of America.

In the memory of my mother

Contents

FOREWORD: RE-INSERTING
HISTORICITY INTO THE CURRICULUM

In a world where ideology has been declared dead and an Orwellian reality has been naturalized into common sense, João Paraskeva's *Conflicts in Curriculum Theory: Challenging Hegemonic Epistemologies* is more than merely timely; it also challenges educators to be agents of change, to take history into their own hands, and to make social justice central to the educational endeavor. By reinserting both criticism and historicity into the current curriculum debate, Paraskeva rigorously unpacks the writing of dominant ideologues and intellectuals who have proclaimed both history and ideology dead.

In so doing, he reveals the ideological manipulation designed to distort history and infuse in the public a paralyzing fear, while at the same time intellectuals have acquiesced their responsibility to speak truth to power and are hiding behind a blind embrace of a "culture of positivism, which [is] fundamentally concerned with 'controlling and dominating the natural and human environment' and thus fostering cognitive passivity" (cf. ch. 1).

How else can one explain the tacit acceptance (and sometimes outright embrace) of a surveillance state under the pretext that it is for one's own good, while in the U.S. democracy, torture is supported by 53 percent of the population? Only in an Orwellian reality disguised as democracy could one rationalize the mass deception whereby former vice president Dick Cheney scared Americans into passivity by spreading the gargantuan lie that Iraq had weapons of mass destruction without providing a shred of evidence. Meanwhile, former secretary of state Condoleezza Rice "spoke menacingly of 'a mushroom cloud' like the cloud caused by the atomic bombing of Hiroshima" (H. Zinn, 2007, p. 194). The dehistorization process as ideological manipulation is so complete that Rice had no reason to worry that Americans would make the link or see the irony in the fact that the only nation responsible for releasing a mushroom cloud, with its resulting carnage and human misery, was not Iraq or any other nation, but the very United States that promotes the illegal invasion of sovereign nations in the name of security, democracy, and peace. It apparently mattered little to Rice that restraint could have prevented the United States from dropping "atomic bombs on the cities of Hiroshima and Nagasaki in August 1945. The bombs killed as many as 150,000 people [including women and children] and left countless others to die slowly of radiation poisoning" (p. 61).

Although American intelligence had broken the Japanese code and learned that the Japanese were ready to surrender, President Harry Truman went ahead, perhaps unnecessarily, with the bombing of two densely populated Japanese cities, stating that "the world will note that the first atomic bomb was dropped on Hiroshima, a military base. That was because we wished in the first attack to avoid, insofar as possible, the killing of civilians" (H. Zinn, 1980, p. 8). According to Howard Zinn (1980),

> This was a preposterous statement: the 100,000 killed in Hiroshima were almost all civilians. The U.S. Strategic Bombing Survey said in its official report, "Hiroshima and Nagasaki were chosen as targets because of their concentration of activities and population...The dropping of the second bomb on Nagasaki seems to have been scheduled in advance, and no one has ever been able to explain why it was dropped. Was it because this was a plutonium bomb whereas the Hiroshima was a uranium bomb? Were the dead and irradiated of Nagasaki victims of a scientific experiment? (p. 8)

This does not explain why we continue to denounce the despicable use of Jewish prisoners in concentration camps in inhumane scientific experiments but know next to nothing about the scientific experiment conducted by the United States in the atomic bombing of Hiroshima and Nagasaki. Many believe the two bombs were dropped to determine the differing impact on humans of plutonian and uranium bombs. That is why even a sanitized exhibition of the Enola Gay, the plane that carried the first atomic bombs dropped on a civilian population, eventually disappeared from the Smithsonian Museum, bringing about major protests by veterans and interested patriots who prefer to live with a lie. This lie has been perpetuated in schools by the teaching of a distorted history. According to Howard Zinn (2005), teaching "the history of war is dominated by the very story of the battles, and this is a way of diverting attention from the political factors behind a war. It's possible to concentrate upon battles of the Mexican War and to talk just about the triumphant march into Mexico City and not about the relationship of the Mexican War to slavery and to the acquisition of territories that might possibly be slave territories" (p. 189). It is also possible, for example, to concentrate on the battles of World War II without mentioning the carnage witnessed in the firebombing of Dresden, Germany, where more than one hundred thousand civilians were incinerated by the Allies' brutal, and some say unnecessary, bombing of the city.

In the same vein, future teaching of the Iraq War will probably be presented in terms of the battles to control Baghdad, establishment of the safe "green zone," with much celebration of U.S. technological wizardry and its massive firepower, meanwhile reducing the killing of over half a million Iraqi civilians (and the body count continues to climb) to the gutless euphemism, "collateral damage." The story that will never be told from the victor's perspective is that the Iraq War was illegal, having been based on falsehoods to justify the U.S. invasion, which led to the slaughter of hundreds of thousands of innocent civilians, including women and children. In fact, we can count on historians to rewrite history to create a detached, objective curriculum that leads students through a bank of facts to be memorized. As Robert Fields wrote about Vietnam, for example, future students will learn that "[Iraq] hurt our country badly...[The Iraqi] people fought for their freedom. [Saddam Hussein's terrorists] took advantage of the fight...they hid and ambushed the Americans" (p. 20), substituting Iraq for Vietnam and terrorists for communists.

Field's history of the Vietnam War remains intact, and good students will recite verbatim the lies told by their teachers. Noam Chomsky (Barsamian, 2004) suggests that "not everyone accepts this. But most of us, if we are honest with ourselves, can look back at our own personal history. For those of us who got into good colleges and the professions, did we stand up to that high school teacher who told us some ridiculous lies about American history and say, 'That's a ridiculous lie. You're an idiot.'? No. We said, 'All right. I'll keep quiet, and I'll write in the exam and I'll think, yes, he's an idiot'" (p. 39). When not telling outright lies, history teachers engage in a more insidious form of lie, which is the omission of historical events. In other words, the story of resistance to the Iraq War will not be told and the voice of Patricia Riggs, a student at East Central Oklahoma State University, will never be heard, her political clarity never rewarded:

> I don't think we should be over there [in Iraq]. I don't think it's about justice and liberty, I think it's about economics. The big oil

corporations have a lot to do with what is going on over there...We are risking people's lives for money. (Zinn, 2007)

In fact, Patricia Riggs is right, to the degree that the United States had been determined to control the Middle East since the end of World War II in 1945. Even liberal Democratic president Jimmy Carter minced no words in his Carter Doctrine, in which the United States claimed the right to defend its interest in Middle East oil "by any means necessary," including military force (Zinn, 2007, p. 195). Thus, the Carter Doctrine is nothing more and nothing less than a continuation of President Eisenhower's CIA-sponsored coup d'état against the democratically elected government of Iran in 1953, which enabled the United States to install as its puppet the Shah of Iran, Mohammad Reza Pahlavi, who for decades oversaw a cruel dictatorship that, for all practical purposes, declared civil war on its people through the torture, killing, and disappearance of citizens, meanwhile obeying the golden rule that guaranteed the U.S. oil corporations total access to what some politicians and oil executives at the time referred to as "our oil." By the same token, we will never read in history books the painful, courageous voice of Cindy Sheehan, "whose son died in Iraq...[and who,]...in a speech to a Veterans for Peace gathering in Dallas, addressed President Bush: 'You tell me the truth. You tell me that my son died for oil'" (p. 201).

What you will hear ad hominem is how great Americans sacrificed their lives to protect our freedom and liberty. If fighting for freedom and liberty is the reason the United States has sent innocent Americans to die in foreign lands, we would also expect the United States to invade Saudi Arabia, whose brutal autocratic royalty is not dissimilar to the regime of Saddam Hussein, whom we once fully supported even as he was gassing Iranian soldiers and his own people. We also would expect the United States to protect the freedom and liberty of East Timor's citizens, who were fighting against the tyranny of Indonesia, a country committed to the genocide of East Timorese people that was aided by U.S. intelligence, arms, and helicopters. According to Daniel Patrick Moynihan's memoir, *A Dangerous Place,* in which he discussed the Indonesian invasion of East Timor and also shed light on his role as U.S. ambassador to the United Nations, "The U.S. government wanted the United Nations to be rendered ineffective in any measures that it undertook. I was given this responsibility and I filled it with no inconsiderable success" (quoted in Chomsky, 1991, p. 8). Moynihan later described his success, stating that "within two months, reports indicated that Indonesia had killed about 60,000 people. That is roughly the proportion of the population that the Nazis had killed in Eastern Europe through World War II" (p. 8).

Victors are always guaranteed impunity, even when, like Moynihan, they callously and arrogantly write about their war crimes and other atrocities because they will never have to face trials like those held in Nuremberg to exact justice for Nazi crimes against humanity. Because victors cannot be tried for their crimes, it is not a coincidence that the U.S. government aggressively opposed the creation of the World Court. This opposition is demonstrated by the United States' arrogant dismissal of the World Court ruling in favor of Nicaragua in the case of the illegal United States mining of Nicaragua's harbor.

As João Paraskeva demonstrates in this illuminating book, the history that students are asked to read in school is devoid of conflicts because policy makers do not want students to realize that "the curriculum, as a political, ideological, cultural, and economic project, must be understood as a document that is determined by the dynamics of conflict. Such a document really shows a cultural capacity. It is mandatory, then, to go beyond simply demystifying the notion of conflict; we must treat it without affections of any kind, especially since the social reality is basically determined by conflict and flux, not by a closed functional system" (ch. 1).

By and large, most conservative and many liberal educators who want to avoid all forms of conflict in the curriculum criticize Paulo Freire's educational proposals, due to his insistence that educators understand the dialectical nature of conflict between the oppressor and the oppressed. For instance, Gregory Jay and Gerald Graff have argued that Freire's proposal in *Pedagogy of the Oppressed* to move students toward "a critical perception of the world [that] implies a correct method of approaching reality" so they can develop "a comprehension of total reality" assumes that the identity of the oppressed is already known. As Jay and Graff point out, "Freire assumes that we know from the outset the identity of the 'oppressed' and their 'oppressors.' Who the oppressors and the oppressed are is conceived not as an open question that teachers and students might disagree about, but as a given of Freirean pedagogy" (Freire & Macedo, 1995). Hence, even Graff's seemingly liberal proposal to teach to the conflict assumes an objective position that discourages the inherent dialectical relationship between objectivity and subjectivity. The virtue of a radical democratic project is that it provides an ethical referent, both for engaging in a critique of its own authority and as part of a wider expression of authority. In my view, what needs to be engaged pedagogically is not merely who is really oppressed, but the social, economic, and cultural conditions that lead to the creation of savage inequalities, such as the misery of ghetto life in East St. Louis, where African-Americans and other oppressed groups materially experience the loss of their dignity, the denial of human citizenship, and, in many cases, outright violent and criminal acts committed by the very institutions responsible for enforcing the law. Those who materially experience oppression have little difficulty identifying their oppressors. Adopting a relativistic posture toward the oppressed and the oppressor points to Graff's privileged position, this enables him to intellectualize oppression so as to make it abstract, and is not unlike the position of individuals who attempt to rewrite the history of oppression as mere narratives. I believe being suspicious of one's own politics should not be an excuse to attempt to understand and address how power can work to oppress and exploit.

What makes *Conflicts in Curriculum Theory. Challenging Hegemonic Epistemologies* an indispensable read for all educators is that Paraskeva's brilliant analysis of past and present—and the future path of—curriculum theory goes beyond a language of critique that, in some instances, discourages "epistemological diversity" and "socio and cognitive justice" while naturalizing what Sousa Santos called "espistemicides—a lethal tool that fosters the commitment to imperialism and white supremacy" (cf. ch. 8). Ethically, as Paraskeva argues, those really concerned with social and cognitive justice need to complexify critical approaches and to move beyond the fixed borders of terrain that assumes a permanent deterritorialized approach and itinerant position. Both Paraskeva and Sousa Santos embrace an ethical radicalism that denounces educators who, according to Freire, "(even with the best intentions) carry out the revolution for the people" (Freire, 2000, p. 127)—a process through which indigenous knowledge is filtered out by the imposition of the "official" knowledge infused in the curriculum "by the same methods and procedures used to oppress them" (p. 128). Hence, Paraskeva insightfully argues that "the target should be fighting against the coloniality of power and knowledge" (cf. ch. 8) that continues to undergird the very conception of West-centric knowledge—a conception that fails to appreciate the essence of "a rich and paradoxical engagement with the pertinence of what lay in an *oblique* or alien relation to the forces of centering" (Bhabha, 1994, p. xi). In other words, an alien relation constitutes knowledge itself and without which, as Freire posited, the development of new knowledge can never take place, since knowledge construction is predicated on the "perception of the previous perception [and] knowledge of the previous knowledge" (Freire, 2000, p. 115). Thus, an ethical radical pedagogical project that invariably also implies an ethical radical political project must lay bare the notion of the blind glorification of a "Great Tradition, a touchstone of Taste." According to Homi Bhabha, such glorification necessarily requires the skill "to survive, to produce, to labor and to create, within a world-system whose major economic impulses and cultural investments are pointed in a direction away from you, your country, your people" (Bhabha, 1994, p. xi) This hollowing out of what constitutes indigenous knowledge gives rise to a dehumanizing, toxic pedagogy that "spurs you to resist the polarities of power and prejudice, to reach beyond and behind the invidious narratives of center and periphery" (p. xi).

As a scholar entrenched in a language of possibility, Paraskeva unabashedly embraces the pedagogy of hope championed by Paulo Freire, whereby men and women become conscious of their capacity as agents of history who can intervene in the world so as to make it less discriminatory and more humane. It is a pedagogy of hope that was further elaborated by Henry Giroux as "educated hope"—a process through which, while dreaming of utopia, we critically understand both the possibilities and limitations of our dreams—dreams that are a sine qua non for imagining that another world is possible, as daringly stated by Howard Zinn (2007):

> Imagine the American people united for the first time in a movement for fundamental change. Imagine society's power taken way from giant corporations, the military, and the politicians who answer to corporate and military interest…Two forces are rushing toward the future. One wears a splendid uniform. It is the "official" past, with all its violence, war, prejudices against those who are different, hording of the good earth's wealth by the few, and political power in the hands of liars and murderers. The other force is ragged but inspired. It is the "people's" past, with its history of resistance, civil disobedience against the military machine, protests against racism, multiculturalism, and growing anger against endless wars. (p. 212)

DONALD MACEDO
Distinguished Professor of Liberal Arts and Education
University of Massachusetts Boston

REFERENCES

Barsamian, D. (2004) "The Progressive Interview," *The Progressive*, May.

Bhabha, H. (1994) *The Location of Culture*. London and New York: Routledge, p. xi.

Chomsky, N. (1991) "On the Gulf Policy," *Open Magazine*, Pamphlet Series, p. 8.

Freire, P. (2000) *Pedagogy of the Oppressed*. New York: Continuum, p. 127.

Freire, P. and Macedo, D. (1995) "A Dialogue: Culture, Language, and Race," *Harvard Educational Review*, Vol. 65, No. 3, Fall, pp. 377–402.

Zinn, H. (1980) *A People's History of the United States*. New York: Harper Perennial.

Zinn, H with Macedo, D. (2005) *Howard Zinn on Democratic Education*. Boulder, Colorado: Paradigm Publishers.

Zinn, H. (2007) *A Young People's History of the United States* (adapted by Rebecca Stefoff). New York: Seven Stories Press.

ACKNOWLEDGMENTS

This book would not have been possible without a great deal of help from many people. I owe a great deal to Donaldo Macedo, James Beane, Sheila Macrine, Boaventura de Sousa Santos, Lília Bartolomé, Jurjo Torres Santomé, Shirley Steinberg, Gustavo Fischman, Henry Giroux, and David Hursh for their constant care, friendship, encouragement, crucial comments, and challenges related to my work. Special thanks to Dwayne Huebner for the countless hours of interviews and fruitful conversations, but above all for his care, hospitality, humanity, and critical feedback. My debt will be forever open. Also, I would like to acknowledge the debt I owe to colleagues, friends, and mentors, namely, Barbara Broadhagen, Herbert Kliebard, Michael Apple, Thomas Popkewitz, Peter McLaren, Steve Selden, Mariano Enguita, José Gimeno Sacristán, José Félix Ângulo Rasco, David Gabbard, Angela Valenzuela, Bernadete Baker, Tero Autio, Eero Ropo, Bob Jessop, David Gillborn, Tristan McCowan, Michael F. D. Young, Tom Pedroni, António Nóvoa, Ana Sanches Bello, Cathryn Teasley, Jarbas Santos Vieira, Júlio Diniz Pereira, Beth Macedo, Alice Lopes, Inês Dussel, António C. Amorim, Alfredo Veiga Neto, Nilda Alves, Maria Cecília, Flávia Vieira, Maria Alfredo Moreira, Lia Oliveira, Manuel Silva, Viktor Kajibanga, Paulo de Carvalho, Narciso Benedito, António Soares Marques, Joao Rosa, Cristina de Novais, and Elizabeth Janson. A word of thanks to Dody Riggs for the oustanding support, friendship, and solidarity in editing the manuscript.

During my time at Miami University, I was fortunate to meet several colleagues with whom I interacted in very insightful ways. My thanks to Richard Quantz, Kate Rosmaniere, Dennis Carlson, Kathleen Abowitz, Lisa Whim, Aliya Rahman, Denise Baszile Taliaferro, **and** Jamal Abu-Attiyeh. Dennis, Denise, Lisa, and Aliya thoroughly read substantive parts of the book and their critical input was inestimably precious. In addition, my numerous interactions with the serious scholar and critical pedagogue Richard Quantz helped me to complexify my readings of educational and curriculum theory and policies. I really miss Miami, for it is a place that cultivates humanity. Also, I cannot forget my undergrad and grad students (at the University of Minho and the University of Porto in Portugal; the University of Coruña, Spain; the University of Florence, Italy; the Federal University of Pelotas, Brasil; Miami University, Ohio; and the University of Massachusetts, Dartmouth) with whom I have learned a lot. A word of thanks to southern Africa people, especially those in Angola, Mozambique, South Africa, Swaziland, Zimbabwe, and Namíbia. Also special thanks to Samantha Hasey and Burke Gerstenschlager, Palgrave Macmillan editors, for their care, humanity, and constant support.

A great deal of thanks must be reserved for my wife Isabel and my daughter Camila. Last but not least, a word of profound gratitude to my father and my mother, great references in my life. Unfortunately, my mother did not live enough to see the completion of this book, which resulted from many of our interesting discussions that are quite visible in this volume. The reader will inevitably identify in this work silences, omissions, and oversimplifications, for which I take absolute responsibility.

INTRODUCTION

The field of curriculum is theoretically shattered and profoundly disputed, to the extent that disputes have become an endemic part of the field's DNA. In some cases, such quarrels have been intellectually sanguinary. Sometimes the field appears to be an estuary of ideological debris upon which new cultural battles will be fought. As Carlson (2005) accurately argues, curriculum can no longer be considered "a distinctive field, with a unique history, a complex present, and uncertain future, because the category does not become reified" (p. 3). The field, Carlson argues, needs to be understood as "an historical construct assembled out of cultural battles over power and knowledge, and...it needs to be treated as a 'slippery' category whose meaning is unsettled and even contested." Curriculum theorizing is indeed a "challenging undertaking [framed] by the total rational potential of man" (Macdonald, 1967, pp. 166–9). To face these challenges, I attempt in this book "to develop alternatives" (Kliebard, 1975a, p. 49) to the way we think about the field. In fact, what this book aims to do is to (1) put into historical context the emergence and development of the history of the field; (2) unveil the emergence of a group of critical theorists within the curriculum field; (3) offer a new metaphor of the field as "a critical curriculum river" that meanders extensively to help understand these theorists' complex journey, including the battles fought for control of the field; and (4) examine and lay out a critique of the reconceptualist movement. Furthermore, I argue in this book that the future of critical curriculum theory needs to overcome such tensions, twists, and contradictions and engage in the creation of an itinerant curriculum theory (ICT) that must be committed to the struggle against epistemicides.

Current tensions inside the curriculum field demand an analysis that is framed within the complex social frameworks—economic, political, cultural, religious, and ideological—that emerged in the United States at the end of the nineteenth century. During the last two decades of that century, the crystallization of the Industrial

Revolution brought about significant transformations in the social fabric and revealed that schooling was an outdated institution facing the pressures of a newly emergent social order. This marked the beginning of a profound and intricate struggle for control of school knowledge, and of its social and cultural functions.

The theoretical ebb and flow of the critical intellectuals at the very core of such political, ideological, and cultural debates over school knowledge cannot be minimized. Their multidirectional roots extend from the turn of the twentieth century to the present day. To promote a better understanding of the work of this divergent group of critical scholars, this book provides the reader with a road map for tracking their theoretical contributions—what I refer to as the critical curriculum river. This metaphor, which is based on Vincent Harding's novel *There Is a River,* is a methodological tool used to reveal the various critical tributaries that have taken critical curriculum theorists in many different directions. While critical theorists come from a number of traditions, the river metaphor helps show how these traditions flow both together and individually in the history of the field. Although this group of scholars has never occupied a dominant position in the field, it is undeniable how much they have contributed to the struggle for a more just curriculum. In fact, their critical curriculum platforms not only have challenged both dominant and counterdominant positions, they also have capably edified a great deal of politically coded analyses in the field.

One of the most powerful leitmotifs of this critical curriculum river is the struggle for curriculum relevance—that is, for a just curriculum that can foster equality, democracy, and social justice. At the forefront of this struggle are the valuable contributions of intellectuals such as Dewey, Washington, Du Bois, Bode, Counts, Rugg, Huebner, Macdonald, Wexler, Aronowitz, Giroux, McLaren, and Apple, among others. The civil rights movement, the so-called romantic critics, and the Highlander Folk School also have had a profound impact. Grounded in different epistemological terrains, each of these scholars and movements was able to construct sharp challenges to an obsolete and positivistic functionalist school system, despite receiving severe criticism from counterdominant perspectives. Each one was in fact quite successful in claiming the need to understand schools and curriculum within the dynamics of ideological production.

This book lays out a map of the curriculum river, and in so doing lays bare the major arguments at the core of the political struggle for a democratic curriculum. It also proposes a possible path for future critical curriculum theorists, analyzing the general tensions that emerged in the curriculum field at the end of the nineteenth century and exposing how different groups were able to edify a hegemonic position in the curriculum field throughout the last 100 years. In examining such struggles, the conflicts within the counterdominant tradition, the dead ends, and the challenges faced by a critical curriculum river begin to be unveiled.

In this sense, and as a way to overcome dead ends, the book also proposes a promising future path for critical theory and challenges critical curriculum theorists to deterritorialize their approaches and assume a critical itinerant position. This would allow these theorists to complexify the struggle for curriculum relevance, thus fully engaging them in the struggle against epistemicides. To put it simply, epistemology can be defined as the study of knowledge, its justification(s), and its vast theories. It seeks to address issues related to the fundamental conditions of knowledge, its sources, structures, and borders, as well as the mechanisms related to the creation, dissemination, and legitimization of knowledge. Epistemology helps us understand that the knowledge of reality is inevitably limited by the level of development of the (technical/scientific) means and methods used to investigate and discern what actually is true; this is the case in all areas of knowledge about natural and social reality. As I claim in this book, the future course of the critical curriculum river will depend on the struggle against the epistemicides—that is, the way hegemonic epistemologies, predominantly that of the Western male, have been able to violently impose, both secularly and religiously, a coloniality of knowledge (cf. Sousa Santos, 2009). In other words, this is how particular kinds of knowledge and "science" have been able to acquire a dominant position, while at the same time too many others outside the Western realm of rationality have been silenced. The epistemicide needs to be seen as a world *tout court* Western secular rationality spreading from the hard sciences to the social sciences and on to the humanities, and gradually being dominated by the prestigious Anglophone discourses (and practices), due no doubt to its associations with the power structures of modernity (slavery, eugenics, technology, industry, and capitalism) that impose a positivist worldview, ignoring other non-Western epistemological platforms (cf. Bennett, 2007).

This task is not a laudable romanticization of indigenous cultures. In fact, it is precisely the opposite. It is a struggle against what I call "indigenoustude"—the mystification of indigenous cultures and knowledge. Moreover, it implies non-Westernizing the West and avoiding any kind of Eurocentrism in the anti-Eurocentric struggles—something that some postmodern and postcolonial approaches have ignored (Sousa Santos, 2009). Such a move is the potential future for critical curriculum theory—that is, to go beyond the struggle for curriculum relevance and fully engage in the struggle against a "social fascist" view of epistemology. The promising future for such a critical curriculum river is the struggle against curriculum epistemicide. This is the real struggle for social justice, which consciously assumes that there is no social justice without cognitive justice.

Such a dynamic allows us to go well beyond the tensions between critical and postcritical perspectives. It claims the need to assume an itinerant position, one that pushes the struggle for curriculum relevance to a different and more just path. In other words, the struggle against the Western eugenic coloniality of knowledge is the best way to transform schools and its social agents into real leaders in the struggle to democratize democracy. As this book reveals, (an)other knowledge is really possible. It also demonstrates the existence of a southern theory (Connell, 2007) and of a multifarious platform of southern epistemologies (Sousa Santos, 2009) that have been silenced by the dominant Western epistemologies. In so doing, this book attempts to show how critical theory re-ideologicizes and repoliticizes the educational agenda. As Cabral (1974, p. 16) would put it, this is not an act of courage but of intellectual honesty. Moreover, as Kemmis (1992) claims, we need to reconsider and perhaps modify our theoretical categories and our methodological tools, since most of the approaches we now employ are the product of modernist perspectives and epistemologies.

This book comprises eight chapters, which are preceded by the foreword and this introduction. Chapter 1 begins by setting the groundwork for examining some of the most important challenges that have beset the curriculum field historically, and aims to correct the schools' presentation of curriculum content as devoid of conflict, tensions, and struggles. Against this backdrop, we can trace how critical progressive curriculum theorists such as Apple and Giroux were able to challenge the dominant traditions, which were fueled by positivist creeds and counterdominant perspectives. As I point out in this book, an accurate examination of the nature of conflict enables one to explicitly experience the profoundly political nature of curriculum content, and also unveils the overt and intricate nexus between the hidden curriculum and the knowledge relayed via school dynamics, which is frequently repressive and actually preserves a particular culturally dominant platform (cf. Williams, 1976).

In doing so, we see how these critical scholars challenge curriculum relevance and at the same time retrieve the secular Spencerian question, "What knowledge is of most worth?" We also identify the bitter and poisonous tensions that flowed through the very center of the critical curriculum river.

The next chapter provides a history of curriculum thought in the United States from the 1890s to the beginning of the twentieth century, tracing the general tensions found within the emergent curriculum field. I examine the battle over knowledge that is controlled by educators who are humanists, developmentalists, social efficiencists, and social meliorists. In so doing, I emphasize the work, thoughts, and role of specific curriculum pioneers—Eliot, Harris, Hall, Rice, and Ward, among others—and the conflicts they engaged in. As demonstrated in this chapter, no single movement was able to claim a total victory in the struggle of knowledge control. This chapter lays out the foundations that allow the reader to undertake the deep exegesis in the subsequent chapters of the impact of Bobbitt, Charters, and Snedden's curriculum perspectives, and the importance of the civil rights movement and the romantic critics in the struggles over the U.S. curriculum. It also offers powerful tools to better understand not only Tyler's emergence and the subsequent developments that challenged his dominant position, but also the emergence of yet another group, the social reconstructionists, who fermented a nonmonolithic critical curriculum river.

In Chapter 3 I unveil the curriculum conflicts produced by a new cycle that was under way in U.S. society in the early part of the twentieth century. This cycle was propelled by the fresh and volatile demands imposed by a speedy and frenetic industrialism. I examine the political tangles between the humanist hegemonic tradition led by Harris and Eliot, Prosser's manual education, Snedden's vocational education, and Bobbitt's and Charters's pilgrim cult of social efficiency. Such a creed, profoundly influenced by Taylorism and Rossism, was about to become the dominant tradition in the field, a position that is quite evident today. It was an epoch in which the field was confronted with a plethora of important analyses, including those of Inglis, Kilpatrick, and Ayres. In this context, the noteworthy works of Dewey, Bode, Falgg Young, and others were not minimized. In Chapter 3 I also analyze the serious resistance these dominant traditions were facing.

In Chapter 4 I analyze Tyler's arrival on the scene and his rise to a predominant position in the field. I describe how Tyler (and Tylerism) was able to incorporate behavioral and testing traditions in his approach while at the same time speaking to both the Deweyan and the social reconstructionist traditions. As a result, Tyler maintained his leadership in the field while incorporating both dominant and nondominant traditions.

The fifth chapter describes how the social efficiency movement was gradually losing its dominance of the field as the social consequences of World War II pushed it in seemingly different directions. The field was facing new demands, and the dominant curriculum used from before World War II through the postwar period called for "life adjustment education." This curriculum was an incarnation of Bobbitt's and Charters's models, yet in a more humanized form that focused on social problems—something Bobbitt and Charters had done, but in a regressive, conservative way.

Chapter 6 reviews the social, cultural, and political turmoil that U.S. society was facing in the 1960s as a result of the Vietnam War, which instigated a new wave of change in education in general, and in curriculum in particular. I examine how the field of curriculum and the critical curriculum tradition were profoundly influenced by the civil rights movement, and by the so-called romantic critics and the student revolt. This network of dynamic organizations and individuals was able to laudably refute and openly challenge a segregated society while making demands for a more just society, equal rights, real democracy, and the eradication of eugenic policies and practices. It is in this context that we highlight the Geneseo Conference, one of the towering events in the secular struggle for a more culturally relevant curriculum.

The chapters to this point provide a fairly exhaustive analysis of the conflicts that dominated the curriculum field since the end of the nineteenth century. Our analysis in Chapter 7 begins by bringing forward the tensions and clashes around the absence of conflict within the curriculum field and the need to make the claim that schools lack curriculum relevance. To understand such tensions and clashes, this chapter returns to the beginning of the nineteenth century as it frames and contextualizes the current struggles within the larger curriculum field. This strategy, anchored by the noteworthy thinking of Kliebard and others, goes beyond their vision and analysis by incorporating minute analyses of the romantic critics of the civil rights movement, and of the singular political project called the Highlander Folk School. In addition, the role that Horton played in this respect cannot be erased from the historical curriculum debate. Such critical historical exegesis, which is fundamental to our understanding, situates the curriculum field within the progressive contemporary critical river. The book engages in a discussion to understand the source of this curriculum river, thus exposing another heated tension that was sparked by the reconceptualists.

In the final chapter, I accomplish two things. First, I establish the need for a more culturally relevant curriculum and for the recognition that this struggle should be seen as one against the coloniality of knowledge, as well as a fight against epistemicides. In essence, I argue that the struggle for social justice is a struggle to achieve cognitive justice and to democratize knowledge. Second, I advocate for an itinerant theoretical posture as the future for the critical curriculum river, a posture that celebrates and goes beyond the obstacles created by the tensions between critical and poststructural approaches.

CHAPTER 1

THE NATURE OF CONFLICT

The problem of conflict abstinence in the curriculum was at the center of the debate among scholars who were situated in different progressive political perspectives. These groups of scholars were engaged in powerful analyses that addressed both the dominant and counterdominant perspectives. They were challenging the culture of positivism (Giroux, 1981a), which was fundamentally concerned "with controlling and dominating the natural and human environment" (Wexler, 1976, p. 8), thus fostering cognitive passivity (Kincheloe, 1993). These scholars saw the urgent need, as Wexler (1976) puts it, to "turn from science as the single standard of knowledge in favor of a plurality of equally ways of knowing" (p. 8). Learning, Giroux (1983) claims, "takes place in a variety of public spheres outside of the schools" (p. xxviii).
Apple (1971), who was strongly motivated by his academic background,[1] claims that:

> there has been, so far, little examination of how treatment of conflict in the school curriculum can lead to political quiescence and the acceptance by students of a perspective on social and intellectual conflict that acts to maintain the existing distribution of power and rationality in a [given] society. (p. 27)

As a political, ideological, cultural, and economic project, curriculum must be understood as a document that is determined by the dynamics of conflict and exhibits a cultural capacity. It is mandatory, then, to go beyond simply demystifying the notion of conflict and to treat it without affectations of any kind, especially since, as Dahrendorf (1959, p. 27) notes, the social reality is basically determined by "conflict and flux, and not by a closed functional system." The creed of the absence of conflict in the curriculum was, to use Giroux's (1981a) argument, a flight from history, which is in reality the suppression of history. Conflict must be seen as a stimulus because it is a fundamental element of the social transformation framework; in other words, conflict, in a Marxist perspective, is actually a major source of social change and innovation.

Just as incidental learning contributes "more to the political socialization of a student than certain forms of deliberate teaching of specific value orientations" (Siegel, 1970, p. xiii; cf. also Giroux, 1983), so too must conflict be understood not as a social obstruction but as a dialectic instrument, as a creator of the dynamics of legitimization and of social progress. In fact, there is generally a tense compromise between the hidden curriculum and conflict. Such a compromise, as we will examine later on, was overtly visible in the works of the so-called romantic critics, and Jackson (1968) felicitously "curricularized" it. While on the one hand it is impossible, as Giroux (1983) claims, to ignore "the way in which the structure of the workplace is replicated through daily routines and practices that shape classroom social relations, or in other words, the hidden curriculum of schooling" (p. 4), on the other hand, such a notion, "as it currently exists in the literature, fails to provide the theoretical elements necessary to develop a critical pedagogy based on a concern with cultural struggles in the schools" (p. 70).

Ultimately, the curriculum cannot be analyzed in isolation from the social dynamics that construct themselves daily around constitutive and preferential rules (McLure & Fisher, 1969). As a social institution, the school is not insensitive to this dualism. The school thus functions as the distributor of a concrete rationality, which as it is assimilated by the student empowers him or her to function and to accept the institutional mechanisms and their complex dynamics that contribute to the stability of the interests of an industrialized society (cf. Dreeben, 1968).

The dominions of science are presented as a corpus of knowledge without being analyzed as human constructs. Science must be perceived as a dominion of knowledge achieved by means of specific techniques of discovery or formulation of hypotheses. It reflects a human community and, as such, is ruled by norms, values, ambitions, and ideals that translate a historical perspective of struggles and quarrels at the personal and the intellectual level. Such conflicts habitually catalyze the emergence of new knowledge paradigms that question formerly unquestionable knowledge conceptions.

Students are introduced to a science that lacks conflict in its methodology, its objectives, the foundation of paradigms, and the choice of specific criteria to the detriment of others (cf. Dreeben, 1968).

This kind of teaching impedes the possibility of determining the conflict and the discord that are the real sources of scientific progress. Students are similarly introduced to a science in which the political compromise that marks the scientific world is silenced. In the majority of schools, conflict, although a propelling mechanism of scientific progress, is almost nonexistent for students.

Science, which demands behavior shaped by organized skepticism (Storer, 1966), cannot be amputated from its own historical dynamics, which have been carried out on the basis of competition between distinct paradigms and which, although marked by a significant degree of objectivity and neutrality, should not be analyzed without considering concrete social synergies. Science must be regarded and taught as a complex field of argumentation and counterargumentation that is based on a theoretical and procedural framework, according to which the conflict between the different paradigms may be legitimized. Science, in Gramscian terms, is not an objective notion but an ideology that expresses a union between objective facts and formulated hypotheses (Manacorda, 1970).

In fact, it is difficult to determine a separation between conflict and competition in (what is called) the field of science, especially since competition over priority and recognition in new discoveries is a characteristic of all established sciences (Hagstrom, 1965). Another important aspect is the objectivity that emerges to circumscribe (what is called) the field of science taught at schools, and which may lead to a relinquishment vis-à-vis a political compromise (Apple, 1971). Such objectivity may not be as neutral as it is said to be, and instead be concealing moral, intellectual, and political conflict (Gouldner, 1970). Educational theory and research are both profoundly submersed in a dangerous functionalist platform.

> American educational theory and research became firmly entrenched within an instrumentalist tradition that defined progress as technological growth and learning as the mastery of skills and the solving of practical problems...Educational research surrenders its capacity to question and challenge the basic imperatives of the dominant society to a functionalist ideology fuelled by the politically conservative principles of social harmony and normative consensus. (Giroux, 1981a, p. 5)

Like the scientific field, society is portrayed in the school as a cooperative system rather than a space of constant strife and compromise. Social studies attempts to legitimize the idea that society is based on felicitous cooperation, conveying the idea that social conflict is not in itself an essential part of the framework of the Constitution and embedded in the maintenance of the social tissue. It is thus relevant that the school—subject to a conservative perspective—transmits an idea of a society that is based on a functional dynamic of consensus (conflict is seen as dysfunctional).

If the social order is legitimized by the regularity of change (Dahrendorf, 1959), and if the social tissue is not a static social web but a realm in which "continuous change in the elements and basic structural form of society is a dominant characteristic" (Apple, 1971, p. 35), then social change and progress emerge and are propelled by the dynamics of conflict—dynamics that must not be dissociated from the curriculum as a mechanism of knowledge construction. Should the opposite occur, "there [will be] no union between the school and society" (cf. Gramsci, 1971, p. 35).

As Freire (1990), Apple (1971), Giroux (1981a, 1983), Wexler (1976), Willis (1977), Bernstein (1971), Young (1971), and others have amply demonstrated, the school sells itself to a system of beliefs and the students are offered very specific pictures. Both serve to legitimize the existent social order, for they systematically neglect change and conflict and do not portray humans as creators or recipients of values and institutions. We are faced with what Freire (1990) calls a dehumanizing pedagogy, a pedagogy that actually oppresses both the oppressed and the oppressor. This scenario becomes all the more perilous in an era when, in many countries, education has become compulsory for every child.

Given these omissions and silences, the school as an institution cannot adequately fulfill the needs of local communities and is powerless to ignite a transformation of the existing social order. The school thus functions as a political field of socialization that competes with the family and assumes compromises as students adjust to authority (Siegel, 1970). Therefore, it is not controversial to admit that "the public schools are a choice transmission for the traditional rather than the innovative, much less the radical" (p. 316). This is very much in line with Freire's (1990) critique of the banking model of education, where students are viewed as empty vessels to be filled with the teachers' knowledge. In this approach to education, students are, by and large, domesticated rather than liberated—a vision that views "knowledge is a gift bestowed by those who consider themselves knowledgeable" (p. 58).

By criticizing certain programmatic approaches to the sciences and social studies, Apple (1971), Giroux (1981a), and others adamantly declare that the alternative must be conducted by political activity and "through the construction of a new educational discourse and mode of analysis about the nature of schooling" (Giroux, 1988, p. 3).

To divorce the educator's educational existence from his political existence is to forget that education, as an act of influence, is inherently a political act, as has been insightfully argued by some of the major exponents of the critical curriculum river. A close analysis of the nature of conflict allows us to understand the manner in which it enables the students (and educational agents) to deal with the political realities and complex power dynamics that are frequently repressive in a way that preserves the institutional modes of interaction (Eisinger, 1970). In problematizing the nature of conflict as an alternative form of conscience, a critical approach to education should not only question the knowledge presented in the history books and social studies texts, it also must uphold the schools as organisms that systematically distort the functions (social, intellectual, and political) of the conflict within the communities. Such functions are fundamental to their ideological genesis and serve as an orientation for the individual, as Zinn (2005) clearly points out:

> The educational system taught about the Founding Fathers and the Constitution and it taught us pride in the American Revolution and the Civil War, the great presidents and the great military leaders. There was nothing in my education that suggested that there was anything wrong with the existing arrangements. (p. 37)

In considering this issue, one finds a combination of concerns that constitute the embryo of one of the great arguments—an argument that has permeated the curriculum thinking of a number of progressive educators—that emerged during the civil rights movement regarding the policy of textbook adoption. Without a broad analysis and understanding of the dimensions of what is at stake—knowledge—educators will continue to run the risk of being dictated to by these institutional values and of losing their creative, participative capacity (Huebner, 1962). The need to fight for an education system that would challenge savage social inequalities (Kozol, 1992), that would provide the proper political tools to "read the word and the world" (Freire, 1998), that would challenge the pedagogy of the big lies and the positivist trap that has been dominating the educational apparatus (Macedo, 2006) was inevitable. Thus it was crucial to challenge forms of pedagogy that built a "semi-intransitive consciousness [in which students] cannot apprehend problems situated outside their sphere of biological necessity, [in other words,] their interests center almost totally around survival and they lack a sense of life on a more historic plane" (Freire, 1974, p. 17). Teaching the social dialectic of change, thus giving students better conceptual tools and politics to deal with the complex social reality, became an imperative (cf. Spencer, 1902). What is at stake, as I address later on, is a challenge to epistimicides (cf. Sousa Santos, 2005, 2009). The call was for the emergence of a critical transitive consciousness, one

> characterized by depth in the interpretation of problems; by the substitution of causal principals for magical explanations; by the testing of one's findings and by openness to revision; by the attempt to avoid distortion when perceiving problems and to avoid preconceived notions when analyzing them; by refusing to transfer responsibility; by rejecting passivity; by rejecting passive positions; by soundness of argumentation; by the practice of dialogue rather than polemics; by receptivity to the new for reasons beyond mere novelty and the good sense not to reject the old just because it is old—by accepting what is valid both in old and new. (Freire, 1974, p. 18)

In essence, one cannot minimize the powerful relation of conflict that is established between the hidden curriculum and the knowledge relayed in schools. The fact is, while questioning the knowledge handed out by the schools—knowledge that is transmitted and influenced and indoctrinated by significant others in the students' lives (parents, teachers, media)—critical educators evoke an old question raised by Spencer (1860) at the end of the last century. This question was already a cause for concern in the classic period of antiquity, and it would prove to be "the most central of all the questions that can be raised about curriculum" (Kliebard, 1999b, p. 5): "What knowledge is of most worth?" (Spencer, 1860, pp. 84–85).

According to Spencer (1902), "not science, but neglect of science, is irreligious" (p. 45); science was different from the study of languages because of its efficacy, clarity, and rigor, and because "its truths are not accepted on authority alone" (p. 44). Thus Spencer (1860, pp. 84–85) provides one uniform answer to his question:

> Science. This is the verdict on all the counts. For direct self-preservation, or the maintenance of life and health, the all-important knowledge is—Science. For that indirect self-preservation which we call gaining a livelihood, the knowledge of greatest value is—Science. For the due discharge of parental functions, the proper guidance is to be found only in—Science. For that interpretation of national life, past and

present, without which the citizen cannot rightly regulate his conduct, the indispensable key is—Science. Alike for the most perfect production and present enjoyment of art in all its forms, the needful preparation is still—Science, and for the purposes of discipline—intellectual, moral, religious, the most efficient study is, one more—Science.

Spencer, who pioneered a functional curriculum design based on identifying and classifying the human activities that sustain life, proposed a curriculum constructed around five major human activities: "Those directly needed for bodily and self-preservation. Those related to employment and earning a living that indirectly supported self-preservation. Those needed for parenting. Those needed for political and social life. Those of an aesthetic and recreational nature that related to leisure" (Gutek, 1991, pp. 249–50).

Spencer's thinking was to become predominant on the U.S. educational scene (Kliebard, 1999b). It is possible to trace his influence in some of Eliot's works, namely, in Eliot's crusade for the New Education, wherein he upheld the study of the pure sciences, modern European languages, and mathematics, and, with the Committee of Ten, "parity to the natural sciences in the secondary-school program" (cf. Cremin, 1964, pp. 92–93). Moreover, the Spencerian conception of a worthwhile curriculum had repercussions for the path the U.S. curriculum would take by the end of the nineteenth century (Kliebard, 1999b).

Contrary to what was subsequently found, particularly in the *Yale Faculty Report* (cf. Silliman, 1829), the study of the sciences was valued more highly than the subjects considered traditionally humanistic. This reformative curriculum proposal was praised not only because it was directed, as Kliebard (1988) notes, "consciously or unconsciously, to a rising middle class that saw the traditional curriculum as exclusionary and remote from practical affairs and the interests of a modern industrial society" (pp. 21–22), but because the process of curriculum development itself was seen "as scientific" (p. 21).

The character of education is not necessarily determined by the knowledge deemed most valuable but by the knowledge that confers the greatest social respect and honor, and that leads to prominent social positions (Spencer, 1902). Spencer argued above all that before there could be a rational curriculum, "we must settle which things it most concerns us to know, or . . . we must determine the relative values of knowledges" (p. 6).

This argument continued to be debated, and by the end of the 1960s and the beginning of the 1970s, the U.S. curriculum field was inflamed—not only by the works of the so-called romantic critics (Henry, 1963; Kohl, 1988; Kozol, 1967), but at a later stage by the work of Jackson (1968), Bowles and Gintis (1976), and Jencks (1971). These later works were related to theories of reproduction and they saw the school as one of the key social institutions needed to reproduce the existing economic relations of a particular society. In keeping with this perspective, the fundamental role of education is directly related to the socialization of students, with the purpose of contributing to the reproduction of existing social relations.

Before that time, the majority of investigations into teaching and learning were oriented to principles relevant to classrooms in a stricter sense—the acts of explaining, reminding, and reinforcing, which contribute more directly to the learning process and focus more on individual aspects than social ones (Doyle, 1986). Reducing the dynamics of conflict to an individual level eliminates the opportunity to being able to resolve other problems at the social level.

According to Wexler (1976), both Jackson and Jencks were "urging their colleagues to examine more closely the experience of education and to study the social organization of schooling itself with less emphasis on its 'efficient output'" (p. 9). Jackson (1968) attempted to reveal the interior of the "black box" that is the schooling institution, affirming the existence of a correspondence between the institutions of production in an industrialized society and in a schooling institution. He continued by asserting that the school is ruled by inner codes that are characterized by a strong inequality of power between teachers and students, which facilitates the shaping of students into the molds imposed by the adults. The students thus tacitly learn specific social norms, which are principally identifiable by confronting the urgencies of the day-to-day and the classroom tasks. These norms serve to structure their future life, which demonstrates how the school contributes to individual adaptation to a (continuous) social order (Dreeben, 1968).

The school performs its role implicitly through the organizational modalities and routines that determine the day-to-day activities in the classroom. This establishes a territory with very particular principles, wherein the learning processes that constitute fundamental parts of the production chain are processed (Torres Santomé, 1998). The academic demands of the official curriculum are considered directly related to an adult's productive life by means of the hidden curriculum.

Bowles and Gintis's (1976) analysis would later repoliticize the hidden curriculum (with Jackson this issue was somehow depoliticized) by conferring on it a vital political importance. They saw it as an instrument for the reproduction, cohesion, and stability of the social relations of production and distribution. Notwithstanding Jackson's depoliticizing perspective, his approach allows us to discern the meaning of certain practices that hereto had appeared to have gone undetected and were diluted within the daily school routine, namely, the maintenance of order, the attention-seeking strategies of the teachers and others representing authority, the acceptance of sanctions, the submission to those in power, and evaluation.

We cannot ignore the fact that any analysis of the processes of learning and teaching within schooling institutions should not be limited to the physical space of the institution; we must proceed further, taking into account the economic, social, political, and cultural contexts through which teaching and learning acquire a more complete meaning (Torres Santomé, 1990). Jackson (1968), who agrees with Doyle's (1986) thinking in characterizing classroom practices, describes the process of curriculum development in the classroom by comparing it to the difference between a butterfly and a bullet. This particular metaphor gives us more awareness of the depth and the complexity of practices at the classroom level, especially because they are known to be based on a logic determined by the dominant individualism in the teacher's behavior.

However, as I mentioned above and as Dale (1977) observed, Jackson does not examine the hidden curriculum in terms of its ideological and political importance in the perpetuation of a particular social stratification. The analysis conducted by Jackson and other similar writers reveals them to be idealistic, inasmuch as they fail to criticize the immense injustice that underlies the data placed on the table, thus ignoring their degree of dependency on the stratified social forms (Torres Santomé, 1998). The manner by which the objectives, the contents, the methodology, and the evaluation are involved with (and implicated in) power relations and built on the economic, political, and cultural spheres is ignored. Moreover, as stressed by Young and Whitty (1977), the analysis of how the forms of power within a particular society function in accordance with and in favor of concrete interests, ideologies, and forms of knowledge, which ultimately help guarantee the economic and political priorities of specific social groups, is marginalized.

Despite admitting to the possibility of resistance against the established norms, Jackson fails to understand that such postures of protest—which are often passive—may eventually contribute to the transformation of the practices of dissimulated objectives, or reproduction. Jackson minimizes the importance of what one might refer to as the metaphor of the stone, as formulated by Dewey (1916) at the beginning of the twentieth century. In Jackson's analysis, the possibilities for the emancipation of daily classroom practices are (almost) annulled. The politics of conflict are ignored by not deepening the possibilities of transformation that both students and teachers possess.

Jackson's analysis demonstrates a clear concern with and respect for practice, but the fact is that one is able to comprehend and better intervene in the schooling reality only by establishing a relation between what occurs within the classroom and the wider and more flexible frameworks, which are sensitive to social, cultural, economic, and political contexts (Atkin, 1983).

In the end, Jackson's analysis—and, later, the theory of correspondence traced by Bowles and Gintis (which, as we will see later on, is severely challenged by, among others, Apple and Giroux)—appears circumscribed, not only by economically based determinism but by a functionalist dimension that imposes an a-critical vision of day-to-day schooling and ignores the people, dismissing them as passive beings incapable of altering an adverse destiny (Torres Santomé, 1998). These are reductive analyses, which ignore the relational and the more encompassing vision of the educational phenomenon and do not accept it as a producer of the dynamics of transformation or of strategies of resistance. It is increasingly urgent to continue to separate oneself from an economic-formalist conception, which considers the economy to be composed of invariable elements brought together through diverse means of production of an almost Aristotelian nature and essence that are auto-reproducible and auto-regulated by a kind of internal combination (Poulantzas, 1980).

Fundamentally, notwithstanding the fact that the works that proliferated in that period demonstrated a great advance in the curriculum field, none of those mentioned delved into how knowledge was determined (i.e., made socially valid). In other words, there was a reductionism in the study of the teaching and learning behaviors and the processes of the interveners in the educational practice that limited itself to an exclusive comparison and verification of certain forms of knowledge, thus ignoring the real and more encompassing value of the curriculum, which remained hidden. Along these lines, it is mandatory to interpret curriculum issues within a wider, more organic dimension, denouncing the school as a mechanism of social segregation and perpetuating the established logics of power.

As McLaren (1994) claims,

> the hidden curriculum deals with the tacit ways in which knowledge and behavior get constructed, outside the usual course materials and formally schedule lessons. It is a part of the bureaucratic and managerial "press" of the school—the combined forces by which students are induced to comply with the dominant ideologies and social practices related to authority, behavior and morality. (p. 191)

Giroux (1981a) in turn reveals that

> the hidden curriculum represents one of the most important conceptual tools by which radicals can explore the dialectical relationships and tensions that accompany the process of reproduction at the level of day-to-day classroom interactions...to make sense of the hidden curriculum means that schools have to be analyzed as agents of legitimating organized to produce and reproduce the dominant categories, values, and social relationships necessary for the maintenance of the larger society. (p. 72)

It is this preoccupation that one finds throughout particular critical approaches, some of them showing the distinctive influence of Gramsci. Education, according to a Gramscian perspective, must submit to a wider form of analysis:

> The crisis of the curriculum and organization of the schools, i.e. of the overall framework of a policy for forming modern intellectual cadres, is to a great extent an aspect and a ramification of the more comprehensive and general organic crisis. (Gramsci, 1971, p. 40)

The peculiarity of the context in which schools and their agents are to be found must not be ignored. The curriculum serves to construct a web of assumptions, which are legitimized once they are constituted and incorporated into an intimate relation with the contexts—social, political, cultural, and ideological—in the socialization practices and knowledge formulation processes.

The nature of the conflict plays out around the field of knowledge. Consequently, the dynamics subjacent to the field of curriculum may not be dissociated from what Dahrendorf (1993) defines as modern social conflict determined by binominal citizenship and economic growth. In other words, the great social modern conflict (to which the school and the curriculum are not insensitive) plays out between sociopolitical developments on the one hand and economic developments on the other. The future is made up of a plural existence based on a conflict that is itself an icon of openness and vigor for societies, especially since the true question is not how conflict might be abolished but how humanity might learn to live with it and transform it into a productive step forward for freedom.

Many critical educators initiate a unique and intricate journey through the field of education by challenging curriculum relevance, based on a particular kind of Marxist/neo-Marxist perspective (or in reaction to such perspectives) on the theme of the (absence) of conflict in curriculum. The urgent need for school and curriculum relevance became a non-negotiable claim for critical progressive curriculum scholars. For them it was the fundamental issue in the complex struggle for social justice and equality (Wexler, 1976). On the front lines of educational reform in the 1970s and 1980s, critics were claiming the need for a political reading of education in general and the curriculum in particular. They also were challenging the nonpolluted curriculum perspective and its social relevance. One cannot minimize the influence of Huebner, Macdonald, Apple, Giroux, Wexler, and McLaren, who themselves were strongly influenced, albeit in different ways, by complex epistemological zones, such as analytical philosophy, symbolic interactionism, hermeneutics, phenomenology, critical theory, and (neo-)Marxism, and by the developments emerging from what would be coined the new sociology of education/curriculum and the works of Willis, Bernstein, Young, Dale, and Whitty, among others. They were able to bring to the fore towering concepts that would reshape the field, namely, ideology, hegemony, common sense, hidden curriculum, power, reproduction, resistance, transformation, emancipation, class, gender, and race, among others.

Some of these educators faced severe criticism from both conservative and progressive liberal platforms. The more severe and devastatingly heated (and juicy) debates occurred precisely within the very marrow of so-called progressive liberal and critical platforms. Although in different ways, Apple, Giroux and Freire were not able to avoid straightforward, incisive criticism from Bowers, Wexler, and Ellsworth, and also Pinar, that (unintentionally, I believe) helped create a heated atmosphere within the reconceptualization movement. We will return to these issues later on.

Despite such fiery tensions, Apple and Giroux were able to lead the political approach(es) in the field:

> Wexler emerged [in the seventies] as the most sophisticated critic on the Left of Apple and Giroux, and quite possibly the most sophisticated

theoretician on the Left in contemporary field" (p. 44), [but]...one
cannot ignore the massive dominance portrayed by Apple and Giroux.
The effort to understand curriculum as a political text shifted from
an exclusive focus upon reproduction of the status quo to resistance
to it, then again, to resistance/reproduction as a dialectical process,
then again—in the mid-1980's—to a focus upon daily educational
practice, especially, pedagogical and political issues of race, class, and
gender. The major players in this effort continued to be Apple and
Giroux, Apple through high voluminous scholarship and that of his
many students, and Giroux through his prodigious scholarly production. (Pinar, Reynolds, Slattery, and Taubman, 1995, p. 44)

However, these are not similar approaches. According to Aronowitz
(1981), Giroux was able to go "further than many of his contempo-
raries such as Apple and Willis who grasp the contradictory character
of schooling but have not conceptualized the moment when the classroom becomes open to change" (p. 3). Thus we confront two different approaches and arguably distinct political projects. I see such
differences, upgrades, and detours as part of the critical history of
the field. While Apple and Willis target the same issues, they actually
end up showing different ways to understand them, and in so doing
they end up edifying distinct yet powerful curriculum approaches.
Although each in his own way was able to semantically stretch particular critical pedagogy insights to the limit, it seems that Giroux
pioneered the will to play and explore new poststructural and postmodern perspectives (cf. Apple, 2010; Giroux, 1981a).

The main goal for critical progressive educators should be social
justice and real democracy, while acknowledging that there is no social
justice without cognitive justice (Sousa Santos, 2005; cf. Paraskeva,
2010a). In a spaceless world (Bauman, 2004) profoundly segregated
by neoliberal globalization doctrine (Paraskeva, 2010b; 2010c), critical pedagogy, in its different windows (Kincheloe, 1991), more than
ever before needs to win the battle to democratize democracy. The
schools and the curriculum have a key role in such a struggle (cf.
Counts, 1932)—in fact, the reinvigoration of the Left, as Aronowitz
(2001) argues, depends on this.

Having as its epicenter the theme of conflict, a number of critical
theorists restructure the question formulated by Spencer, complexifying it but also making it more just. Apple, for example, asks not *what*
knowledge is of the most worth but *whose* knowledge is of the most
worth. In other words, the predominant issue is not knowledge itself
but precisely whose knowledge. Whose vision did it represent? Who
benefits? Faced with a school system that can be defined, as Giroux

(1981a) claims, as a social construct that serves to mystify rather than illuminate reality, one cannot deny the importance of challenging meaningless curricula.

In short, what is at stake—and always has been—is knowledge (selected, diffused, and evaluated). It is around this framework that the great lines of thought, which by the end of the nineteenth century had already burst forth with the metaphor of the mind as a muscle, attempted to impose a new social order via the curriculum. In fact, the nature of conflict is determined by the dynamics—of form and of content—inherent in the ways socially valid knowledge is diffused throughout the schools.

In the remaining chapters, I address particular aspects of the history of the curriculum field from the end of the nineteenth century through the 1980s in order to identify and understand the general tensions, conflicts, and compromises within the field of curriculum knowledge. My aim is to help the reader understand and situate a particular flow of critical progressive curriculum—what I call the critical progressive curriculum river.

CHAPTER 2

THE STRUGGLE OVER KNOWLEDGE CONTROL

MIND-AS-MUSCLE

In the early days of the country, one cannot fully understand U.S. history "without some appreciation of the centrality of education" (Perkinson, 1968, p. 1) and the principal objective of education was "to convert men into republican machines" (Rush, 1965, p. 16). In a nation of immense fertile territory (Verplank, 1836), a "thoroughly American curriculum would help unify the language and culture of the new nation and wean America away from a corrupt Europe" (Kaestle, 1983, p. 6). The increasing population density increased social tensions as well, stigmatizing certain groups and creating festering social sores, thus allocating to the school the function of inculcating morality in the hope of maintaining social order. Hence, the school was to play a profound role in the diffusion of discipline and behavior models: As Kaestle (1983) writes:

> The emphasis on school discipline to influence adult behavior overlooks the purposes of discipline in childhood. There were two compelling reasons for training children to be obedient, punctual, deferential and task-oriented. The first is simply that discipline was needed for the orderly operation as a school...The second reason for encouraging childhood discipline is that most parents wanted children to behave in a deferential and obedient manner. (p. 69)

With an excessive number of students per class and a teacher growing increasingly weaker professionally, the school would strive to achieve a "cultural conformity and educational uniformity" (Kaestle, 1983, p. 71). For this reason, textbooks such as the *McGuffey Reader* were the "more influential standardization" (Kliebard, 1995, p. 2) mechanism of the nineteenth-century school curriculum, thereby contributing significantly to the sedimentation and crystallization of a number of behaviors demanded by industrialization (Perkinson, 1968). McGuffey's textbooks covered a myriad of issues and are profoundly politically coded. If, as McGuffey argued (1839), "in our haste to be rich and mighty, we outrun our literary and religious institutions, they will never overtake us...we must educate or we must perish by our own prosperity" (pp. 150–152).

In the midst of this reformative spirit (cf. Lipscomb, 1903; Philbrick, 1885; Wood, 1988), the *Report on Courses of Liberal Education* (Silliman, 1829; also known as the *Yale Faculty Report*) emerged. It analyzed the plan of education at the college level, as well as the importance of studying ancient languages:

> We are decidedly of the opinion that our present plan of education admits of improvement. We are aware that the system is imperfect. We believe that changes may, from time to time, be made with advantage to meet the varying demands of the community, to accommodate the course of instruction to the rapid advance of the country, in population, refinement and opulence. We have no doubt that important improvements may be suggested, by attentive observation to the literary institutions in Europe. (p. 299)

The *Report* determined that the object of a collegiate course of study should have as its basis the aim to "lay the foundation of a superior education" (Silliman, 1829, p. 300). Quite naturally, the *Report* defends a teaching scheme that is grounded in an (inflexible) mental discipline and a call for memorization:

> The two great points to be gained in intellectual culture are the discipline and the furniture of the mind; expanding its powers, and storing it with knowledge. The former of these is, perhaps, the more important of the two: A commanding object, therefore, in a collegiate course, should be to call into daily and vigorous exercise the faculties of the student. (p. 300)

In this manner, a wide uniform plan of studies was promoted, one in which all the mental faculties would be duly exercised, especially since the (total) perfection of the mind depended on the incessant exercise of its various powers (Muelder, 1984; Tyack, 1974). Thus, the "mental discipline by which mind-as-muscle could be strengthened" (Beyer & Liston, 1996, p. 3) would not actually depend on the isolated study of mathematics, nor on an isolated study of classical languages, but on a perfect symbiosis between "the different branches of literature and science, as to form in the student a proper balance of character" (Silliman, 1829, p. 301). In fact, "the success of each is essential to the prosperity of the other" (p. 323).

This is "the most famous document of nineteenth century mental disciplinarism" (Kliebard, 1995, p. 5); its "lineage could be traced in some respects to the classical university of the Middle Ages" (Beyer & Liston, 1996, p. 3), with its emphasis on the *artesliberales* and *sermonicales* (cf. Paraskeva, 2001). Contrary to Spencer's endorsements, the *Report* defended classical languages as the guarantors of mental exercise, dictating rigor and discipline by means of recitation and memorization. However, with the rapid growth of an immigrant population, it was impossible to maintain the mental disciplinarian philosophy, and teaching (both theory and practice) was radically altered. In the nineteenth century, Kliebard (1995) argues,

> at the heart of America's educational system in the nineteenth century was the teacher. It was the teacher, ill-trained, harassed and underpaid, often immature, who was expected to embody the standard virtues and community values and, all the same ripe, to mete out stern discipline to the unruly and dull-witted. (p. 1)

The school, as a specific political social project, demonstrated its weakness by showing that it was impotent in meeting the new challenges imposed by society, which was controlled by the rhythms and compasses of industry and technology (cf. Tyack, 1974). Clearly, as Kaestle (1983) points out, certain aspects of economic development would affect schooling in multiple ways:

> By fostering commerce, geographical mobility, and communication, capitalism encouraged schooling for literacy, mathematics, and other intellectual skills. By creating more wage labor, capitalism contributed to the demand for work discipline although other factors also account for school discipline. By creating more tightly coordinated productive hierarchies, such as in factories, industrialization promoted the values of punctuality, subordination, and regimentation that came also to characterize schools. (p. 63)

By around the 1890s, "the signs of change were unmistakable" (Kliebard, 1995, p. 4). High industrialization, as Urban and Wagoner (1996) argue, "highlighted urbanization dilemmas (demographic crescendo of approximately 14 million immigrants), as well as visible extremes of wealth and poverty" (pp. 159–160). It also created the opportunity for an increasingly stronger U.S. "proletariat class" (Kaestle, 1983, p. 66) to emerge.

Kliebard (1995) claims that "with the change in the social role of the school came a change in the educational center of gravity; it shifted from the tangible presence of teacher to the remote knowledge and values incarnate in the curriculum" (p. 1). Naturally, he continues, "by 1890 visible cracks were noticed in mental discipline" (p. 3). Fundamentally, the collapse of mental discipline "as a theory of curriculum" (p. 6) was due to the transformation of the existing social order, which brought on the new problematization of knowledge (Apple, 1999; Kliebard, 1982; Kolesnik, 1979; Krug, 1969).

THE STRUGGLE OVER KNOWLEDGE CONTROL

Industrialism and the concomitant complex social transformation led to a large increase in admissions to secondary school. This also led to a redefinition of the essence and aim of schooling as the forum for the diffusion of knowledge (Tyack, 1974). In this sense, the problematization of the knowledge reflected in the curriculum (a quite ancient concern; cf. Aristotle, 1945) would come to be an extremely complex question, especially in a society that was experiencing the "massive new influx of students into secondary schools" (Kliebard, 1995, p. 7; cf. also Troen, 1976). The economic crisis of 1893, which motivated the growing disbelief in obsolete social institutions (among which the school was no exception), accelerated people's awareness of the imminence of a new world and of the need for a new school and curriculum (Kliebard, 1988).

The trajectory between knowledge and social values and their incorporation in the curriculum became an increasingly complex task, particularly since "different segments in any society will emphasize different forms of knowledge as most valuable for that society" (Kliebard, 1995, p. 7). Social trends began to emerge with regard to education in general and to curriculum in particular, led by various interest groups with the aim of controlling the knowledge disclosed in the curriculum. Each represented "a force for a different selection of knowledge and values from the culture and hence a kind of lobby for a different curriculum" (p. 7).

Thus, the rupture with the curriculum premises prescribed in the *Yale Faculty Report*, which in the interim had been revealed to be incapable of meeting the challenges of an increasingly culturally polychromatic society, inaugurated a new era in the struggle for control of knowledge in schools. In 1892, the National Education Association's *Report of the Committee of Ten* emerged.

FITTING FOR LIFE IS FITTING FOR COLLEGE

Chairman of the Committee of Ten was Charles W. Eliot, president of Harvard University. This appointment, according to Kliebard (1995), recognized "the great influence [Eliot] had exercised not only in higher education but in elementary and secondary schools as well" (p. 9), and it foregrounded "the humanist interest group which, though largely unseen by professional educators in later periods, continued to exercise a strong measure of control over the American curriculum" (p. 9).

In the 1880s and 1890s, Eliot (1905a) later remarked, "no State in the American Union possesse[d] anything which can be properly called a system of secondary education" (p. 197). Moreover, "between the elementary schools and the colleges [was] a wide gap very imperfectly bridged by a few public high schools, endowed academies, college preparatory departments and private schools" (p. 197), which were not subject to common standards and did not portray a uniform matrix.

The Committee of Ten searched for uniformity in both "secondary school programs and in college admission prerequisites" (Eliot, 1894, p. 107; also cf. National Education Association, 1894). At the end of the nineteenth century, the chaos in secondary schooling was an unquestioned reality (Krug, 1969), and inherent in the need to improve secondary schools were both the creation of new schools and the implementation of common and more elevated standards for existing ones, so that colleges might find "in the school courses a firm, broad, and reasonably homogeneous foundation for their higher work" (Eliot, 1905a, p. 202). As Eliot declared, "A single common course of studies, tolerably well selected to meet the average needs, seems to most Americans a very proper and natural thing" (p. 11). Uniformity was thus the path for American schools to follow, although Eliot (1892, 1905a) was a fervent supporter of the system of elective studies in which "the choice offered to the student does not lie between liberal studies and professional or utilitarian studies, [since] all the studies which are open to [the student] are liberal and disciplinary, not narrow or special" (1905a, p. 13).

The Committee of Ten, after a project of coordinating and correlating the recommendations assembled from the various conferences (Eliot, 1894), concluded that all students, regardless of their destination, were entitled to the best ways of teaching the various subjects (Kliebard, 1995). Thus they proposed a curriculum matrix for secondary schooling based on four programs or courses of study that were separately designated as classical, Latin-scientific, modern languages, and English (Krug, 1969). It was assumed that education for life was education for college ('Report of the Committee on Secondary School Studies', 1894). One should not forget, however, that very few students at that time went to high school.

This document spurred a wide range of heated reactions (Sizer, 1964). The report's social importance was undeniable for some (Sachs, 1894), in that it not only showed that "the present weakness of our schools was due to the fact that there is very little substantial recognition of the sciences of education" (Parker, 1894a, p. 490) but also "disseminated a praiseworthy educational theory which attempted to create greater complicity between the secondary school system and colleges" (Eliot, 1894, pp. 105–10), thus illustrating the "progressive spirit in American education" (Bradley, 1894, p. 370). For others, however, "practically everything about the Committee of Ten has been controversial" (cf. Krug, 1969, p. 45), especially because there was something very strange about the unanimity behind the conclusions presented in the report (Sachs, 1894, p. 75). Whereas the report for some was "the first classic in American pedagogical literature" (National Education Association, 1894, p. 142), for others it not only revealed a conspiracy on the part of the colleges—and it needs to be seen as a rather too conservative document (Kasson, 1893–1894) in which teachers are the silent majority (Greenwood, 1894)—but also ignored "the art either as a historical inheritance or as a spirit-inspiring individual expression" (Clark, 1894, p. 376). The report was, DeGarmo (1894) claims, a "poor mess of pedagogical pottage" (p. 276) that sacrificed the dearest principles of social and political equality. The Committee of Ten was a victim of a well-spent popular psychology, which defined education merely as a preparation for the faculties of the mind (Schurman, 1894).

Moreover, the American Philological Association raised its voice against the report and formed a Committee of Twelve, which claimed that if the report were put into practice, standards would drop, and argued that secondary schools and colleges should oppose a scheme that threatened their own degradation (cf. Sizer, 1964). According to Small (1896),

> our business as teachers is primarily, therefore, not to train particular mental powers, but to select points of contact between learning minds

and the reality that is to be learned...Our business as teachers is to bring these perceptive contacts of pupils' minds with points of objective reality into true association with all the remainder of objective reality, i.e., we should help pupils, first, to see things, and second, to see things together as they actually exist in reality. (pp. 176–178)

Ultimately, if the Committee of Ten on the one hand manifested a profound belief in the creation of a standardized educational process and the need to institute the one best system (Marble, 1894), on the other it is a graphic example of the dynamics of gender, power, cultural segregation, and differentiation that are found in the discourse that structures the report. In the text, which indicates the major intentions of the Committee of Ten, profound conflicts between the various social factions circulate around what is promulgated as "legitimate culture" (Apple, 1999, p. 76). Quite naturally, "the kind of subject matter that was to be taught and many of the methods of teaching subject matter remained relatively limited to the cultural resources of dominant groups" (pp. 78–79).

The Report of the Committee of Ten is a strategic political document that tries to perfect the existing social order rather than to reform it. It is testament to the reorganization of cultural capital, to a redefinition of what is understood to be legitimate culture, and to a transformation of the curriculum that has inevitably brought about compromises and concessions.

According to Sisson (1910), no school in the United States remained unaffected by the report. Eliot (1905a), who for a period of time assumed leadership of the humanist movement, had the reputation of a reformer. While arguing for mental discipline, he was not exactly a defender of the established social order. In fact, says Kliebard (1995),

> Eliot differed from most mental disciplinarians in that he thought that any subject, so long as it were capable of being studied over a sustained period, was potentially a disciplinary subject...Although [he] did not emphasize education for the purpose of direct social reform, he remained optimistic with respect to human capabilities. The right selection of subjects along with the right way of teaching them could develop citizens of all classes endowed in accordance with the humanistic ideal. (p. 10)

Despite his influence, Eliot (1905a) ended up having to concede and compromise, especially in terms of substantive strategic options, such as the system of electives in which he staunchly believed. In this regard,

Eliot "had to settle for a choice of four different courses of study in the high school rather than the system of electives" (Kliebard, 1995, p. 10). According to Eliot, the great objective was much deeper than uniformity of programs for the students. The great aim was the search for uniformity of "topics, methods, and standards of attainment for any subjects that might be offered or taken" (Krug, 1969, p. 46), an objective that ended up "lay[ing] comparatively too much emphasis on facts and too little upon ideals" (cf. Clark, 1894, p. 375).

Five Windows of the Soul

The credibility of the *Report of the Committee of Ten* fell amid growing criticism of its recommendations. Its obsession with uniformity would lead, although Eliot denies it, to giving minimal attention to substantive issues that required much greater thought, such as those related to elementary schools. For example, as Krug (1969) writes, "the high school did not live unto itself. Its fortunes and destiny were linked not only to college but also to the elementary school" (p. 93). But the elementary schools, according to Krug, had their own issues and difficulties and were targets of repeated criticism, namely, the problems of waste and dropouts, which had been ignored by the National Education Association. Krug noted, moreover, that the "elementary school people felt they were hampered by domination from the high schools" (p. 94) and that they "were indeed the overworked and oppressed proletariat of the pedagogical enterprise" (p. 96). Therefore, an awareness of the need for a "special project of their own, comparable to the Committee of Ten in scope and especially in the possession of a substantial expense account" (p. 97), developed quite naturally.

It is in this context that, in 1893, the Committee of Fifteen on Elementary Education "was authorized to divide the members of the committee into three sub-committees—one on the training of teachers, one on the correlation of studies in elementary education, and one on the organization of city school systems" (Maxwell, 1895, p. 8). Of these three subcommittees, the one to attain greatest prominence was the one linked with the correlation of studies in elementary education (Marble, 1895). Harris was its chairman, and he was soon to be "wearing the mantle of the humanist position" (Kliebard, 1995, p. 14; cf. also Maxwell, 1895, p. 14).

Harris proved to be more sensitive than Eliot to social transformation. However, despite having embraced certain reform causes such as women's access to higher education (Harris, 1896), Harris gained a name in the education field as a great conservative. As Kliebard explains (1995), Harris's "lukewarm reaction to manual training [and] deep reservations about the virtues of child-study as a basis for determining what to teach," his clear opposition to vocational education, and his staunch support for a "curriculum constructed around the finest resources of Western civilization" (p. 15) confer on Harris the image of a man who would mark the education field as the great defender of humanist studies who mistrusted the predominance that the natural sciences were beginning to enjoy.

To implement his approach, Harris (1889a, pp. 96–97) stressed that "school education should open five windows of the soul (arithmetic, geography, grammar, history, literature)" five provinces that would remain the means by which the culture would be propagated and perpetuated to the majority of citizens (Kliebard, 1995).

Harris (1880) argued further that the course of study for schools and colleges should have two functions:

> It must furnish the best range of studies for discipline—or the subjective training of the powers of the mind, and it must present the objective world of nature and humanity in outlines complete enough to give to the youth a general survey of his relations to both aspects of the world. (p. 167)

Curiously, the convenient association that Harris established between formal and substantial development contributed to the antagonism and consequent dissociation vis-à-vis the doctrine of mental discipline proposed by Eliot, and to the reservations Harris expressed about Eliot's desired elective system.

According to Harris (1880), "as long as these electives are so arranged that the symmetry of the course of study is preserved, and each department is represented in a proper manner, there is no great injury to the pupil" (p. 173). Harris believed that the content of the subjects, rather than their form, was crucial in determining their value. By emphasizing the virtue of an effective focus on content of what was learned, instead of disciplinary value, Harris argued for a curriculum that would uphold the humanistic ideal (cf. Krug, 1969).

In 1895 in Cleveland, the Committee of Fifteen began to face severe criticism, principally with regard to the report that emerged from one of its subcommittees, *The Correlation of Studies in Elementary Education*. This criticism came in particular from a group of U.S. educators who, in 1892, had founded the National Herbart Society (cf. Krug, 1969); this occurred at the same meeting of the National

Education Association at which the Committee of Ten had been founded. Among the notables attending was "a 35-year old professor from the University of Chicago named John Dewey" (Krug, 1969, p. 107). By associating with names like De Garmo, Frank and Charles McMurry, Brown (who later would succeed Harris as commissioner of education), Butler, and Rice, Dewey affiliated himself with an intellectual movement that "had undertaken to challenge the existing order in American education" (Kliebard, 1999c, p. 69).

Like the other two subcommittees, the Subcommittee on the Correlation of Studies in Elementary Education (1895), which was headed by Harris, acted in response to a string of questions that had been submitted by educators "throughout the country whose opinions might be considered as of value" (Maxwell, 1895, p. 9). From the seventeen questions submitted, the fifth (in the order in which they appear in said report) alluded explicitly to the correlation of the studies: "What should be the purpose of attempting a close correlation of studies? a) to prevent duplication, eliminate non-essentials, and save time and effort? b) to develop the apperceiving power of the mind? c) to develop character—a purely ethical purpose?" (p. 11). In this manner, the subcommittee began to trace the concept of correlation, and as Kliebard (1995) stresses, Harris used the terms "correlation"—crucial in Herbartian curriculum theory—and "concentration," but not in the sense proposed by the Herbartians.

To the Herbartians, correlation was an umbrella concept that would promote the "interrelationship among the subjects themselves" and not, as mentioned by Harris, an instrument of "correlating the pupil with his spiritual and natural environment" (Kliebard, 1995, p. 16). With the concept of concentration, Harris similarly related it to his five windows of the soul; in other words, he maintained that the course of study in elementary school should be concentrated around its five provinces. For the Herbartians, the concept of concentration was in fact related to "a particular subject, such as history or literature, as a focal point for all subjects" (p. 16), thus achieving a certain unity in the curriculum they had conceptualized. The obvious adulteration of the meaning of these two Herbartian concepts—correlation and concentration—forced the movement to react against the report of the Subcommittee on the Correlation of Studies in Elementary Education (cf. De Garmo, 1895).

Frank McMurry (1895, p. 165), whose ironic sarcasm is obvious in his references to the report, observed that the subcommittee had "four points in their definition of correlation", stressing that the fourth still concurred with the "old idea of study, in which, from the adult standpoint, we decide that what the child will use as a man shall constitute his course" (p. 165). McMurry concluded by emphasizing that "knowledge is not primarily for the sake of knowledge, but for use, and the only condition under which the ideas will be active is that they shall appeal to the child and shall fit his nature. Child study, interest and apperception demand that the chief factor shall be the nature of the child" (p. 165).

Parker (1895) had a similarly reaction to the report: "The failure of this report is that the Herbartian doctrine and all other doctrines of concentration are ignored in their fundamental essentials" (p. 165)—which is precisely what the committee left out. Parker added that it is an old story, like the "play of Hamlet with Hamlet left out, or to put it a little more mildly, Hamlet kicked out" (p. 165).

Harris (1895) reacted to these interventions by reiterating that "to make Herbart of use in pedagogy, we must ignore his philosophy" (p. 166). He posed the following question: "Without educational values, what are you going to do with all your studies?" (p. 166). Aligning himself with Parker's stance, he added, "I am amazed to think that in appointing this committee there was any such notion as Parker's. Correlation has no business to mean what they make it to mean" (p. 166).

Charles McMurry (1895), responding to Harris, mentioned that there is no dictionary that offers an alternative synonym of correlation—"The analysis and isolation of subjects of study" (p. 166)—since there is no one other than Herbart who could have expressed his educational principles.

Dewey (1899) contended that the five windows of the soul proposed by Harris did not present any principle of cohesion between them. In other words, the symmetry that was so ardently defended by Harris—a study course that might mention the whole human experience—did not exist. For Dewey, the major objection to Harris's report was not specifically rooted in the foregrounding of Western civilization, but in the fact that such a concept did not appear to be sensitive to the way a child perceives his world and the role he performs in it. For Dewey (1895), the major problem facing education resided in the difficulty of reconciling psychological and social factors.

Notwithstanding the criticism directed at his report, Harris (1895) reiterated that his study had a scientific dimension that allowed him to claim that "child study is not the only thing" (p. 167). He expressed his concern with the problematic of correlation; that is, "to find what there is to be correlated, and then correlate it" (p. 167). Despite some criticism of the *Report of the Committee of Ten,* the *Report of the*

Fifteen was "an American idea against the world" (Winship, 1895, p. 128).

However, Krug (1969) notes that Herbartianism "was not the only evangelical movement at this time. One representing far greater numbers of people was the child study movement" (pp. 107–8), and with "Herbartianism losing its early potency as a reform movement" (Kliebard, 1995, p. 35), it was the child study movement that soon posed the most direct threat to the principles defended by Harris and by Eliot.

THE GREAT ARMY OF INCAPABLES

On the front lines of the criticism directed at the recommendations disseminated in the *Report of the Committee of Ten* one could find Hall, "a person who had early on assumed unquestioned leadership of the child study movement in the United States" (Kliebard, 1995, p. 11), and one who would come to reveal himself to be a "pivotal figure in the second of the four interest groups seeking to influence the curriculum at the end of the century, the developmentalists" (p. 11). Their ideology rested on the recognition of a natural order of child development, which they believed should serve as the scientific platform for determining what should be taught. Interesting to note is that developmentalists' initial criticisms of the report "did not involve adolescence or any aspect of child study, but were based on their admiration of secondary schools in Germany and France" (Krug, 1969, p. 116).

Hall (1894) believed that the child study movement rested on three major pillars: first, it benefited the teacher by educating, stimulating, refreshing, and reinvigorating him; second, it had the child as its referent and enabled teachers to adapt their methods to the children in order to make alterations in the course of the teaching-learning process that were positively received; and third, the child study movement was an added value for science, since it involved contact between the best science and the best education of the time. Furthermore, according to Hall, human development "followed the general psychonomic law which stated [that] ontogeny recapitulates phylogeny" (Perkinson, 1968, p. 188).

In his first great investigation, influenced significantly by Adams (1879) and Burnham (1897), Hall (1883) maintained that taking a systematized inventory of the contents of the minds of children would enable us to determine more systematically what should be taught in schools. In 1890, "the child study movement was [already] in full blast, enrolling thousands of disciples among teachers and others interested in education" (Krug, 1969, p. 110). It was consolidated in 1894, at the annual meeting of National Education Association. With Hall at the forefront, not only did "the cause of child study became identified with scientific and hence valid ways of addressing the great educational issues of the day" (Kliebard, 1995, p. 37; cf. Hall, 1892), but the "efforts of the humanists to preserve in the curriculum the great accomplishments of Western culture were increasingly being regarded as speculative and old-fashioned" (Kliebard, 1995, p. 37). Hall (1901a) criticized the Committee of Ten for the increased enrollment in Latin and the decline in physics enrollments; he also (1904a) accused the report of being constructed on the basis of three extreme fallacies.

First was the fallacy that all students should learn the same way and for the same period of time, independently of their hypothetical destiny. Hall (1904a) pointed to the fallacy of uniformity, noting that there is a "great army of incapables, shading down to those who should be in schools for the dullards or subnormal children" (p. 509). Second was the fallacy that all subjects are of equal importance and, therefore, should be taught in the same manner, which implies an overlapping priority of form over content. Third was the fallacy that preparation for college is essentially the same as preparation for life. In Hall's (1901b) opinion, the established educational order should be inverted so that "the college depends on the high school, and *not vice versa*. The latter should declare its independence, and proceed to solve its own problems in its own way" (p. 487).

Eliot (1905b) reacted to Hall's accusations by reiterating that the report's recommendations, "far from being fallacies, are sound and permanent educational principles, on which alone a truly democratic school system can be based" (p. 326).

Eliot argued that all students should learn the same way and for the same amount of time, independently of their hypothetical destiny. He stressed that among the various issues included in the agenda to be discussed at the different conferences, one was the following: "Should the subject be treated differently for pupils who are going to college, for those who are going to a scientific school, and for those who, presumably, are going to neither?" (cf. National Education Association, 1894). This issue was subjected to the same treatment as all the others by "ninety-nine honest and intelligent teachers," who unanimously declared that

> every subject which is taught at all in the secondary schools should be taught in the same way and to the same extent to every pupil so long as

he pursues it, no matter what the probable destination of the pupil may be, or at what point his education is to cease. (Eliot, 1905b, p. 328)

As for the second fallacy pointed out by Hall in the report—the assumption that all subjects are of equal importance if they are taught in the same manner—Eliot (1905b) counter-attacked by stating that "this dogma is nowhere explicitly stated in the Report of the Committee of Ten, [rather, it was] implied in some of the opinions expressed by the several Conferences and by the Committee" (p. 333). Finally, in response to the third fallacy Hall pointed out— the assumption that preparing for college is essentially the same as preparing for life—Eliot (1905b) also reiterated that such a doctrine was nowhere laid down in the *Report of the Committee of Ten*, or in the reports from several of the committee conferences.

Hall was the target of a great deal of criticism from a wide range of authors who worked in various sectors of the field of education. Dewey (1897) believed that the child study movement had created great expectations for its capacity to significantly transform curriculum practice; Judd (1909) argued that there was "so much mythology in Dr. Hall's books that one can hardly wonder at the reluctance of high-school teachers to read or follow their teachings" (p. 570); and Harris (1900) felt that the child study movement exposed itself to "the dangers of arrested development" (p. 455)—in other words, the children lost too much time studying something they had already learned.

Fundamentally, the major divergence between Harris and the child study movement was the fact that Harris defended a curriculum that stemmed from the nature of the actual child, whereas Hall interpreted the child study movement as a means of teaching a curriculum determined on other grounds. In other words, Harris was more worried about "the content of studies in relation to human experience and wisdom" (Krug, 1969, p. 112). Despite some criticism, Hall was able to earn the admiration of and have a strong influence on thousands of teachers (Lancaster, 1905; Shorey, 1909).

Paradoxically, although Hall "had covered himself in the armor of science, it is significant that his curriculum ideas were drawn, not so much from the scientific data so diligently collected by him and his fellow psychologists, as from his metaphysical, even mystical, assumptions about the alleged relationship between the stages in individual development and the history of the human race" (Kliebard, 1995, p. 38). It would be unwise to ignore how the power of slavery and eugenics interfered quite dynamically with the typology of the mainstream curriculum (cf. Popenoe and Johnson, 1918; Selden, 2000; Watkins, 2001, 2010; Winfield; 2010). Hall believed "that the child recapitulates in his or her development the stages that the whole human race traversed throughout the course of history" (Kliebard, 1995, p. 38; cf. Hall, 1904b). In essence, the issues addressed by Hall also swirled around the attempt to control the knowledge that should be disclosed via the curriculum.

The child study movement soon saw the beginning of its end, given its obvious impotence in significantly altering schooling practices. Hence, at the end of the penultimate and the beginning of the last decade of the nineteenth century, both Herbartianism and the child study movement "had lost their driving force" (Krug, 1969, p. 115). Moreover, due to the loss of credibility of the humanist perspectives defended by Eliot and Harris, coupled with the absence of sharpness in terms of an effective alteration of schooling practices, there developed an increasingly stronger belief in the need for education reform, having as background the efficiency and efficacy of the school system. Heading this new approach was a "young New York pediatrician," whose interest in prophylaxis had led him to some searching questions about the city schools (Cremin, 1964), and who had witnessed the memorable meeting at Cleveland where the confrontation between Harris and the Herbartians took place: his name was Rice.

THE SCIENTIFIC RAZOR BLADE

Returned from Germany in 1890, Rice undertook a survey of American elementary education "sponsored by the influential journal, *The Forum*" (Kliebard, 1995, p. 17). From state to state, from city to city, Rice noted that "public apathy, political interference, corruption and incompetence were conspiring to ruin the schools" (p. 4).

According to Rice (1969, p. 176), four elements exerted a profound influence on the conditions of schools:

> The public at large; it must unfortunately be said that in the large majority of instances the people take absolutely no active interest in their schools the boards of education, [since they] were elected according to whims; the superintendent and his staff [who] could be regarded as the central figures; [and] the teachers, [who were,] after all, the greatest problem.

The criticism directed at the first in a series of nine articles by Rice, published in *The Forum,* were soon forthcoming, especially from the "professional press—a reaction that ranged from chilling disdain to near-hysteria" (Cremin, 1964, p. 8). Some argued that Rice was not an authority because he lacked any experience in the classroom (Schneider, 1893), while others accused him of being a snobbish intellectual who, by means of radical analyses of university quality, had entirely foregone the notion of U.S. public education. While dealing with this criticism, Rice embarked on his next investigation, seeking comparative data for the reasons why certain schools were able to achieve significant levels of success while others were not, which would lead to a shift in the focus of his investigation. Rice (1912) made his intentions crystal clear: "Teachers and administrators must be made to do the right thing" (p. v).

Having defined the problems within the school system with "relative facility," Rice (1912) stressed that the level of crisis the education system had reached forced the imposition of a "scientific system of pedagogical management [that] would demand fundamentally the measurement of results in the light of fixed standards" (p. xv). He argued further:

> The school has but a single purpose, which is that of educating children. Consequently, in the strict sense, scientific management in education can only be defined as a system of management specifically directed toward the elimination of waste in teaching, so that the children attending the schools may be duly rewarded for the expenditure of their time and effort. (p. viii)

According to Rice (1912), there was a direct proportionality between time and results, which never should be belittled. Such proportionality would prove to be a polemical issue because, as Rice stated, educators could not reach a consensus on the two questions that dominated schooling practice: "How much time shall be devoted to a subject? and What result should be accomplished?" (p. 5).

Rice proceeded with his crusade, arguing loudly for scientific management of the schools, marked by criteria of efficiency and efficacy, and calling attention to the difficulties permeating rational education reform. For Rice (1912), "politics in school boards, incompetent supervision, insufficient preparation on the part of teachers [were not] the ultimate cause" (p. 20) of public indifference and obstacles to educational progress; they merely constituted "the symptoms of a much more deeply hidden disease which permits all sorts of havoc to be played with the schools" (p. 20). The nation needed a professional teacher-training program because the "incompetence and negligence" (Rice, 1969, p. 15) that permeated the teaching profession at the time was malignant.

According to Rice (1969), a school subjected to unscientific or mechanical management meant that it assumed as its principal function the practice of "crowding into the memory of the child a certain number of cut-and-dried facts—that is, that the school exists simply for the purpose of giving the child a certain amount of information" (p. 20). Conversely, "the aim of the new education was to lead the child to observe, to reason, and to acquire manual dexterity, as well as to memorize facts—in a word, to develop the child naturally in all his faculties, intellectual, moral, and physical" (p. 21).

Rice (1969, pp. 17–18) highlighted three general principles, which underlie his theory of scientific management:

> The school system must be absolutely divorced from politics in every sense of the word so that all the elements of the board of education do not feel obligated or coerced into giving opinions about what they think best for the school. The supervision of the schools must be properly directed and thorough, [which translated into] creasing the professional strength of the teachers. Teachers must constantly endeavor to grow both in professional and in general intellectual strength.

Rice, both despite and because of being associated with Herbartianism, diverged from the perspectives disseminated by Eliot and Harris and increasingly distanced himself from Hall. Rice ended up becoming the leader of the "third of the major curriculum interest groups that was to appear just before the turn of the century, the social efficiency educators" (Kliebard, 1995, p. 20), a doctrine that, by its intention to depoliticize the education system, seemed to cast a common shadow with the notion of survival of the fittest, a leitmotiv of social Darwinism.

THE DENIZENS OF SLUMS VERSUS THE GRADUATES OF HARVARD

The last decade of the nineteenth century was highly significant in the development of U.S. education. It was an epoch in which the field of pedagogy witnessed the emergence of various profoundly significant works—*Principles of Psychology* by James, *Talks on Pedagogics* by Parker, *Animal Intelligence* by Thorndike, and *The School and Society* by John Dewey—which ultimately expressed the many faces of an era that strove to construct a large theoretical field for an increasingly urgent pedagogical transformation, and which had, in the thinking of Spencer, one of the great, if not the principal, motivators. As mentioned previously, Spencer's thinking and social Darwinism infuse the *Report of the Committee of Ten*. Fundamentally, Spencer (1969) introduced the concept of survival of the fittest, amplifying its significance and conferring to it a link to human civilization.

At the front line of challenges to the social Darwinist perspective was Ward. According to Ward, "the laissez-faire position that the social Darwinists had advocated was...a corruption of Darwinian theory because human beings had to develop the power to intervene intelligently, in whatever were blind forces of nature, and in that power lay the course of social progress" (Kliebard, 1995, p. 21). Ward maintained that social Darwinists ignored "the crucial fact that with the emergence of mind the very character of evolution changes" (Cremin 1964, p. 96), since "the mind is *telic*," [it] has purposes, [it] can plan [in other words, it is able to supplant] the relatively static phase of genetic evolution with a new dynamic phase" (p. 96).

In this sense, Ward (1883) maintained that "moral progress would largely depend on the intellectual direction of the forces of human nature into channels of human advantage" (p. 216). Spencer would transform his theory of knowledge evolution into a principle of curriculum (Kliebard, 1999b) in which "the genesis of knowledge in the individual must follow the same course as the genesis of knowledge in the race" (p. 6). In contrast, Ward saw education as the great panacea for all social ulcers (Cremin, 1964) and believed that social progress would be achieved by the construction of a just and adequate education system (Kliebard, 1995). Moreover, Ward (1883) maintained that social inequality was merely a reflex of the misdistribution of the social inheritance. Unlike Spencer and the social Darwinists, Ward saw public education not as a cause of the erosion of parental responsibility, but as the "only feasible device for turning evolution to the larger social good" (Cremin, 1964, p. 98).

By understanding education as a powerful instrument of social transformation, Ward distanced himself similarly from the humanist movement in general and, most particularly, from Eliot; however, it is important to note that, just like Eliot, Ward demonstrated an unwavering belief in the power of human intelligence. In addition to denoting the nonexistence of class variations in the intellect, Ward (1893) characterized himself as a paladin of egalitarianism, fervently defending education as an instrument of diffusion and consolidation of social harmony. He strongly criticized the doctrine of the survival of the fittest and declared that the "denizens of slums are not inferior in talent to the graduates of Harvard College" (p. 290). According to Kliebard (1995), Ward proved to be not only the "prophet of the welfare state in the twentieth century" (p. 23) but also "the principal forerunner of the fourth and last of the major interest groups that were struggling for control of the curriculum in decades ahead, the social meliorists" (p. 23). In the words of Ward (1893), in social meliorism was the remedy for the increasingly acute social dilemmas, "which could not be explained as mere ethical or moral conflicts" (p. 290) but instead needed to be explained as resulting from the profound and complex friction in the social fabric. Ward attacked the discourse of segregation, the generator of social injustice, which was an increasingly complex challenge, given the strength and acceptance the Spencerian doctrine seemed to enjoy.

Small (1896), like Ward, perceived education as an instrument of vanguardism for social amelioration and was sure that it would place the forthcoming generation in contact with three main realities: interdependence—the conviction that in an industrial society nobody survives alone; cooperation—correlated with interdependence; and progress—the awareness that new people and new events require new social approaches.

In essence, Small (1896) upheld a broad perspective of education in which "the rational center is the student himself" (p. 178) and pedagogy was seen as the science that would help the children organize their contacts with reality. Consequently, the teacher was perceived not as a leader of children but as a maker of society. For Ward (1883), a fundamental corrosive truth began to crystallize, a truth that is perhaps as basic as the actual concept of formal education's social segregation: "Intellectually considered, social differentiation has always been far in advance of social integration" (p. 397). By striving arduously for a curriculum that could lead to social transformation, thus creating the necessary equilibrium and social harmony, Ward assumed a borderline position in the curriculum debate at the end of the nineteenth century. He stressed that in the distribution of knowledge there rests all social reform, and that this reform should be an inherent function of the state. Ward and Small deserve credit for having transformed "the harsh Spencerian doctrine of social Darwinism into a full-fledged philosophy of meliorism" (Cremin, 1964, p. 99).

In considering the general tensions within what has been called the curriculum field since the end of the nineteenth century, I have highlighted the roles of specific curriculum pioneers—Eliot, Harris, Hall, Rice, Ward, and Small, among others—and the conflicts in which they were engaged. We will next examine how these particular embryonic tensions expanded and were disseminated, and how they influenced the field throughout the twentieth century. In so doing, we will undertake another deep exegesis of the impact of Bobbitt's and Charters's and Snedden's scientific curriculum fever, the importance of the civil rights movement and the romantic critics in the struggle for the U.S. curriculum, the emergence of Tyler, and subsequent developments that challenged Tyler's dominant position. We will also build a path along which to analyze the emergence of a specific critical progressive curriculum river, in which the works of Dewey, Counts, Rugg, and others cannot be marginalized.

CHAPTER 3

A SIMPLISTIC TOOL FOR A LETHAL PHENOMENON

At the dawn of the twentieth century, the United States of America was pulsating with the rhythms of a multifaceted transformation of the social fabric. This transformation, already begun in the last decades of the nineteenth century, was spurred on by a new industrialism—and, consequently, by the new dynamics of capitalist exploration—that not only brought about "a transformation in America's economic arrangements and in its social institutions [but also] precipitated a moral crisis" (Kliebard, 1999a, p. 3). In fact, "westward expansion and the growth of industry, agriculture and population put vastly increased demands upon existing schools and required the building not only of new schools, but of whole new educational systems" (Pulliam, 1991, p. 83); in other words, "society demand[ed] much more of the schools than ever before" (Good, 1956, p. 17).

In response to these successive changes, which were occurring at an alarming rate, an awareness of the need for a national movement to train manual laborers began to consolidate. Such a movement had already begun to emerge around 1876, propelled by the Russian tool exhibit at the Philadelphia Centennial Exposition (Cremin, 1964). We are confronted by a movement that was, in fact, emerging as a cure for delinquent children, children of the poorer class, immigrants and racial minorities, and as the "socially correct" answer for how to integrate the American Indians and African-Americans who continued to work for the actualization of the freedom they nominally had won in 1865. In this crusade, three stand out: Armstrong, who maintained that manual training was a way to correct the character defects of African-Americans; Washington, who believed that manual training gave credible economic independence to the African-American community; and Du Bois, who argued that manual training had abandoned its true obligation—to contribute to social equality.

At the turn of the twentieth century, U.S. education initiated a new cycle in the social project of Americanization, which was in accordance with the new and volatile demands imposed by an industrialism that was taking its first steps. This "project" obviously ran counter to the humanist thrust supported by Harris and Eliot. The former perceived manual training as dangerous, given the fact that it served "to unite the critics of the educational system already existing" (Harris, 1889b, p. 417). Harris categorically refused to accept that manual training had the same importance as the so-called subjects of science and literature. Eliot did not believe that vocationalism—the last stage in the manual training process—warranted mention in his *Report of the Committee of Ten* (1894). This was one aspects of his position that received a great deal of criticism, although Eliot would admit much later that manual training constituted "a very useful element in the curriculum" ((1908, p. 10).

However, aware of the enormous power held by the humanist view and conscious that Harris would not easily relinquish his "windows of the soul," Woodward (1885, p. 614) considered it important not to annihilate traditional education. He thus demonstrated his awareness that it was imperative to highlight the fact that a " 'new' education includes the 'old,' " keeping the essential parts of traditional education intact while advancing an educational structure that incorporated two areas: "the wing of natural science which the humanistic curriculum had undervalued [and] manual training which completes the old education" (Kliebard, 1995, p. 113). Furthermore, Woodward believed that a compromise with Harris was not out of the question, especially since his "full-fledged pedagogical rationale for manual training" (Kliebard, 1999a, p. 6) was powerful "in furnishing the knowledge and experience [and] in establishing the major premises essential to logical reasoning" (Woodward, 1890, p. 204), an opinion that is corroborated by Butler (1888), for whom "manual training is mental training through the hand and eye" (p. 379).

Notwithstanding the criticism, manual training was seen as a way to establish a bridge between the past and the future. However, this was a movement that had been constructed around ambiguity. For example, whereas some defended manual training as being anchored to a specific moral code—Armstrong's case—and others assumed that the fundamental character of manual training was to lead to better economic conditions—Washington's case—the fact is that others who "were capable of crafting their messages to their audiences" (Kliebard, 1995, p. 22) also contributed to the ambiguity of the movement. This permeability would, in fact, contribute to its wide acceptability. Thus, "manual training as a curriculum reform achieved first respectability, then prominence, and finally acceptance in the councils of educational leaders and with the public generally because it was associated with moral redemption and pedagogical renewal, but the economic message was never absent" (p. 24). The seeds for the "social efficiency ideal" (p. 27) were thus planted.

However, as Prosser (1912) stressed, "manual education has not met and cannot meet the needs of industrial education" (p. 928). Faced by constantly changing social demands, manual training evolved, step-by-step, into vocational education, "the most dramatic and...the most far-reaching of the successful curriculum innovations" (Kliebard, 1995, p. 111). While the first, as an educational reform, had the virtue of not forgetting the past—"the era of the independent artisan and the dignity of the work associated with pre-industrial America" (Kliebard, 1999a, p. 24)—and of looking to the future—"the society that was being wrought by the new industrialism" (p. 24)—the second "projected a distinctly more explicit commitment to economic benefits both to the individual and to the nation" (p. 25) without ignoring the restoration of the virtues of the past and the reinforcement of certain traditional images. The appeal to vocationalism increased progressively and, quite naturally, by 1895,[1] in the darkest pits of the economic depression that had exploded two years earlier, the National Association of Manufacturers (NAM) emerged, which, along with the American Federation of Labor and the National Society for the Promotion of the Industrial Education, would place vocational education in the center of the curriculum debate. In this context, NAM "made school policy a centerpiece of their deliberations" (Kliebard, 1995, p. 117), which, by following the German model, was nearer to what some enterprises such as General Electric and Allis Chalmers had already begun doing around 1870. These corporations transformed worker training with a process of vocational formation that was organized and directed toward the needs of the actual enterprise (Nelson, 1975).

Vocational education would endure moments of criticism and upheaval similar to what happened with manual training. Although most people professed to be convinced of the German model's effectiveness as applied to the U.S. reality, explosive conflicts between employers, employees, and unions resulted from the fact that vocationalism was controlled by the employers; that salaries were reduced because of the greater availability of qualified manual labor; that the workplace was increasingly insecure; and because of the constant need for workers to requalify. Furthermore, there were conflicts between the supporters of industrial and of agricultural education, and it became important to stress the social and economic costs that such reforms would entail, especially since "vocational education has always been more expensive than the ordinary types of education" (Snedden, 1912, p. 126).

In 1906, the Commission on Industrial and Technical Education (the Douglas Commission) emerged to "investigate the needs for education in the different grades of skill," declaring that the education system proved inadequate to the "modern industrial and social conditions" (Report of the Massachusetts Commission on Industrial and Technical Education, 1906). Fundamentally crystallized at the commonsense level was the notion that the "public school curriculum with its traditional emphasis on academic subjects was meeting the needs of only a small minority of youth" (Kliebard, 1999a, p. 32), thereby concluding that "traditional education did not need to be supplemented; it needed to be replaced, at least for large numbers of America's schoolchildren" (p. 35).

Thus, federal support was needed to finance the new teaching structure, and "the question of federal aid to vocational education, the joining of industrial trade training with farmers' interests was almost a political necessity" (Kliebard, 1995, p. 124).

The first steps toward implementing a national system of industrial education were thus taken, born of a strategy promoted by the National Society for Promotion of Industrial Education, which, having formed a coalition, incorporated the interests of the National Association of Manufacturers, the American Federation of Labor, the American Bankers Association, the United States Chamber of Commerce, the National Metal Trade Association, and even local unions (Fones-Wolf, 1983). In 1917, as a consequence of the compromises reached by these various societal forces, the Smith-Hughes Act was passed. The act guaranteed economic federal support for "vocational agriculture as well as trade and industrial education and home economics" (Kliebard, 1999a, p. 113). As Kliebard (1995) noted, "With money, powerful lobby groups, energetic leadership in high places and a sympathetic public, vocational educational was well on its way to becoming the most successful curriculum innovation of the twentieth century" (p. 124).

In the forefront of the vocationalist trend, in addition to Finney, Ellwood, and Peters, we come across Snedden and Prosser, respectively commissioner and deputy commissioner of education in Massachusetts. Prosser, as we shall see later on, would later position himself as a pivotal figure in the life adjustment education movement.

To Snedden (1925), the "curriculum [was], of course, simply a well-documented series of plans and specifications expressive of the educational purposes of policy-makers on behalf of a specified group of learners" (pp. 259–260). The vocational educational movement would come to align itself perfectly with Snedden's understanding of the school "as an agency of social control with social efficiency as the all-inclusive aim for education" (Drost, 1967, p. 81). Snedden noted the importance of understanding the term "objective," arguing that it should imply "not merely direction, aim, or qualitative character of expected attainment, but also amounts, degrees of excellence, or other quantitative measures of the same" (p. 54). As a curriculum innovation, the roots of Sneddism can be found in the thought of Spencer, Ross, and Ward—although Snedden rejected Ward's optimistic vision, according to which "knowledge would mitigate the unequal condition among men" (p. 28). Snedden accepted, as did Ward (1883), the development of intellect in the educational process as subordinate to the acquisition of knowledge.

It is in Dutton, who in 1908 published *The Administration of Public Education in the United States*—an extensive work that would be prominent in the first two decades of the twentieth century—that Snedden identifies the four major objectives of education: physical well-being, moral and social efficiency, personal culture, and vocational education (Drost, 1967). Snedden, who saw "education, more than ever, as a kind of 'treatment' rather than the transmission of the cultural heritage" (p. 77), believed that the "the ultimate aim of education" was "the attainment of the greatest degree of efficiency," an efficiency that could only be achieved through the school. To Snedden, as for Spencer, science was like a religion (cf. Bode, 1924).

The demand for vocational education, according to Snedden (1910), "is rooted in the social and economic changes of the age [and] vocational education is not in conflict with liberal education, but is a supplemental form, and may be expected to reinforce it" (pp. 81–82). Thus he defined a liberal education as "that which aims to broaden the intellectual and emotional horizon of the individual…and may be interpreted as that which concerns itself with the consuming, as opposed to the productive process in life" (pp. 4–5). He continued, stating that vocational education "is older than liberal education, for the simple reason that men have always had to have occupations involving more or less skill, by which they could earn a livelihood" (p. 9), and that it is much more directed toward production rather consumption and therefore presents distinct objectives (Snedden, 1920). The function of the school, Snedden concluded, is not necessarily trans-formative (Snedden, 1934).

Snedden (1921) considered vocationalism one of the premises for solidifying a democratic society, in that it is not only a socio-educational proposition that is sensitive to the vocations adopted by each individual, but also guarantees the effective specialization of a citizen. The best work of our age "is that which is dominated by the tendency toward specialization...The division of labor is the key to modern efficiency" (Snedden, 1905, pp. 301–305). In essence, Snedden upheld the desirability and the feasibility of uniformity with an increasingly greater flexibility in the curriculum field. In other words, the "system of 'fitting for a probable destination'" was Snedden's definition of "flexibility," which would imply that mobility "rested in the more adequate preparation one possessed for one's place in life"—in short, in "vocational efficiency" (Drost, 1967, pp. 121–122).

However, vocational education would encounter significant resistance, from movements in the educational field in general and in the curriculum field in particular. Although Dewey "never outlined an explicit plan for vocational education, nor did he write extensively on the subject" (Kliebard, 1999a, p. 232), he was opposed to the fact that the vocationalization of the curriculum seemed to "undermine the most important function of education, the fostering of intellectual and moral growth." Moreover, Dewey (1916) proposed that a curriculum directed only toward technical efficiency makes education "an instrument of perpetuating unchanged the existing order of society instead of operating as a means of its transformation" (p. 369). Dewey (1915) added that "the kind of vocational education I am interested is not one which will 'adapt' workers to the existing industrial regime; I am not sufficiently in love with the regime for that" (p. 42). Moreover, for Bagley (1914), Flagg Young (1915), and Du Bois and Dill (1912), the vocationalization of the curriculum was an instrument for perpetuating and reinforcing race, gender, and class divisions.

Bagley (1914), although a believer in social efficiency, disagreed with Snedden in that he perceived the dichotomy of liberal/consumer education versus vocational/producer education as simplistic divisions with a restricting perspective. He proposed a distinction between "specific education and general education" (Drost, 1967, p. 130). Hullfish (1924) similarly believed that Snedden had completely mixed up the true sense of the meaning of democracy and of democratic education by fragmenting liberal education from vocational education, thereby failing to perceive the mind as a unit.

Finney and Ellwood, who shared so many points of view with Snedden, would come to take a critical position as well. Finney (1917) moved away from the essentialist and segregationist perspective of the school, arguing that Snedden should fight for the dilution of social injustice and for the consolidation of a democratic culture. Ellwood perceived the foundation of the educational objectives proposed by Snedden as reductive and restricted to "practical educational problems" (Drost, 1967, p. 136). Kilpatrick argued that Snedden's efficiency-based centralism led to the construction of an educational atmosphere described as a "leveling, stupefying, deadening drift toward uniformity and bureaucracy" (p. 136). Bode (1924) found Snedden's proposal reductive and undemocratic; he felt that the separation of the vocational from culture was a lethal plan that would lead to the multiplication of a race/class/gender elite. Furthermore, Bode (1927) refused to accept that the scientific approach was the only valid source to determine educational aims, stressing that democracy should be understood as "a progressive humanization of the social order" (p. 14). To Bode, instead of the curriculum being limited to scientifically determined objectives as proposed by Snedden, it was important that the curriculum did not ignore the "historical perspective" (p. 119). Counts (1930) associated himself with the perspective proposed by Bode, denouncing the selectiveness of Snedden's curriculum proposal, arguing that the "school will become an instrument for the perpetuation of the existing social order rather than a creative force in society" (p. 126). Snedden (1935) replied to this round of criticism soon thereafter, arguing that the society, the school, and the curriculum were going through a complicated period: "The times are out of joint. America is sick" (p. 48).

With the galloping advance of industrialization, vocationalism was to evolve into an increasingly social efficiency–based doctrine. In the words of Judd (1923), "Business has in recent years demanded sweeping changes in education in order to prepare more efficient workers" (p. 281). Furthermore, "business is eager to see a revision of the school curriculum" (p. 287). According to Davenport (1909), "The most significant educational fact today is that men of all classes have come to look upon education as a thing that will better their condition; and they mean by that, first of all, something to make their labor more effective and more profitable; and second, they mean something that will enable them to live fuller lives" (p. 11). Fundamentally, as reiterated by Krug (1964), "the spirit of reform in American society demanded an explicit social mission for the schools, and many sought to supply its definition" (p. 245). As forewarned by Kliebard (1995),

"Of the varied and sometimes frenetic responses to industrialism and to the consequent transformation of American social institutions, there was one that emerged clearly dominant, both as social ideal and as an educational doctrine. It was social efficiency" (p. 77). Quite naturally, "efficiency became more than a byword in the education world: it became an urgent mission" (p. 77), one that runs through the metamorphoses of the premises of Ross's and Taylor's doctrines.

Ross "provided Snedden with the doctrine of social control" (Drost, 1967, p. 28). Ross argued that "society is always in the presence of the enemy, and social control is, in a significant sense, a compilation of the weapons of self protection in the arsenal of society... Education was one of the most effective of those weapons in society's arsenal" (Kliebard, 1995, p. 80). Furthermore, according to Ross, the U.S. school was infected by an intellectual bias that prevented the assumption of an efficient system of social control.

Taylor personifies the other ingredient of the social efficiency ideology: "efficiency itself" (Kliebard, 1995, p. 81). Actually, Taylor believed in social efficiency as a mechanism, which permitted the reduction of human error and the consequent increase in production (cf. Taylor, 1911). In fact, and according to King (1913), "no discussion of education for social efficiency would be complete without some attempt to view it in its relation to these broad problems... race-welfare and race-improvement" (p. 282). As Bobbitt (1918) argues, "Never before have civilization and humanization advanced so swiftly" (p. i).

Social efficiency was thus presented through a rigorous discourse, especially since, as Taylor and Ross both emphasized, the human being has a natural tendency for laziness that must be fought mercilessly (cf. Copley, 1923). According to Emerson (1917), "This national inefficiency, this national wastefulness, this national squandering of current and future material" (p. 10) can be remedied by means of recourse to the principles of efficiency. In the words of Davenport (1909), "No man... educated or uneducated, has a right to be useless" (p. 15). Here we find a social movement that began to have repercussions in various sectors of society. Actually, as documented by Wilentz (1997), "what began as a blueprint for rearranging authority in the workplace turned into a design for modern living itself" (p. 32).

It was through a belief in the struggle against wastefulness that the doctrines of Ross and Taylor begin to permeate the education system. Bennett (1917) perceived that the combat against wastefulness in the schools entailed the "reorganization of the curriculum by the elimination of all antiquated materials and all that is not essentially practical" (p. 215). Education for efficiency is not exactly a "sentiment, it is business; it is not charity, it is statesmanship" (Davenport, 1909, p. 12). In 1918, "social efficiency as a curriculum theory was almost at its zenith" (Kliebard, 1995, p. 99), and in 1920, the U.S. curriculum was vocationalized and the background issue was no longer what form would be taken on by the curriculum but who would control it. Kliebard (1968) stated that "1918 was a vintage year in curriculum,

> not only because of the appearance of Franklin Bobbitt's *The Curriculum*, which was the first full-length book on curriculum, but also because of Alexander Inglis' brilliant *Principles of Secondary Education*, which, although not exclusively a curriculum book, was concerned primarily with curriculum questions. In 1918 too, the Teachers College Record published an article by one of the younger members of the Teachers College faculty, William Kilpatrick. That article, "The Project Method," was later to have a profound effect on the activity movement in curriculum. Finally, the Commission on the Reorganization of Secondary Education issued its Cardinal Principles of Secondary Education with its widely quoted seven aims, a report which set the fashion for the consideration of curricular objectives. (p. 71)

Along the same lines of thought, one finds Schubert (1986), for whom "the year 1918 marks a time of certainty that the curriculum field was likely to be quite permanent on the education horizon" (p. 75), thanks to three major contributions: "William Herald Kilpatrick published an article entitled *The Project Method* in *Teachers College Record*...the publication of *The Curriculum* by Franklin Bobbitt...and NEA's Commission on the Reorganization of Secondary Education (1918) report entitled *Cardinal Principles of Secondary Education*" (p. 75). Also noteworthy is that for Tyler (1987), "the first time curriculum-making was viewed as a profession was in the twenty-sixth *Yearbook of the National Society for the Study of Education*. Both parts, one and two, in 1927, were devoted to curriculum-making theory and practice. That's where it first became a recognized specialization" (p. 389). Notwithstanding the fact that many authors credit Bobbitt with being the author of *The Curriculum*, which dates the birth of the curriculum field, the fact is that the constitution of the curriculum as a "self-conscious field of study" actually does not owe itself exclusively to this or to that other work, to this or to that other author, but to a combination of studies, works, intellectuals, and social events that would take determining steps toward what would constitute the curriculum field in the twentieth century.

In the first two decades of the twentieth century, the explosion of secondary school students "who had no aspirations to college attendance...led to increasing interest in finding principles for curriculum organization based on perceived student needs rather than on the logical organization of the academic disciplines" (Cruikshank, 2000, p. 178). The "break came with the 1918 report Cardinal Principles of Secondary Education" (p. 178), which was "a major landmark in secondary education in United States" (Kliebard, 1995, p. 96). The document—prepared by a commission led by "Snedden's protégé, Kingsley" (p. 97), a mathematics professor—is "perhaps the most widely [and powerful] list of educational aims...based on Spencer's approach" (Levine & Ornstein, 1981, p. 333). According to Pulliam (1991), the seven "cardinal principles" became standard objectives for teachers, school boards, and administrators: "(1) health, (2) command of fundamental processes, (3) worthy home membership, (4) vocation, (5) civic education, (6) worthy leisure, and (7) ethical character" (Commission on the Reorganization of Secondary Education, 1918, pp. 11–15). As is highlighted by Kliebard (1995), Kingsley "produced the document that proved to be the capstone of the quarter-century of furious efforts at curriculum reform that began with the Committee of Ten" (p. 97). In essence, Kingsley translated the conception of general education proposed by Snedden (vocational education for the producer and liberal education for the consumer) into "the famous seven aims [that] followed in rough outline the conclusions of the effort of Spencer of more than a half century before to base the curriculum on categories of vital life activities" (Kliebard, 1999b, p. 20). Snedden (1919) would nevertheless come to criticize the report, classifying it as "almost hopelessly academic" (p. 522), having been produced in an atmosphere of "serene scholastic aloofness" (p. 522), and accusing the commission of being concerned with "the liberal education of the youth" (p. 526).

Three years after the *Douglas Commission Report,* Ayres published *Laggards in Our Schools.* Unlike the *Douglas Report,* which expressed some concern for the well-being of 25,000 children to whom school meant little or nothing, Ayres's (1909) study concerned itself with retardation and elimination of waste from an efficiency perspective. The major concerns expressed in the *Douglas Report* were reduced in Ayres's treatise to a logic of "simple efficiency and cost-effectiveness" (Kliebard, 1995, p. 89). The reduction of waste required the application of standards used in industry (Ayres, 1909). As a curative measure, Ayres elaborated an index of efficiency "by which school systems could measure their rates of productivity as a prelude to curriculum and structural change" (Kliebard, 1999a, p. 51).

A year after the publication of Taylor's *Scientific Management Comprising Shop Management*, Bobbitt (1912) published "The Elimination of Waste in Education," an article that conveyed the importance of scientific management to schooling. Bobbitt described how Taylor's principles were applicable to the model drawn by Wirt, whom Bobbitt described as an educational engineer. In addition to relating scientific management to time management, Bobbitt stressed that Taylor's fourth principle—"work up the raw material into the finished product for which it is best adapted"—could be applied to education in general and to Wirt's model in particular. Bobbitt (1912) argued that educating "the individual according to his capabilities [required] that the materials of the curriculum be sufficiently various to meet the needs of every individual in a community; and that the course of training and study be sufficiently flexible that the individual can be given just things he needs" (p. 269). Wirt, a former student of Dewey's in Chicago, attempted to construct a school model in accordance with the principles proposed by Dewey (1900), in which the school was understood as an "embryonic community life, active with types of occupations that reflect the life of the larger society and permeated throughout with the spirit of art, history and science" (p. 44).

Bobbitt theorized that

> if the school were a factory, the child raw material, the ideal adult the finished product, the teacher an operative, the supervisor a foreman, and the superintendent a manager, then the curriculum could be thought of as whatever processing the raw material (the child) needed to change him into the finished product (the desired adult). (Seguel, 1966, p. 80)

In 1918, Bobbitt published *The Curriculum,* in which he insisted that "it was not enough to develop new curricula: there was also a need to learn more about how new curricula can best be developed" (McNeil, 1977, p. 287).

Bobbitt (1913), one of the proponents of the social efficiency ideology, saw the school as a space for the production of individuals, just like a factory. He proclaimed that "education is a shaping process as much as the manufacture of steel rails; the personality is to be shaped and fashioned into desirable forms" (p. 12). He viewed education as "a social process...the process of recivilizing or civilizing anew, each new generation...and society's performance of this recivilizing function we call education" (Bobbitt, 1925, p. 453). To Bobbitt (1924), the more prominent characteristics of man are not "his memory reservoir, whether filled or unfilled, but action, conduct, and behavior" (p. 45). The curriculum developer has, consequently, two important functions to perform. She or he must first determine the finished products the consumer market desires, and then determine the most efficient way to produce them. These functions are intimately linked to the notion of standards control, which is referred to in the first two of the eleven principles of management proposed by Bobbitt (1913): "(1) definite qualitative and quantitative standards must be determined for the product and (2) where the material that is acted upon by the labor processes passes through a number of progressive stages on its way from the raw material to the ultimate product, definite qualitative and quantitative standards must be determined for the product at each of these stages" (p. 11). In other words, the curriculum developer must act as a social agent who determines the needs of society, and the final product of schooling must coincide with those needs. Consequently, Bobbitt added, "the standards must of necessity be determined by those that use the product, not by those who produce it" (p. 35); in other words, "standards are to be found in the world of affairs, not in the schools" (p. 35).

In 1922, Bobbitt published *How to Make a Curriculum*, wherein he enumerated more than 800 objectives and activities connected with the needs of students, such as the "ability to care for teeth, eyes, nose and throat; ability to keep the heart and blood vessels in normal working conditions, [as well as] spelling and grammar" (pp. 14–28). Fundamentally, Bobbitt (1918) understood the importance of the curriculum-making process as the first step in the implementation of efficient curriculum management: "We need principles of curriculum making...We had not learned that the studies are means not ends" (p. 283). According to Schubert (1986), Bobbitt advocated that "the curriculum should be formulated...by analyzing activities of adult life and transferring them into behavioral objectives" (p. 75), a process that would come to be known as activity analysis.

Bobbitt elaborated a method that essentially helped to define the curriculum-making process as a step-by-step approach: "The first step in curriculum-making...is to separate the broad range of human experience into major fields;...the second step is to break down the fields into their more specific activities;...the third step is to derive the objectives of education;...the fourth step is to select from the list of objectives those which are to serve as the basis for planning pupil activities; [and] the fifth step is to lay out the kinds of activities, experiences and opportunities involved in attaining the objectives" (McNeil, 1977, p. 290).

As Bobbitt (1918) explained,

> the curriculum may, therefore, be defined in two ways: it is the entire range of experiences, both undirected and directed, concerned in unfolding the abilities of the individual; it is the series of consciously directed training experiences that the schools use for completing and perfecting the unfoldment. Our profession uses the term usually in the latter sense. But as education is coming more and more to be seen as a thing of experiences, and as the work-and-play-experiences of the general community life are being more and more utilized, the line of demarcation between directed and undirected experience is rapidly disappearing. Education must be concerned with both, even though it does not direct both. (p. 43)

To Bobbitt, the curriculum clearly was a "mosaic of full-formed human life" (p. 43).

Charters (1923) similarly perceived the curriculum as a series of objectives that students must achieve through a series of learning experiences. However, "it was through the improvement of teaching that Charters became interested in the curriculum, unlike Bobbitt, [for whom it was] through the improvement of the management of education" (Seguel, 1966, p. 94). Charters "analyzed the life activities for their knowledge content, not for needed human abilities as did Bobbitt" (p. 94). Although he delineated a method of curriculum-making that was very similar to Bobbitt's, the fact is that Charters would come to diverge from Bobbitt with his emphasis on "ideals and systemized knowledge in determining the content of curriculum" (McNeil, 1977, p. 291). Charters's (1923) ideal curriculum combined ideals and activities and, unlike Bobbitt, he paid special attention to knowledge in his method of curriculum-making.

Charters (1901) denounced the crisis of the curriculum, appealing to a reform in accordance with the principles upheld by the doctrine of social efficiency, namely, what was useless should be removed from the curriculum and replaced with what would be socially useful. Charters argued that the survival of certain knowledge depended on the fact that that same knowledge met human needs, which entailed the development of a rigorous method of acquiring that knowledge. In Kliebard's (1968) words, "The modus operandi that became associated with the major curriculum leaders like Bobbitt and Charters can easily be identified as activity analysis, but beyond the technical process lay a social doctrine sometimes vigorously proclaimed, sometimes half expressed. The doctrine was social efficiency" (p. 75), which would come to impose on the curriculum the need for school subjects to have social utility. Consequently, the ideology of social efficiency rested on the curriculum dichotomy of school subjects: "the academic and the practical" (p. 77).

Nevertheless, advocates of social efficiency would face extensive criticism. According to Bode (1927), the social efficiency ideology failed to present an ideal alternative for the education system. He believed that the proposals of Bobbitt, Charters, and Snedden silenced "the ideal of progressively changing [the] social order" (p. 79). Bobbitt, Charters, and Snedden perspectives express a direct application of Taylor's principle to education and a perspective of sociological determination of the educational objectives, aspects that are questionable since, as Bode (1927) highlights, democracy should not lead to schooling which only meets existing social conditions. According to Bode (1927) democracy is the progressive humanization of social order. Counts (1930), like Bode, condemned the way the selection of educational objectives was conducted, stressing that the objectives only reflected the dominant interests of American culture. According to Counts, "The inevitable consequence is that the school will become an instrument for the perpetuation of the existing social order rather than a force in society" (p. 126).

Kliebard (1995) maintained that Bobbitt revealed some ambiguity in his curriculum theorization. For example, in 1926, Bobbitt mentioned that "education in not primarily to prepare for life at some future time. Quite the reverse; its purpose is to hold high the current living. (...) In a very true sense, life cannot be prepared for. It can only be lived" (p. 43). However, in 1934, Bobbitt admitted that "while there are general guiding principles that enable parents and teachers to foresee in advance the long general course that is normally run, yet they cannot foresee or foreknow the specific and concrete details of the course that is to be actualized" (p. 4).

Moreover, the social efficiency ideology was infused with patterns of segregation. As Levine (1917) argued, "We must stop teaching the 'average' child; the genius and the laggard cannot learn willynilly. We must also formulate a curriculum for these types of children" (p. 594), thus crystallizing the notion of school as a selective agency. King (1913) noted that "there are many forces at play in society that it is not desirable should appear in the school. This is partly due to the fact that society is far from perfect" (p. 178). Such segregation would come to pass not only at the level of class dynamics, but also in terms of gender. In fact, Bobbitt (1912) would also come to advocate for the need for a certain kind of gender segregation, since boys and girls require different types of leadership; that is "boys require masculine leadership in many of their activities and the girls feminine leadership" (pp. 270–271). Both Bobbitt (1912) and Charters (1926a, 1926b) believed that men and women had very distinct social destinies. Charters (1926a) argued that curriculum should be defined "on the basis of what people are going to do" (p. 327); in other words, "the social efficiency educators were primarily concerned with efficient performance in a future social role" (p. 327). This position was quite distinct from that assumed by Hall, who believed that interest should be considered a crucial criterion in determining a curriculum. This was also true of Taylorism. In fact, one function of a "human engineering" perspective in curriculum was to provide a place for a new class of experts. Hence, we need to think about Taylorism in class terms, and as an ideology of social control. Approaches portrayed by scholars like Counts, Apple, Wexler, and Giroux teach us a great deal here. As Apple (1986) argued, "As a management technology for deskilling workers and separating conception from execution, Taylorism was less than fully successful" (p. 40).

Moreover, Apple highlighted the fact that "many of the techniques now being proposed in or standing behind the reports for evaluation and testing, for standardized curricula, and for 'upgrading' and rationalizing teaching, e.g. systems management and management by objectives, competency-based testing and curriculum development, reductive behavioral objectives, and so forth come from similar soil" (p. 40). Taylorism, as Apple stressed, "perhaps the archetypical attempt by capital to control people's work, [did] not come 'directly' from dominant groups in an unmediated fashion. It's been much more complicated than this and requires a more subtle appraisal of class dynamics both outside and inside education" (p. 140).

That is why it is important, as Giroux (1981a) argues, to look "at the dialectical tension that exists between teacher-education programs and the dominant society through a set of concepts that link as well demonstrate the interplay of power, ideology, biography and history" (p. 143). Taylorism—as a classed, raced, and gendered ideological form—cannot be detached from the ideology of social control, although "teacher education programs and their respective schools of education provide appearance of being neutral" (p. 143). Giroux continues:

> Teacher education programs are caught in a deceptive paradox. Charged with the public responsibility to educate teachers to enable future generations to learn the knowledge and skills necessary to build a principal and democratic society, they represent a significant agency for the reproduction and legitimation of a society characterized by high degree of social and economic inequality. Teacher education programs embody structural and ideological contradictions that are related to a larger social order caught in a conflict between the imperatives of its social welfare responsibilities and its functional allegiance to the condition of capitalism. (pp. 143–144)

As Wexler (1976) argued, Taylorism is profoundly linked with the cult of efficiency, and this cult is not dissociated from a creed of professionalism that invaded the educational field, contaminating inclusively educational research. Popkewitz (1979a) is quite aware of this:

> Technical definitions of educational problems and the procedural responses to reform in teacher education are legitimized by much of the research in the field. Most research tends to view teaching as a problem of human engineering and teacher education as the most efficient way to provide new recruits with specific behaviors and attitudes of the people who practice teaching…the conduct of schooling, the system of status and privilege of the occupation, and the social and the political implications of institutional arrangements are obscured through a process of reification. Teaching and teacher education are treated administratively. (pp. 1–3)

As Counts (1932) argued, and as I will address later on, the Taylorist/capitalist social efficiency model that dominated the education system needs to be destroyed. According to Counts, teachers need to assume unprecedented social responsibilities, and the lack of freedom and creativity in schools need to be challenged.

In fact, at the very beginning, those with capital rejected Taylorism because they knew it would lead to social crises. Thus, Taylorism often was about creating and legitimating a new class of people, of professional engineers. Previously, engineers were craftsmen working on the shop floor who, when they became really skilled, were given managerial responsibilities. However, they were still workers based on the shop floor and had the workman's full range of knowledge. Thus, one of the things that efficiency and human engineering wanted to secure was a place between capital and labor for a newly emergent middle-class occupation—the professional expert. Taylorism was undeniably really about creating and legitimating a class of professional experts.

In September 1918, "the most dramatic event in the evolution of the movement to reform the curriculum" (Kliebard, 1995, p. 137) took place with the appearance of an article by Kilpatrick in *Teachers College Record:* "The Project Method." As we will see later, Kilpatrick, who was "sharply critical of traditional education, [presented a] clear alternative to the reforms being promoted by the social efficiency interest group" (Cremin, 1964, p. 217; cf. Kilpatrick, 1926).

However, the more elaborate and more powerful criticism comes from Kliebard (1968; 1995). He draws from Lovejoy (1936), who observed that the men who determined the intellectual patterns in the first two decades of the twentieth century were characteristically "esprits simplistes—minds which habitually tend to assume that simple solutions can be found for the problems they dealt with" (p. 7). This presumption of simplicity causes extremely complex issues, such as what knowledge is of most worth to be treated "by easy means as observing and counting and measuring, and, if worse comes to worst, by consensus" (Kliebard, 1968, p. 73). Kliebard continues to draw on Lovejoy, noting that "if anything characterizes the thinking of early curriculum specialists and, to some extent our own thinking, it is the desire to enumerate and particularize, hence our faith in *the* six principles of good school-community relations or *the* four or five or nineteen steps in curriculum development" (pp. 73–74). Examples of this perspective are Bobbitt's books—*How to Make a Curriculum*, which lists hundreds of objectives, and *The Curriculum*, in which the entire social efficiency doctrine is laid out:

> The central theory is simple. Human life, however varied, consists in the performance of specific activities. Education that prepares for life is one that prepares definitely and adequately for these specific activities. However numerous and diverse they may be for any social class, they can be discovered. This requires only that one go out into the world of affairs and discover the particulars of which these affairs consist. These will show the abilities, attitudes, habits, appreciations, and forms of knowledge that man needs...They will be numerous, definite, and particularized [objectives]. The curriculum will then be that series of experiences which children and youth must have by way of training those objectives...that series of things which children and youth must do and experience by way of developing abilities to do the things well that make up the affairs of adult life; and to be in all respects what adults should be. (Bobbitt, 1918, p. 42)

As Kliebard (1968) writes, "In one passage is the quintessence of early curriculum thinking: the simplistic approach to a complex problem, the strong emphasis on specification and enumeration, even the suggestion of a differentiated curriculum for different social classes" (p. 74). In essence, the social efficiency ideology struggled against what Ellwood (1914) derided as "education...as soft affair" (p. 572)—in other words, an education that is "very far from furnishing the discipline which life requires" (p. 572). To Levine (1917), "Education is a mass of conflicting principles...a strange welter of incongruous theories and educational aims that are hardly recognizable because of the painful lack of a common terminology, and yet, psychology is a science everybody knows—only it is told in the language that nobody understands" (p. 594). The advocates of social efficiency, when confronted by a social and cultural instrument such as the curriculum, opted for simplistic solutions and ignored the fact that they had in hand dangerous tools, which cut off the present and future of thousands of generations. In this sense, we perceive that the curriculum in the hands of social efficiency educators was converted into a lethal weapon constructed on the linearity of the imposed arguments, arguments that still influence curriculum. Curiously such simplicity in opposing, for example, Dewey's and Hall 's conceptual models (namely the theory of recapitulation and the theory of the culture-epoch, respectively), contributed to the implementation of social efficiency notions in the twentieth century (cf. Kliebard, 1968; 1995). It was simple: there was only the need to determine objectives and reduce them to a series of stages, an idea that was a clone of Taylorism. This notion of simplicity that is well embedded in the *Cardinal Principles of Secondary Education* would prove to be "a fundamental assumption in subsequent work in curriculum" (Kliebard, 1968, p. 75).

Fundamentally, Bobbitt and Charters—who witnessed the decadence of mental discipline as a theory for curriculum (Kliebard, 1975b)—established themselves as the major promulgators of the behavioral and scientific movements in the curriculum. Both continued the work developed by Spencer and Rice, establishing a bridge between their work and what years later would come to be known as the Tyler rationale, an issue that we will examine in the next chapter.

As Kliebard (1999a) wrote:

> Proceeding from the root metaphor of the school as a factory and the curriculum as a production process, school children became "raw material" and the teacher the overseer of the production process, making

sure that the products were constructed according to the specifications laid down and with a minimum of waste. (p. 53)

Nonetheless, the opposition was increasingly strong. This refers to the social reconstructionist movement, which will be dealt with in greater detail later on and which, as we have flagged previously, needs to be seen as a catalyst of what I call the critical curriculum river.

CHAPTER 4

THE EMERGENCE OF RALPH TYLER

Although opposition to the creation of a scientifically controlled curriculum was increasing, Bobbitt was able to introduce "a potent new vocabulary into curriculum discourse, and this metaphorical language came to control what was deemed to be right and proper in curriculum design. Derived directly from the manufacturing process, that language also served to define the overarching purposes of schooling" (Kliebard, 1995, p. 53). This perspective was consolidated by 1930, when the National Society for the Study of Education (NSSE) published its *Twenty-Sixth Yearbook*, which had two parts: Curriculum Making: Past and Present, and The Foundations of Curriculum Making. The first part delivered strong criticism of traditional schooling, while the second came to be seen as a point of reference with regard to curriculum-making (Whipple, 1930). The committee, which included some relevant names—Rugg (chairperson), Bagley, Bobbitt, Charters, Counts, Judd, and Kilpatrick—recognized the need for curriculum reform and to create a guideline for curriculum-making. The characteristics of an ideal curriculum were laid out, some of which are still relevant today. These included the ideal curriculum, which, as Rugg (1930) explains,

> focuses on the affairs of human life; deals with the facts and problems of the local, national and international community; enables students to think critically about various forms of government; informs and develops an attitude of open mindedness; considers students' interests and needs as well as opportunities for debate, discussion and exchange of ideas; deals with issues of modern life and the cultural and historical aspects of society; considers problem-solving activities and practice in choosing alternatives; consists of carefully graded organization of problems and exercises; deals with humanitarian themes, and purposeful and constructive attitudes and insights. (pp. 3–16)

It is worth noting that over the course of the twentieth century, no single doctrine was able to obliterate the others. In fact, as Kliebard (1995) notes, "by 1930 curriculum reform had become a national preoccupation...[however,]...many of the curriculum reforms that were emerging in the decade of the thirties represented not so much a victory for one position over the other as a hybridization of what were once distinct and easily recognizable curriculum positions" (pp. 179–80). As a curriculum document, the *Twenty-Sixth Yearbook* of NSSE would determine the future course of the field. It had a profound influence on the *Eight Year Study*, which was carried out by the Progressive Education Association from 1932 to 1940 and was "probably the most ambitious of the efforts to stimulate curriculum reform at the local level" (p. 182). This most pertinent and powerful curriculum experiment ever carried out in the United States of America (Tanner & Tanner, 1995) started with the aim of resolving the overwhelming social crisis. Tyler (1976a) explained:

> With the onset of the Great Depression in 1929, new demands for change came with such force that they could no longer be denied. Youth in large numbers, unable to find work, enrolled in high school. Most of these new students did not plan to go to college, and most of them found little meaning and interest in their high-school tasks. But still they went to school; there was no other place for them to go. (p. 38)

Not surprisingly, an old issue emerged. After the work of the Committee of Ten, "complaints were being voiced about alleged domination of the high school curriculum by the colleges" (Kliebard, 1995, p. 183). This complaint gained momentum by the early 1930s; in other words, it "became clear in the minds of curriculum reformers that the colleges were the principal impediment to curriculum reform at the secondary school level" (p. 183). An increasingly large division between colleges and high schools caused the Progressive Education Association to attack the problem. According to Tyler (1987), the "Progressive Education Association appointed a Committee on the Relation of School and College, to recommend what they could do to reduce the rigidity of the high school curriculum and to make it more effective for the wide range of students they were getting" (p. 71). This recommendation was a landmark in the field of curriculum research; it attempted to demonstrate that students can be successful in college even if they come from a secondary system that opts for a curriculum organized around the needs and interests of the students.

With the exception of Fordham, which never accepted the idea of shifting its entrance requirements, "for eight years, schools would be permitted to develop curriculum that they believed to be appropriate for their students,...[and] during that time, their graduates would be admitted to college without prejudice because of not having met the typical college entrance requirements" (Tyler, 1987, p. 71). However, "in exchange for that freedom, there would be an evaluation program," based on a concept that would come to be known as formative evaluation; in other words, it meant that "what we had to do in evaluation was to provide information, as best we could collect it, which would help the schools to continue to revise and improve their programs as we went along" (p. 71). In fact, it was due to the difficulty experienced in the evaluation of the study (the schools actually were allowed to abandon the project) that Bode, as a member of the directing committee, suggested that Tyler could lead the evaluation process. Bode told the committee, "We've got a young man at our university who approaches testing quite differently. He starts out with 'What are your objectives? What are you trying to do?' instead of starting out with 'I've got the test already for you'" (quoted in Tyler, 1987, p. 72). The *Eight Year Study* satisfied the most profound wishes of the social efficiency ideology, which increasingly led the crusade against waste in education, although critics believed that the students would not perform well in college (cf. Worthen & Sanders, 1987).

In fact, Tyler "became nationally visible in 1938 when he carried on his work with the *Eight Year Study*" (Goodlad, 1976, p. 8) and "gave strong impetus [to the] infusion of behaviorism in curriculum thinking" (Kliebard, 1995, p. 184). It was assumed that "education is a process which seeks to change the behavior patterns of human beings" (Smith & Tyler, 1942, p. 11; cf. Tyler, 1931). Consequently, Tyler (1978) stated that "the educational system is...more than the school system" (p. 123) and that it has three major functions in society: "(1) to enable young people to acquire the understanding, skills, and attitudes required for constructive participation in the economic, political, and social life of a democracy; (2) to allow for mobility within society; and (3) to help each person to achieve all that he is capable of achieving" (p. 122). Thus, despite Tyler's (1989a) denial that he had constructed a rationale, the fact is that he confessed that the *Eight Year Study* not only stimulated him "to construct a comprehensive outline of the questions to be answered and the steps to be taken in developing a curriculum," especially since it was a "monumental curriculum project for that time" (p. 201), it also stimulated the emergence of later studies, such as "The Michigan Study, headed by Parker, The Southern Association Study, The Negro High School Study" (Tyler, 1978, p. 65). The *Eight Year Study* led to some significant conclusions, including

> widespread acceptance of the idea that schools could develop educational programs that would meet the needs of all students, recognition by colleges that the entrance testing was a viable selection tool, and the recognition by educational practitioners of the value of defining educational objectives in terms of the behavior patterns students are encouraged to acquire. (Pagano, 1999, p. 96)

Odd as it might seem, the roots of the "Tyler Rationale" (1987) can be found not only in scholars like Judd, his adviser, but also in the thought and work of intellectuals like Counts, who "was helpful as a professor in one course in which [Tyler] did the studies of the immigrants, in this case the Polish coming to Chicago and their education" (pp. 396–402), and in the practices of Dewey, whom Tyler "met with...several times to discuss *The Eight Year Study*" (pp. 396–402). According to Tyler, Judd insisted that "the substance of education is going to come from the observation and work with persons learning, not from books. You can write books about what you learn but the substance comes from the observation and experiment with people learning" (p. 398). While Thorndike had formulated a "theory of very specific associations" (p. 41)—in other words, the need for a meticulous specificity in the learning tasks ("adding 9 to 8 is a different task from 8 to 9" [p. 41])—Judd advanced a theory of generalization: "The important thing was helping the student to seek to generalize" (p. 41). Judd's words to Tyler at his dissertation defense somehow demonstrate not only Judd's thinking but his influence over Tyler: "Tyler, we at Chicago don't count units and things; we count what you know and what you can do" (p. 399). Thorndike had formulated "a theory of learning which involved the idea that learning consisted of building up connections between specific stimuli and specific responses...At about the same time Thorndike was stating his theory, [Judd] formulated a theory of learning called generalization which viewed learning as the development of generalized modes of attack upon problems, generalized modes of reaction to generalized types of situations" (Tyler, 1949, p. 42).

Despite having written hundreds of documents reflecting on the problems of the curriculum field, Tyler would mark the field not only by his participation in the *Eight Year Study* and in the conference called Toward Improved Curriculum Theory, which was held in

1947 at the University of Chicago, but also by the publication of a small book of 128 pages, entitled *Basic Principles of Curriculum and Instruction*. The conference participants included Herrick, Caswell, and Tyler, among others. Its objective was to "develop a more adequate theory of curriculum" (Herrick & Tyler, 1950, p. iii)—not an easy task, because "the writers in the field of curriculum, when considering the problem of curriculum theory, hold a number of differing points of view" (p. iii). In fact, the "curriculum of American schools [had] been subject to a wide variety of theoretical formulations during the past half-century" (Caswell, 1950, p. 110). According to Caswell, "one important source of confusion in curriculum theory is the failure of some students to recognize clearly the foundations upon which such theory must rest" (pp. 110–11). Hence, he continues, "the foundations of the curriculum are to be found in the conception of the values of culture and society and of the individual—how he learns and how he develops. This means that philosophy, sociology, and, in particular, psychology are basic to curriculum theory" (p. 111). Quite naturally, then, the task of the curriculum specialist is "to draw from these fields a consistent body of basic principles, to interpret these principles and to apply them to education" (p. 111). It is therefore erroneous to base a theorization of the curriculum on just one specific principle.

For Tyler (1950) too, "without a comprehensive theory for guidance, the organization of the curriculum is likely to be partial, spasmodic, and relatively ineffective" (p. 59). Tyler believed comprehensive curriculum theory should be sensitive to five aspects: "(1) the function of organization; (2) extent of learner's experiences to be organized; (3) the organizing elements; (4) the organizing principles; (5) the organizing structures" (pp. 61–66). Hence, for Tyler, comprehensive curriculum theory was fundamentally an organizational theory, a theory that "should explain what is required for effective sequencing (vertical organization) and effective integration (horizontal organization), and why" (p. 59).

The issue of curriculum theory based on an organizational foundation leads us to another issue: curriculum planning in the development of the curriculum, a theme that was problematized by Herrick (1950). According to Herrick, "curriculum development is essentially the result of corporative effort and by its very nature must draw upon many kinds of competencies" (p. 37). He was quite adamant in calling for clarification about the bases that consubstantiate the curriculum design: "Any curriculum design or plan, if it is to become effective in improving curriculum, must make explicit and clear the bases upon which curriculum decisions are made" (pp. 40, 49).

Tyler (1950), who thought that the "school curriculum [was] commonly defined as all of the learning which is planned and guided by the school, whether or not it is carried on in classes, on the playground, or in other segments of the pupil's lives" (p. 59), entered the educational arena at the peak of the movement centered on objectives. The focus of this movement was set as much by Bobbitt as by Charters, both being concerned about the interpretative reading that was allowed for educational purposes.

Bobbitt (1918) argued that the context of contemporary society demanded precision and specificity, indicating that teachers should determine their objectives in a non-technical language so that students and parents could understand them. Furthermore, there was the need to distinguish between the objectives for the curriculum as a whole and the objectives of progression for each class or age group. This stance was to be taken up by Charters (1923), for whom the need to clarify the purposes of education was a crucial process. Hence, we need first to determine what he called the ideals of education, then to identify the activities such ideals would entail, and, finally, analyze the ideals as much as the activities, both in terms of units of work and in accordance with human capacity.

Bobbitt and Charters thus brought a scientific and behaviorist element to their analysis of the curriculum field, intending to introduce into educational practices precise and scientific methods, which were beginning to show dividends in other areas of human activity, particularly in industry. Interest in the test expanded in an attempt to establish a relationship between pre-specification of the objectives and evaluation of the performance; this relationship would prove to be one of the central curriculum issues (Kelly, 1989). However a major step was taken by the objectives approaches, and not only by Tyler "the next major exponent of the objectives approach" (p. 51). Tyler's "original aim was to design scientific tests of educational attainment and his solution to this problem was to suggest that this could be done most readily and easily if a clear statement had been made of the kind of attainment that was being aimed at" (p. 51). Bloom, who was a disciple of Tyler, later introduced a new dimension into curriculum planning with the division of objectives into three categories—the cognitive, the emotional, and the psychomotor—thus offering a detailed list of the most ambitious classification of the objectives in the cognitive domain that was ever known (Kelly, 1989).

Tyler is situated in a new form of theoretical elaboration of education and of the curriculum (cf. Lundgren, 1983). This new form emerged as the consequence of an epoch (the first half of the twentieth century) that was marked by enormous educational ambition, one in which new and audacious ideals were formed, the relationship between education and society was reformulated, and new practices and experiences emerged that would give rise to substantial transformation at the level of teaching content, methods, and objectives (cf. Connell, 1980). In a society that was increasingly blinded by a belief in an efficient education system, it is not surprising that educating the masses was motivated less by the desire to provide everyone with a worthwhile education and more by the impositions of a society that was increasingly characterized by social inequality and social segregation. Although not without resistance, education was increasingly seen as preparation for the working world. In this regard, Tyler's words (1968) are clearly enlightening: "Today, education is a necessity for everyone in order to participate in our complex social, civic and industrial life" (p. 2).

In 1949, Tyler published *Basic Principles of Curriculum and Instruction*, which had originally served as the basis for the syllabus of a course with the same name that he had supervised at the University of Chicago (cf. Tyler, 1989a). According to Jackson (1992, p. 24) it was "the bible of curriculum making". Neither a "textbook, for it does not provide comprehensive guidance and readings for a course, [nor] a manual for curriculum construction since it does not describe and outline in detail the steps to be taken by a given school or college that seeks to build a curriculum" (Tyler, 1949, p. 1), it is a book that "attempts to explain a rationale for viewing, analyzing and interpreting the curriculum and instructional program of an education institution" (p. 1). However, when his book reached the hands of individuals who were not used to thinking, Tyler's ideas changed into everything that the author himself negated (Kemmis, 1988). In fact, Tyler had offered a clear definition of educational objectives that should have been formulated in terms of content and behavior, a line of thought that was later followed by Bloom.

Tyler's (1949, p. 1) book offers a rationale (although Tyler was opposed to labels) that begins with identifying four fundamental questions which must be answered in developing any curriculum and plan of instruction...(1) What educational purposes should the school seek to attain? (2) What educational experiences can be provided that are likely to attain these purposes? (3) How can these educational experiences be effectively organized? (4) How can we determine whether these purposes are being attained?

Tyler recommends "three major criteria to be met in building an effectively organized group of learning experiences: continuity, sequence and integration" (p. 84). To conclude, Tyler refers to evaluation as "a powerful device for clarifying educational objectives" (p. 124), alerting the reader to the fact that "evaluation becomes one of the important ways of providing information about the success of the school to the school's clientele" (p. 125).

Adopting Kemmis's (1988) thought, Tyler's work, seemingly without "meaning to," provides a pertinent summary of the techniques desired by many teachers for their practical day-to-day activity. Its informative, clear, and coherent character is based on four aspects: (a) the vision of the student (derived from contemporary psychology); (2) the society outside the school (gathered from sociology and the philosophy of education, and based on the conception of the knowledge necessary for the modern industrial society and for the well-being of humanity); (3) the knowledge of the contents (specified by the authority of the particular specialists in each area of knowledge); and (4) the curriculum elaboration process (based on technical knowledge, such as the words, the selection of content, its organization and sequence in accordance with psychological principles, and the determination and evaluation of the adequate methods of transmission, using behaviorist objective specification technology). In fact, for Tyler, "since tests had proved useful in selecting and sorting military personnel, it seemed that similar tests could be developed for civilian conditions, and for children and youth as well as young adults" (Tyler, 1974a, p. 4).

Frequently referred to as "the father of...educational evaluation" (Ridings, 1989, p. 261), Tyler (1989b) warns, however, of the dangers of labels, which, besides being superficial in one way or another, often weaken the true meaning of the terms:

> I invented the term "evaluation" when applied to educational procedures, so if naming the child, as the godfather names babies, makes you father, then I am. And when it began to be a cliché and evaluation meant so many different things to different people, I invented the term "assessment" and that's what we used next...The problem is that something is labeled, like the Tyler rationale, and pretty soon, it is the form that is in people's minds, not the substance. Forms, like cosmetics, are so much easier to adopt than changing your personality. And that kind of business makes it necessary periodically to change labels because the labels became clichés representing something like Dewey's "Do-I-have-to-do-what-I-want-to-do?" sort of cliché—which was not what Dewey said at all, but a way of quickly labeling it. And then it's lost. (pp. 261–2)

Tyler (1949, pp. 44–6), after stressing that certain objectives (to present the theory of evolution, the colonial period; to develop critical thinking") not only fail to define the final purpose of education but also barely suggest what students should do with such elements, indicated that they are so broad that they become quite useless. He reiterated that "the most useful form for stating objectives is to express them in terms which identify both the kind of behavior to be developed in the student and the content or area of life in which this behavior is to operate" (pp. 44–6). In other words, Tyler needed to be more specific in determining to which content a particular behavior is applicable, especially since it is of no use, for example, to talk of critical thought if the content or the types of problems on which the thought will focus are not mentioned.

It was while in the process of analyzing objectives that Tyler positioned himself in opposition to the Committee of Ten. He saw that the committee's report had been prepared by specialists in the different subjects and that the objectives suggested were those sought by many schools:

> It seems quite clear that the Committee of Ten thought it was answering the question: What should be the elementary instruction for students who are later to carry on much more advanced work in the field? Hence, the report in History, for example, seems to present objectives for the beginning courses for persons who are training to be historians. Similarly the report in Mathematics outlines objectives for the beginning courses in the training of a mathematician. Apparently each committee viewed its job as outlining the elementary courses with the idea that these students taking these courses would go on for more and more advanced work, culminating in major specialization at the college or university level. This is obviously not the question that subject specialists should generally be asked regarding the secondary school curriculum. The question which they should be asked runs somewhat like this: What can your subject contribute to the education of young people who are not going to be specialists in your field? (Tyler, 1949, p. 26).

The important and complex question of the curriculum therefore rests on its true essence: What is one to teach? This has always been a problematic issue but, as previously mentioned, with Spencer's (1860) influence, by the end of the nineteenth century it had changed to, "What knowledge is of the most worth?" As Tyler (1987) wrote:

> Curriculum problems tend to be mostly problems of what is to be taught. Why is it important for children to learn these things? What evidence is there that they haven't already learned it or that it is

appropriate to their age? And so on. Then the problems of what the objectives are and so forth. If you have thirty people you'll find most of the kinds of curriculum problems there. Then evaluation problems— the tendency to appraise students without reference to what it was they were supposed to learn. (p. 52)

Tyler (1976b) observed that Thorndike, Bobbitt, and so many others who were products of an "age of quickening interest in the scientific exploration of social and natural phenomena... [and] the widely held belief that science won the day" (p. 18), sought answers to "Herbert Spencer's insistent question 'What knowledge is of most worth?'" (p. 18).

According to Pagano (1999), Tyler's work "dictates an operationalized sequence of linear steps leading from the formulation of goals and specifications of outcomes, identification of classroom experiences presumed to yield desired outcomes, and precise articulation of evaluation procedures to measure achievement or non-achievement of specified goals" (p. 95). As Tyler (1976b) himself wrote, "[If] educational improvement in the later nineteenth century had come largely from the requirements of the American democratic experiment,... better schooling in the earlier twentieth century grew out of the transformations wrought by industrialism" (p. 19), thus positing once more an unshakable belief in the school as the instrument of consolidation of the dynamics imposed by industrialization.

Therefore, if the purposes of the school "are focused on developing certain patterns of behavior that are considered important to help students participate constructively in society and realize more fully their own personal potential" (Tyler, 1974b, p. 145), then "the school curriculum is designed as a set of experiences that are expected to stimulate students to attempt these patterns of behavior, to afford them an opportunity to practice these patterns, to guide their efforts, and to continue the learning activities until the desired patterns of behavior have become established" (p. 145). It is in conformity with this that "the purpose of achievement testing is to ascertain whether, in fact, the students have acquired the desired behavior" (p. 145). Thus the dynamics of evaluation gain strength (something that traversed Tyler's entire life), which, according to Tyler (1974a), "began as a means for selecting and sorting pupils, and the practices of testing that have been worked out since 1918 are largely the refining of means to serve these functions rather than other educational purposes" (p. 4). In other words, "they are based upon the psychology of individual differences rather than upon the psychology of learning…an appropriate development under the societal conditions of the time" (p. 4). However, over the course of the century, the function of education was transformed and "the critical task is no longer to sort students but, rather, to educate a much larger proportion of students to meet current opportunities" (p. 6).

According to Goodlad (1976), "Tyler has been identified with and criticized for his contributions to what is sometimes called 'educational engineering'" (p. 5), despite the fact that he would be the last one to defend his proposal as the only one. Although no isolated form of information may be considered adequate to make comprehensive and sensible decisions about school objectives, the fact is, as highlighted by Kemmis (1988), *Basic Principles of Curriculum and Instruction* indicates that, according to Tyler's vision of the curriculum, a very special authority is ascribed to psychology for providing a certain learning technology. Tyler's work, Kemmis adds, should be understood as a historical marker that succinctly and clearly structured an eclectic theory based on philosophy, sociology, and psychology—with particular emphasis on psychology. Consequently, the meta-theory proposed by Tyler entailed both a curriculum theory—which assumes its guiding framework and its principles of external theoretical sources to be especially, but not only, from psychology—and a curriculum field, which primarily refers to learning and whose perspective about the latter corresponds to technology derived from its mother subject (psychology) or subjects (philosophy, sociology, psychology).

Despite the references to philosophy and sociology, Tyler, with his emphasis on curriculum development, centered his planning efforts around technical issues, and in this sense he obscured the educational principles that guide curriculum practice in terms of actual educators, leaving their development to the scientific work of theorists outside the schools (cf. Kemmis, 1988). By placing the theoretical construct in the hands of psychologists, philosophers, and sociologists, Tyler released teachers and administrators from having to assume such a responsibility. In fact, the curriculum logic proposed by Tyler created a kind of no-man's land (which he attributed to psychology, philosophy, and sociology), a silenced and obscure domain in which many of the fundamental issues of education politics are played out. It is this nucleus of political decisions about education that Tyler silences by omitting a crucial analysis of the role played by powerful interest groups in the determination of the curriculum.

However, Tyler (1987) maintained that people failed to understand that his logic of curriculum construction was based on the idea that the curriculum was an active, not a passive, pursuit. This is clearly referred to in the following passage:

> Mostly they're people who think of the curriculum as something out there that they're looking at, rather than being involved in developing an education program for a school. In the latter case one asks: "How am I going to develop one? I've got to have kids learning something. What is it they'll learn, and how would I select it to be sure that what they're learning is worth learning?" Then there's the question of how we're going to help them learn it. "What do I know about learning? How should I set up an instructional program?" And "How am I going to organize it so that they can build each year on what they've learned last year?" Finally, "How can I evaluate the effectiveness of this educational program?" (p. 388)

Tyler argued that "these are the questions for people who are going to have to make a curriculum or to use a curriculum... The reason for the popularity of my little book is because most people that are really concerned with the curriculum, other than those that are dilettantes sitting around wanting to talk about it, are people who have to make one or deal with one. There are very few books that help them that way" (p. 389). Tyler reiterated, furthermore, that a particular social theory of reform is based in the fact that "you can't reform in a significant way a social service just from the top down" (p. 94), stressing that "you can tell a minor how to do it. You can control it from above, but when it comes to enterprises that involve the individual having to make decisions, you've got to start helping them be able to make decisions" (p. 94).

In response to the bitter criticism of a number of readings and analyses that were made of the curriculum field, Tyler (1987) commented that "it is fashionable to speak of the collapse, even the demise, of the public school in the United States" (p. 94). According to Tyler (1976a), "several best sellers [exploit this situation by holding] titles... which suggest the terrible conditions in some schools as seen by several concerned writers who also appear to be the prophets of doom" (p. 104). Tyler (1987) saw no reason for such an exacerbated pessimism, especially since, as he wrote, "we're moving ahead with it. Look at the tremendous problems we've had with all this immigration. We've reached them bit by bit; they're learning" (p. 413).

So far this book has traced the development of a particular dominant tradition within the curriculum field, the behavioral systems management industrial model. However, it is important to understand that a non-monolithic yet powerful progressive critical curriculum river confronted this tradition, as will be seen later on, and it is in that river that one should understand the work of Huebner, Macdonald, Apple, Giroux, McLaren, Wexler, Aronowitz, Anyon, and many others. Therefore, before we turn our attention to the *Prosser Resolution*, which should be perceived as another benchmark in the field of curriculum studies, we need to emphasize that what really gives Tyler power as the "grand eagle" of the curriculum field is not just that he was capable of incorporating the behavioral and testing tradition in his approach, but also that he was able to speak to the *Deweyan* tradition and to the social reconstructionist tradition without losing his dominant leadership. This is why Tyler was so powerful.

CHAPTER 5

THE PROSSER RESOLUTION

In 1947, as curriculum theory was becoming more visible, a conference called Toward Improved Curriculum Theory was held at the University of Chicago (cf. Herrick & Tyler, 1950). At the same time, curriculum theorists were beginning to lose their power, as a constellation of struggles following World War II (but well before Sputnik) led to the demise of professional curriculum workers. United States *affect of* involvement in World War II profoundly altered thinking and acting *WWII* in education in general, and in the area of curriculum in particular. Not surprisingly, profound alterations in certain courses were beginning to emerge; physics and mathematics, for example, began to be taught with an increased emphasis "upon aeromechanics, aeronautics, auto mechanics, gunnery, and other aspects of modern life" (Smith, 1942, p. 115).

Notwithstanding the fact that social efficiency (theory) was prominent among leaders in the curriculum field, "with the country fighting a war for democracy, the reordering of the curriculum to accommodate the mass of students was equated with the democratization of the curriculum" (Kliebard, 1995, p. 206). Thus, the social efficiency doctrine gradually began to lose its status as the dominant curriculum logic. The dominant form of curriculum right before and throughout World War II was called life adjustment education. Fundamentally, it was Bobbitt and Charters with a smiling face—in other words, the humanization of Bobbitt's and Charters's doctrines. According to Cremin (1964), "of all the postwar refinements of progressive education . . . none achieved the publicity or indeed the notoriety, of the so-called life-adjustment movement" (p. 333). This movement defended using the curriculum to focus on social problems, just as Bobbitt and Charters had done, but now the problems involved brushing teeth, dialing a telephone, and health awareness, but in a retrogressive and conservative way.

However, although life adjustment was the dominant logic, the fact is that "social efficiency was its most potent ingredient" (Kliebard, 1995, p. 206). The transformation was far reaching, and in 1940, the Special Committee on the Secondary School's report, *What High Schools Ought to Teach*, appeared. The committee included Prosser, who, as previously mentioned, had established himself as the pivotal figure in the Smith Hughes Act, and Tyler, who in the meantime was building a notable reputation in the curriculum field, thanks to his participation in the *Eight Year Study*.

Despite recognizing that the creation of the Board for Vocational Education in 1917 represented a major advance in confirming the social function of the school, the document criticized the tendency of vocational education to cultivate highly specialized skills, noting that many of these skills "fail to meet the needs of pupils because [they are] quite as specialized as were the traditional pre-professional jobs" (American Youth Commission, 1940, p. 10). Vocational education was, furthermore, intimately linked to segregation, in that the majority of students steered toward it were already marginalized, leaving them with a curriculum that was inadequate "in preparing [them] to take their place in adult society" (p. 10). The criticism even stretched to the so-called "conventional subjects" (p. 27), although the document was preoccupied to a great extent with the need to prepare students for their future involvement in society.

Two other major reports emerged after the publication of *What High Schools Ought to Teach: Education for ALL American Youth* (Educational Policies Commission, 1944) and *General Education in a Free Society* (commonly known as the *Redbook*; Committee on the Objectives of General Education in a Free Society, 1945). The former, besides highlighting the importance of developing skills compatible with the needs of society (already noted in the first report), stressed that the "academic subject matter surviving in the high school curriculum mainly serves the needs of the chosen few" (Kliebard, 1995, p. 210). The latter argued that the function of education "should be to prepare an individual to become an expert both in some particular vocation or art and in the general art of the free man and the citizen" (Committee on the Objectives, 1945, p. 54), and that curriculum differentiation, therefore, should be a natural consequence of the profound and complex social transformations that had been taking place in society since the end of the nineteenth century. However, the *Redbook* included an analysis of the *Education for ALL American Youth* report, specifically the question of academic subject matter, which, according to Kliebard (1995), "represent[ed] a cautious, almost timid, reemergence of the traditional humanist ideal" (p. 211). The document received both approval and criticism. Bagley (1905, 1945), who argued for social efficiency as the supreme educational ideal, interpreted the report as opposing Eliot's selective doctrine; Bobbitt (1946), however, stressed that it was absolutely correct to emphasize the formation of specialists. Although he approved of the distinction the report made between general education and special education, Bobbitt argued once more for the predominance of science in the resolution of curriculum dilemmas, claiming that it overturned medieval misconceptions.

In 1945, the U.S. Office of Education produced another study called *Vocational Education in the Years Ahead*, which involved more than 150 people. This study repeated the argument that high school did not adequately prepare students for their future lives. There was wide consensus that "the youth of the nation were not being adequately served by the high school" (Kliebard, 1995, p. 212). It was in this context that Prosser, in response to the challenges made by the committee, elaborated what would become known as the Prosser Resolution:

> It is the belief of this conference that, with the aid of this report in final form, the vocational school of a community will be able better to prepare 20 percent of the youth of secondary school age for entrance upon desirable skilled occupations; and that the high school will continue to prepare another 20 percent for entrance to college. We do not believe that the remaining 60 percent of our youth of secondary school age will receive the life adjustment training they need and to which they are entitled as American citizens—unless and until the administrators of public education with the assistance of the vocational education leaders formulate a similar program for this group. (U.S. Office of Education, 1951, p. 29)

The Prosser Resolution was "the opening salvo in the campaign for what became the life-adjustment education" (Kliebard, 1995, p. 212). As Kliebard argues, "What was needed was a curriculum attuned to the actual life functions of youth as a preparation for adulthood, [and] life adjustment education, in the line with its most immediate ancestor, social efficiency education, had to be applied to the total school curriculum" (p. 213).

As we were able to verify, life adjustment education was closely linked to the lack of congruence between social realities and a high school education, and despite having been found at the core of the *Douglas Commission Report* (1949), it "was no longer an isolated concern; it had become conventional wisdom in the educational world" (p. 220). In other words, this is a doctrine whose scope was the adequacy of the high school to meet increasingly complex social demands. According to Douglas, the concept of life adjustment "stands for an adequate program of secondary education for fairly complete preparation for all the areas of living in which life adjustment must be made, particularly home living, vocational life, civic life, leisure life, and physical and mental health" (p. 114).

In 1947, the Life Adjustment Conference was held with the intent of crystallizing the critical points delineated by the Prosser Resolution (Basler, 1947). The conference, according to Prosser, was a "golden opportunity to do something that would give to all American youth their education heritage so long denied" (U.S. Office of Education, 1948, p. 20). The National Association of Secondary School Principals similarly involved itself in life adjustment education. The association promoted some of the issues that were integral to life adjustment, arguing it could combat alarming dropout rates while also dealing with the lack of preparation for life, which, according to Collier (1950), involved "preparation for post-secondary education, preparation for work, doing an effective day's work in school, getting along well with other boys and girls, understanding parents, driving a motor car, using the English language, engaging in recreational activities" (p. 125).

Life adjustment education would come to count on the support of Catholic educators, who read the Prosser Resolution as a document that was appropriate for the creation of a "vast network of terminal high schools" (Townsend, 1948, pp. 363–4), and who understood life adjustment education as the path to "steady and disastrous lowering of purely academic standards which has made a joke of college education" (pp. 363–4). Faced by the imprint of segregation, which was permeating all educational reforms in general and curriculum reforms in particular, "the rhetoric of life adjustment education was infused with a seemingly genuine concern for the mass of students not being served by contemporary secondary education, and this gave it a humanitarian appeal that reached into a variety of different quarters" (Kliebard, 1995, p. 217).

Prosser, despite having been involved in the efforts to implement the Smith Hughes Act, had warned of the dangers surrounding the increasingly discredited vocational education. Prosser (1912) argued that "our enthusiasm for vocational schools will lead us to establish them faster than we are able to secure teachers possessing not only academic and technical education but also the practical experience necessary in order to carry on the work successfully" (p. 153). Prosser saw that a democratic society had begun to demand from the schools a curriculum that was very different from that proposed by vocationalism. In an article published with Allen, Prosser (Prosser & Allen, 1925) argued that "democracy as social organization…as a form of society" has two obligations: "first, to hold itself together; second, to make itself better" (p. 39). Furthermore, they perceived that there was a *décalage* or lag between the demands of democracy and the schools' capacity to meet such demands. For example, whereas citizens in a democracy "are required to meet many and varied demands for which they need help,…the stratification of citizens is vertical and every avenue is open to every man…Occupations are constantly changing in their demands and opportunities,…[and] the interests and opportunities of citizens are constantly changing as they advance in life" (pp. 92–3). The fact is that "most school systems offer virtually a uniform and standardized training,…education is stratified horizontally in most schools,…all advancement is blocked for those who do not follow the regular path of credits and diplomas,…most school systems give no assistance for meeting these changed demands,…[and] most school systems ignore the whole problem" (pp. 92–3). Such a rift was serious, given the fact that education was marked by conflicting creeds,

[handwritten margin note: true today]

> [on one hand] the creed of the reactionary…the belief that education is primarily for the benefit of a limited group of superior individuals, that education is primarily preparation for the enjoyment of life,…that those unable to meet satisfactory standards in this form of education should be allowed without prejudice to go their way; [and on the other hand] the creed of the progressive…the belief that education is primarily for social well being of this democracy and not for individual benefit,…that education is primarily preparation for the duties of life; that is life,…that every one can and should be educated so that he can work for himself and for society. (pp. 154–6)

It is important not to ignore the class division with which Prosser (1912) adorned his social concept, highlighting the fact that "any effective program for the training of the great mass of our factory workers should give careful consideration to certain difficulties growing out of differences in the sex, capacity, employment and economic condition of the wage earner, and in the social and industrial conditions surrounding him" (p. 137).

In essence, life adjustment education "was the desire to transform general education from subjects representing common elements on the cultural heritage, as Harris had advocated since before the turn of the century, to functional areas of living" (Kliebard, 1995, p. 220). However, life adjustment education as a social movement began to experience strong criticism from the various sectors of society. As Cremin (1964) writes:

> The attack on the life adjustment movement was no isolated phenom-
> enon; it came rather as part of a much larger crisis in American educa-
> tion that had been brewing at least since the early 1940's. There were,
> to begin, the prosaic problems of buildings, budgets, and enrollments
> created by the war. Few schools had been built since 1941; teachers
> had deserted the profession in droves; inflation was rampant; and the
> first of a flood of "war babies" began to enter the elementary grades as
> early as 1946. Then too, there were the multifarious difficulties associ-
> ated with deepening public concern over communist expansionism at
> home and abroad. And finally, though perhaps less visibly, there were
> the voracious demands of an expanding industrial economy for trained
> and intelligent manpower. (p. 338)

According to Kliebard (1995), "some of the attacks on the state of schooling in America at mid-century were concentrated on Satan and alleged political radicalism in the public schools" (p. 221); in other words, "it was a frontal attack on the intellectual respectability of what passed for public education in America" (p. 221). Cremin (1964) shared this perspective, stressing that the social conditions of the time, associated with the "growing dissatisfaction among the intelligentsia, [provoked the] deepest educational crisis in the nation's history" (p. 339), adding that a "spate of books, articles, pamphlets, radio programs, and television panels burst upon the pedagogical scene, airing every conceivable ailment of the schools, real and imagi-nary" (p. 339). Cremin noted further that as a consequence of this, the "most vigorous, searching and fundamental attack on progressive education since the beginning of the movement" (p. 339) took place. Giving form to this conflict were two works that appeared in 1949: Bell's *Crisis in Education* and Smith's *And Madly Teach*. The first criticizes pseudo-patriotic complacency, stressing that "the elemen-tary schools had failed to transmit the elemental wisdom of the race; the high schools seemed far more interested in coddling young minds than in strengthening them; and the colleges, by surrendering to a vague utilitarian mediocrity, had deprived the nation of a humanely educated leadership" (Cremin, 1964, p. 339). The second, although it reveals some crucial differences from the former—for instance, "whereas Bell sought to strengthen the teaching profession, Smith directed his ultimate indictment against it" (p. 339)—reiterates some of the positions transmitted by Bell, indicating that the schools "had failed miserably in teaching the most elementary skills, and education itself had been systematically divested of its moral and intellectual content" (p. 339).

Education revealed the symptoms of a profound crisis, which in Fuller's (1951) words were due to the "falsity of the basic assumptions from which education professors commonly proceed in their anti-intellectual activities [and to the] deterioration in the contemporary training of students, particularly in the high schools" (p. 33), as well as to the "substitution of 'societally significant' subjects for sound education in the humanities, the arts and the sciences [and to the] confusions and inconsistencies that dominate the thinking (perhaps my use of this word is inexcusably charitable), the utterances, and the activities of many education professors" (p. 33). Clearly, the explicit criticism directed to the school system came from individuals directly linked to the schools—"Bell wrote as an experienced educator" (Cremin, 1964, p. 339, note 7)—and from those who were not—"Smith wrote as a layman and amateur" (p. 339, footnote 7).

However, as already identified by Caswell (1952) in the Steinmetz Memorial Lecture, the presence of an increasing number of concerned citizens who kept abreast of educational developments demystified any notion of a subversive conspiracy theory. In other words, a growing number of common people were ready for education reform of a nonprogressive variety, which led to a whole rethinking of the progressive education movement. It is in this context at the beginning of the second half of the century that a group of works appeared, namely Lynd's *Quackery in the Public Schools,* Bestor's *Educational Wastelands,* Hutchins's *The Conflict in Education,* Woodring's *Let's Talk about Our Schools,* and Smith's *The Diminished Mind* (among whom Bestor was "probably the most persistent and effective critic") (Kliebard, 1995, p. 222). Bestor (1952) argued that the school does not have the obligation "to meet the common and the specific individual needs of youth" (p. 415), emphasizing that the major objective of education rests on intellectual training—that is, the deliberate cultivation of the ability to think. Bestor went on to say that although learning to think might not be life's major objective, it should be the central purpose of schooling, adding that the school should not be held responsible for what should be the responsibility of other social institutions (for instance, the family). Bestor (1953) argued, moreover, that the supporters of life adjustment education ignored the primordial role of the school in the intellectual training of the masses, and he denounced the statistical index of 60 percent that was mentioned in the Prosser Resolution as an antidemocratic percentage, given the fact that it stemmed from the principle that the majority of people were incapable of benefiting from that intellectual training. Bestor defended the Prosser Resolution's claim that dividing the school population highlighted the power of destiny in determining the social function a subject would perform, with the privileged places in society occupied by the select few.

Life adjustment educators, "in their effort to reach out to a new population of students and to attune the curriculum directly to the many activities that children and youth will need to perform as members of society" (Kliebard, 1995, p. 224), not only relegated the intellectual development of young people to secondary importance, but in some instances also perceived that such intellectual development was confined to the very small number of young people who wanted to go to college. The reaction against life adjustment education grew and the movement revealed its inability to meet the needs of an increasingly demanding society. Thus, "unable to mount a counterattack in sufficient force to overwhelm the enemy, life adjustment education quickly began to lose credibility first with the intellectual community and ultimately with the general public as well" (p. 225).

However, the greatest blow was still to come. On October 5, 1957, the Soviet Union launched the first earth-orbiting satellite, Sputnik. That was the final straw. For the people of the United States, being beaten in the space race by the Russians was more than a mere preoccupation, it was a humiliation. According to Cremin (1964), "when the Russians launched the first space satellite in the autumn of 1957, a shocked and humbled nation embarked on a bitter orgy of pedagogical soul-searching" (p. 347).

Quite naturally, "the road to prosperity, social reform, and even national security . . . was tied not to adjustment to existing conditions, but to intelligent action" (Kliebard, 1995, p. 226). Moreover, the social efficiency movement, which as has been noted was the most potent influence on life adjustment education, "instead of a reconstruction of the existing curriculum for general education" (p. 225) opted for its replacement. The scapegoat for the U.S. social crisis and for the inoperability and inefficiency of the education system in comparison to the Soviet Union's rigorous system was the soft model of life adjustment education. The criticism was not long in following—from right-wing critics who wanted a return to the basics, from discipline-centered academic scientists who claimed that the knowledge being taught was not real knowledge, and from scientific curriculum-makers and cold war warriors who said the nation must prepare scientists and technologists. One of the most notable critics was Vice Admiral Rickover, father of the atomic submarine, who considered the U.S. identity under threat—one of the leitmotivs that had preoccupied education since the end of the nineteenth century. Rickover (1959) wrote:

> Our schools are the greatest "cultural lag" we have today. When I read official publications put out by the men who run our educational system—booklets such as *Life Adjustment Education for Every Youth,* or *Education for All Youth*—I have the strange feeling of reading about another world, a world long since departed if it ever existed at all. I sense the kindly spirit, the desire to make every child happy, the earnest determination to give advice on every problem any young person might ever meet in life—and withal so complete a misunderstanding of the needs of young people in today's world that it frightens me. If I speak out against this mistaken concept of what twentieth-century American education must be, I do so out of no desire to find fault with those who misread the demands of the times from anxiety for the future of our children. (pp. 23–4)

[handwritten: true today]

Rickover's perspective was centered not only on the lack of meaning that life adjustment had conferred on the nation's education but also on Dewey's ideas, which had legitimized a soft education system and even a perversion of the concept of equality that reigned in U.S. schools. According to Rickover (1959), the inevitable change and reforms in education could not be left in the hands of the professional educators:

> The mood of America has changed. Our technological supremacy has been called in question and we know we have to deal with a formidable competitor. Parents are no longer satisfied with life adjustment schools. Parental objectives no longer coincide with those professed by the progressive educationists. I doubt we can again be silenced. (p. 190)

Rickover (1963) believed that "we have at present no clear-cut educational philosophy with firm objectives; scholastic achievements are too low and there is urgent need for some kind of machinery to set national standards which may serve local communities as a yardstick" (p. 3). He added that "Congress has rightly been called the 'potent and omnipresent teacher'" (p. 306), and that the idea of change had leaked through all the pores of society. According to Rickover (1959),

[handwritten: standards objectives]

change meant a "massive upgrading of the scholastic standards of our schools [that] will guarantee the future prosperity and freedom of the Republic" (p. 15) through the reorganization of the schooling institutions, namely,

> 1. Elimination of "ability to pay" from public education; retention of "ability to learn"; separate secondary schools. 2. Highly qualified teachers to whom much freedom is given in their work and whose influence on all aspects of education is great, notably in setting scholastic standards through national examinations. Total absence of nonteaching school principals and administrators. 3. The use of government grants as a means of raising national standards in education, by making acceptance of standards and of inspection to check on standards a condition for awarding grants. 4. National examinations leading to national diplomas designed to permit great variety in selection of test subjects, yet clear-cut indication on the diploma of the type of examination taken and passed. Cooperation of all interested parties in setting up examinations and great care in evaluating them. (Rickover, 1963, p. 308)

With the process of Americanization having been completed, Rickover (1959) adds, the schools could now concentrate "on bringing the intellectual powers of each child to the highest possible level" (p. 31). As Kliebard (1995) argues, "Unlike 1917, when the nation saw skilled workers as the key to prosperity and security, the mood was swung to the intellectual, particularly to the scientists, mathematicians and engineers, as the key to world preeminence" (p. 228). For this to happen, "at different levels of civilization, different degrees of popular education are needed" (p. 228). Rickover (1959) further criticized the problematic nature of school knowledge, stressing that education was a mechanism crucial for the consolidation of democracy, a growing force that "never reaches perfection...[or] ever find its objectives" (p. 24).

However, the attacks on the education system were not merely rhetorical. A year after the launch of Sputnik—more precisely, on September 2, 1958—Congress approved the famous piece of federal legislation called the National Defense Education Act, in which Congress stated that the security of the nation requires the fullest development of the mental resources and technical skills of its young men and women, and that the defense of the nation depends upon the mastery of modern techniques developed from complex scientific principles. The document was fundamentally concerned with curriculum revisions in mathematics, science, and foreign languages, "with additional attention given to strengthening guidance services, an outgrowth of the increasing concern about identifying talented students" (Kliebard, 1995, p. 228). Furthermore, besides warning that "the massive amount of money involved did not fall to professional educators, [Congress] accepted the verdict of the academic critics that educators had foisted a soft, intellectually puerile curriculum on American schools" (p. 228).

Certainly, the National Defense Education Act marked the end of an era in the curriculum field and the beginning of another, in which control of the curriculum went from its "traditional locus in the professional education community to specialists in the academic disciplines" (pp. 228–9), so that one can clearly identify an effort to "replace the academic subjects as the basic building block of the curriculum" (p. 229), and even "the longstanding emphasis on local efforts at curriculum change was replaced by a pattern of centrally controlled curriculum revision" (p. 229). In fact, Congress voted for the first time to pass massive amounts of money to schools and approved major national funding for curriculum development, not for establishing universities. There was a need to have more people scientifically trained in curriculum development. Thus, scholarships were established at universities, and Congress gave the universities huge amounts of money, controlled by the newly established National Science Foundation, to develop a standardized curriculum based on the disciplines. The government funded development of a teacher-proof curriculum and created economic incentives in the school districts that bought the material (the government would pay 80 percent of all costs), a strategy that proved cheaper than the textbooks for the schools.

As previously noted, these developments disconnected the curriculum from theory. Curriculum theory could do what it wanted, but the discipline of education no longer had curriculum workers. Instead it had Rickover in the military field, who advocated that education must return to science and technology; right-wing critics who said that we must return to the basics; and people in psychology, like Bruner, who talked about the process of education—teaching the disciplines by discovery.

In September 1959, 35 scientists, scholars, and educators gathered for ten days at Cape Cod for the Woods Hole Conference, organized by the National Academy of Sciences, to debate how science education could contribute to the development of primary and secondary schools. In essence, aware that a new era was dawning, the conference participants' central objective was to analyze how scientific knowledge should be enforced in the country. The conference was divided into five work groups, each with an issue to debate: (1) the sequence of a curriculum, (2) the apparatus of teaching, (3) the motivation of learning, (4) the role of intuition in learning and thinking, and (5) the cognitive process in learning. Bruner, besides being chairman of the conference's executive committee, also participated in one of the work groups—the cognitive process in learning—where he was joined by Begle, Cole, Friedman, Inhelder, Page, and Steinbach. A final finding emerged from each of these study groups, which, just as expected, did not reach a consensus on the complex and polemical matters at hand.

Acknowledging the benefits of contributions made by Cronbach, Page, Zacharias, and others, Bruner, as chairman, issued a document that would come to be known as *The Process of Education*. Based on the conference work documents and the many comments made by participants, Bruner (1960) described the spirit of the Woods Hole Conference as follows:

> Physicists, biologists, mathematics, historians, educators and psychologists came together to consider anew the nature of the learning process, its relevance to education, and points at which current curricular efforts have raised new questions about our conceptions of learning and teaching. What shall be taught, when and how? What kinds of research and inquiry might further the growing effort in the design of curricula? What are the implications of emphasizing the structure of a subject, be it in mathematics or history—emphasizing it in a way that seeks to give a student as quickly as possible a sense of the fundamental ideas of a discipline? (pp. 2–3)

Bruner, who maintained that "each generation gives new form to the aspirations that shape education in its time" (p. vii), stressed that the main preoccupation of specialists in the education field continued to be the problematic of knowledge ("What shall we teach and to what end?" [p. vii]). For Bruner, it was extremely important to understand the meaning of the structure of a subject, not only because "to learn the structure, in short, is to learn how things are related" (p. 7), but also because it was an incentive for students in the process of learning. Furthermore, given the fact that "the construction of curricula proceeds in a world where changing social, cultural and political conditions continually alter the surroundings and the goals of schools and their students" (p. 8), and since a profound understanding of the structure of a subject permits a comprehensive understanding of the knowledge therein implicated, "good teaching that emphasizes the structure of a subject is probably even more valuable for the less able student than for the gifted one, for it is the former rather than the latter who is most easily thrown off the track by poor teaching" (p. 9).

In short, Bruner stressed that "the curriculum of a subject should be determined by the most fundamental understanding that can be achieved of the underlying principles that give structure to that subject" (p. 31). He added that "teaching specific topics or skills without making clear their context in the broader fundamental structure of a field of knowledge is uneconomical in several deep senses" (p. 31) for three main reasons: (1) it becomes extremely hard for the student to make generalizations; (2) there is little reward in terms of intellectual excitement; (3) the "knowledge one has acquired without sufficient structure to tie it together is knowledge that is likely to be forgotten" (p. 31).

All of this changed the approach to curriculum. The curriculum was not made but purchased. Furthermore, it was cheap, which allowed educators to do anything they wanted because the government was paying for it. However, it is important to stress that in this period (from the late 1940s to the late 1950s), during which curriculum workers were losing all their power, one person kept his writings and currency intact: Tyler, along with the people behind behavioral objectives. In fact, he was the only person in the curriculum field who was truly powerful because he served as the voice of both scientific and rational curriculum-making. He had given birth to the basic principles of curriculum and instruction. The problematic of knowledge that emerged at this time poured into the disciplines, which were the ideal site for knowledge construction and maintenance.

Two books essential for understanding the curriculum in the United Sates are Tyler's *Basic Principals of Curriculum and Instruction* and Bruner's *Process of Education,* the latter not even being about curriculum. However, an issue was emerging that neither Bruner, who struggled for the schooling of the structure of the disciplines, nor Tyler, who argued that knowledge was to be found in the disciplines of knowledge, could answer: What would the structure of the disciplines be?

In an effort to resolve this question, at the beginning of the 1960s, Phenix published *Realms of Meaning,* which would become a major reference for those thinking about knowledge. Phenix was the major theorist of all the people involved in discipline-centered education. However, *Realms of Meaning,* which greatly influenced the curriculum field, should not be understood as a proposal that reinforced Tyler's ideology. On the one hand we have Tyler with scientific curriculum-making; on the other we have Phenix, with his discipline-centered view; and, finally, we have the two coming together. Phenix would later be known as the great theorist of the disciplines.

Phenix (1964) wrote that "it is not easy to sustain a sense of the whole…All too commonly the teacher teaches a particular subject or unit within a subject without any reference to its relationships to other components of the curriculum" (p. 3), adding that the students "may study one subject after another with no idea of what a growing fund of knowledge and skill might contribute to an integrated way of life" (p. 3). As a result, Phenix criticized the fact that both teachers and students "are prone to take the curriculum as they find it, as a traditional sequence of separate elements, without ever inquiring into the comprehensive pattern within which the constituent parts are located" (p. 3). However, "since education is the means of perpetuating culture from generation to generation" (p. 3), Phenix argued that "the special office of education is to widen one's view of life, to deepen insight into relationships, and to counteract the provincialism of customary existence—in short, to engender an integrated outlook" (pp. 3–4). To give substance to this integrated outlook, a unitary philosophy of the curriculum was needed, due to a combination of factors of which Phenix highlighted four: "(1) a comprehensive outlook is necessary for all intelligent decisions about what shall be included and excluded from the course of study; (2) because a person is essentially an organized totality and not just a collection of separate parts, the curriculum ought to have a corresponding organic quality; (3) society, as well as individual persons, depends upon principles of community; corporate life, like the life of each individual, requires some overall plan; (4) a comprehensive concept of the structure of learning gives added significance to each of the component segments of the curriculum" (p. 4).

Education, to Phenix, was one of the processes for constructing these meanings. Hence, he believed that "the modern curriculum should be designed with particular attention" (p. 5) to the sources of what is "meaningless in contemporary life" (p. 5); in other words, the curriculum should be planned so as to oppose skepticism, depersonalization, fragmentation, and rapid transformations. Consequently, education was considered a constant search for meaning, and the objective of a certain curriculum philosophy consisted of an analysis of the nature of that same framework of meanings—the mapping of the realms of meaning. According to Phenix, there are six crucial patterns of meaning: "Symbolics, Empirics, Esthetics, Synnoetics, Ethics, Synoptics" (pp. 6–7).

In essence, Bruner established the problematic (teach the disciplines but teach them by discovery) that joined the discipline of knowledge with progressive education. But this was rhetorical; even if you agree with Bruner you still have to know what the structure of the disciplines are. According to Bruner, the disciplines are like a skeleton, and we add more flesh to the bones as improvements are made. Bruner's logic raises two questions: (1) What is the structure of the disciplines? and (2) What is the pedagogic structure of the discipline? (a question not asked by Bruner). For example, what is the structure of physics or the structure of history, and which theories underlie them? Simply following these questions might not be the wisest approach to teaching. There must be "a logic" of teaching (pedagogy) that is not limited to following the disciplines' own internal logic. So, Phenix answered these two questions by claiming that teaching a discipline of knowledge may require that one change the structure a little bit in order to make sense to the students.

However, this leads to another serious problem: the knowledge explosion. There are hundreds of disciplines: Which does one teach? Does one teach physics and chemistry, and biology? Does one teach sociology, psychology, anthropology, and social geography? How does one determine the realms of meaning, since there are ways of knowing and the disciplines are grouped around ways of knowing? For instance, empirics involve biology, physics, and chemistry; it makes no difference, which one is taught. What is important is the way of knowing, not necessarily just the facts.

With *Realms of Meaning,* Phenix solved one problem. However, taking the structure of the disciplines into consideration, there was also the need for something that would operationalize Phenix's logic, which was to come about with the National Education Defense Act, which, as noted above, guaranteed that the federal government would pay for 80 percent of the cost of adopting what would come to be known as teacher-proof material. Through the National Defense Education Act, *Realms of Meaning* colonized the field of the classroom. It was undoubtedly the act that prevented Phenix's ways of knowing from straying beyond the boundaries of a theoretical framework.

The years from 1947 until 1970 were the most transformative in the history of curriculum since the era of Bobbitt and Charters. It is important to notice the ideological umbrella that was formed, which included scientific curriculum-making, of which Tyler was the major spokesperson, along with the behavioral objectives curriculum, a return to testing, discipline-centered curriculum movements (a return to the disciplines of knowledge), right-wing and reactionary sentiments to remove any progressive elements, and cold war warriors like Rickover. All of this was not simply rhetoric. For example, the National Defense Education Act, which grew out of these ideologies, was enacted at the federal level. The major movement for prepackaged material started at this time, and people working in curriculum—except for Tyler—had no power. In essence, the National Defense Education Act, which operationalized *Realms of Meaning*, can only be understood as part of a long history of events. We must bear in mind that there were separate tendencies in curriculum research and that they all came together in particular ways. After World War II, Tyler led a rebirth of scientific curriculum-making, and he was the only one who could have done so, given his prestige in the sciences, the prestige garnered through his association with the University of Chicago and as a tester, and because he was someone who worked for progressive education, which made him in essence the eagle of the field. For all of these reasons, the Sputnik surprise and subsequent panic were only the tip of the iceberg. Sputnik in itself was not that important, but it was part of a combination of events that helped bring about reforms in the curriculum field.

In this period of transformation, another name comes to the foreground: Schwab. A biologist, Schwab already had power because he was connected with the biological sciences curriculum bureau project and with the discipline-centered movement. He became powerful in part because he was considered different from the other curriculum people, given his identity as a real scientist. For Schwab, the major issue was not really knowledge. In fact, he took for granted what knowledge is—he believed that knowledge is in the disciplines. His first work was on the discipline-centered curriculum, and he then started to think more generally about it. He started writing his work *The Practical* in reaction to some curriculum theorists, having become angry at the "nonsense" he found in curriculum theory. According to Schwab (1978), the existing curriculum theorization led to three main observations:

(1) The field of curriculum is moribund. It is unable, by its present methods and principles, to contribute significantly to the advancement of education. It requires new principles, which will generate a new view of the character and a variety of its problems. (2) The curriculum field has reached this unhappy state by inveterate, unexamined, and

mistaken reliance on theory. On the one hand, it has adopted theories (from outside the field of education) concerning ethics, knowledge, political and social structure, learning, mind and personality, and has used these borrowed theories theoretically, i.e., as principles from which to "deduce" right aims and procedures for schools and classrooms. On the other hand, it has attempted construction of educational theories, particularly theories of curriculum and instruction. (3) There will be a renascence of the field of curriculum, a renewed capacity to contribute to the quality of American education, only if curriculum energies are in large part diverted from theoretic pursuits (such as the pursuit of global principles and comprehensive patterns, the search for stable consequences and invariant elements, the construction of taxonomies of supposedly fixed or recurrent kinds) to three other models of operation. These other modes, which differ radically from the theoretic, I shall call, following the tradition, the *practical*, the *quasi-practical*, and the *eclectic*. (p. 287).

According to Schwab (1978), "the radical difference of the practical from the theoretic mode [was] visible in the fact that it differs from the theoretic not in one aspect but in many: it differs from the theoretic in method. Its problems originate from a different source. Its subject matter is of a distinctly different character. Its outcome is of a different kind" (p. 288). If the result of the theoretical is knowledge, the result of the practical is the decision, the selection, and the orientation toward a possible action. Schwab believed that the quasi-practical implies two major issues: on the one hand, it allows for the making of intelligent and happy choices in the instruction of a heterogeneous group. Thus, the practical orientation for an increasingly heterogeneous group entails passage through the quasipractical. The appropriate methods are "the methods of the practical per se but with heavy special emphasis on the cherishing of diversity and the honoring of delegate powers" (p. 294). Thus the quasipractical is a method of deliberation. This deliberation is a process that is difficult, time consuming, and unsatisfying, since one cannot guarantee that it will be complete, even though one has to ensure that quasipractical decisions are not confused with the directives, be it by those who elaborate them or by those who translate them into practice, into action. On the other hand, the quasipractical is furthermore related with the organic complicity between the different school organisms, the educational community, and the educational system.

The eclectic mode of operation recommended for the curriculum field "recognizes the usefulness of theory to curriculum decision, takes account of certain weaknesses of theory as ground for decision, and provides some degree of repair of these weaknesses" (Schwab, 1978, p. 295). Whether used eclectically or not, Schwab continues, "theory has two major uses in decision making. [First,] theories are used as bodies of knowledge; [second,] the terms and distinctions which a theory uses for theoretical purposes can be brought to bear practically" (p. 296). However, Schwab argued that the theory had weak points (the content and the objects of theories are inevitably incomplete), but that such fragilities could be resolved by the eclectic mode of operation in two ways: "first, eclectic operations bring into clear view the particular truncation of subject characteristic of a given theory and bring to light the partiality of its view. Second, eclectic operations permit the serial utilization or even the conjoint utilization of two or more theories on practical problems" (p. 297).

In fact, Schwab did not note an open rupture with what was occurring in the field of the curriculum. If he did in fact offer a clear problematization of the theoretical fallacy into which the curriculum field had arrived, the fact is that Schwab does not problematize the disciplines as sources of knowledge in any of the points of his thesis—practical, quasipractical, or eclectic. In other words, he begins with the principle that knowledge is poured into the subjects while criticizing the excess of theoricity, an excess that in fact led people outside the field of education to theorize about it. Thus, with some difficulty, one may place Schwab among those who opposed the positivism and behaviorism that determined the rhythms of the majority of classrooms throughout the country. Although Tyler was obviously the dominant spokesperson of the curriculum field, there was also a reactionary antipositivist, antiscience, and antibehaviorist movement. These movements, which were viscerally opposed to the dominance of the discipline-centered material, the dominance of behavioral objectives, the dominance of tests, and the dominance of Tyler, emerged in the late 1960s and early 1970s. It is to them that we turn our attention next. In so doing, we will uncover the struggles for curriculum relevance in which civil rights and the romantic critics, as well as a particular critical progressive curriculum tradition (in which the works of Greene, Huebner, Apple, Giroux, and others could not be minimized), played a substantial role.

CHAPTER 6

THE STRUGGLE FOR CURRICULUM
RELEVANCE

Although the behaviorist and subject-centered movements successfully constructed and controlled a certain curriculum hegemony, especially in the 1950s and early 1960s, the period dominated by the "Tyler Rationale" also encountered significant resistance. This included the works of Sharp (1951), Spears (1951), Corey (1953), Hopkins (1954), Pritzkau (1959), and Miel (1964), among others, which should not be marginalized. Although it is impossible to regard these oppositional positions as a movement in the true sense of the word, they did assume positions divergent from the status quo that were clearly opposed to the reductive notion of the curriculum, which emphasized previously established objectives and defined the teacher's primary function as the stimulation of the learner (cf. Hopkins, 1954; Pritzkau, 1959; Sharp, 1951; Spears, 1951). What was clearly called for was the need to reorient the teacher's work, which would require a reeducation of those already active in the profession (Corey, 1953; Miel, 1964; Sharp, 1951).

Despite the fact that some discipline-centered theorists were not concerned about social efficiency, their resistance to this conceptual fundamentalism, which was centered on a rationale based on social efficiency and effectiveness, stretched to other sectors of society. Their struggle led to the emergence of many critical voices, as demonstrated by the works of Packard (1957), Whyte (1956), Mills (1951), and even Ellison (1952), who in a notable novel denounced the miserable social conditions of many African-Americans. Thus, analysis of this problematic issue should have a wider social context.

It is important to understand that the profound social crisis in the United States during the 1960s had its roots in conditions at the beginning of the twentieth century (cf. Goldman, 1956). The 1960s "appeared to be a time of genuine fracturing in relations between

America's young people and their elders" (Urban & Wagoner, 2000, p. 313). It was "a period of cultural and political change unique in American history" (Button & Provenzo, 1983, p. 316) in which "a major social revolution occurred" (Ignas & Corsini, 1979, p. 111). The emerging postwar society, unable to provide reasonable life options to the less endowed classes, denied them the present and mortgaged their future. However, members of those disadvantaged classes were not willing to accept such conditions, especially since they had helped defend the nation in World War II in the interest of democracy and social justice. Curiously, while World War II managed to create a war economy "that convincingly ended the decade-long Great Depression" (Urban & Wagoner, 2000, p. 279), the fact is that "America's schools emerged from the war showing more continuity than change" (p. 283). In fact, "black leaders were concerned that the ending of the depression had not resulted in any significant increase in employment opportunities for the black people" (Spring, 1976, p. 142).

In a society still marked by segregationist patterns, by an oppressive education system supported by traditional values, by growing opposition to the Vietnam War, and by the imminent danger of a nuclear conflict, social disenchantment was increasingly explosive (cf. Ayers, 2001). It is within this context that we must view the student revolts, which helped reveal the true conditions in America and damaged the country's foreign image. The nation was collapsing into what Myrdal (1944) years before had called the American dilemma, which expressed the profound paradox of the democratic ideals that the country purported to represent and the stigma of racism that ran through U.S. society (cf. United States Commission on Civil Rights, 1962).

With the "historic and controversial Supreme Court decision *Brown vs. Board of Education of Topeka,* which [in 1954] declared segregated public education unconstitutional" (Spring, 1976, pp. 146–7), the Fourteenth Amendment was belatedly recognized. However, the American nation was forced to further confront the problem of segregation with the Rosa Parks incident on December 1, 1955, and the subsequent Montgomery bus boycott that stretched throughout most of the following year. The controversy escalated further with the events that took place in Little Rock, Arkansas, in 1957.

Seventy years after Homer Plessy "had been arrested for refusing to ride in the 'colored' coach of a train as required by Louisiana Law" (Urban & Wagoner, 2000, p. 298; cf. Hessong & Weeks, 1991; Spring, 1986; Strike, 1982), which led to the U.S. Supreme

Court's "separate but equal" ruling in *Plessy v. Ferguson* (Blaustein & Ferguson, 1957), and after Oliver Brown's daughter "was denied the right to attend a white elementary school within five blocks from her home" (Spring, 1976, p. 147), the Supreme Court, pressured by the collapse of "America's foreign image during the Cold War" (p. 141) and by important social studies by Clark (1952) and Myrdal (1944), ruled that racial segregation was unconstitutional. Nevertheless, opposition to the politics of integration persisted (Bullock, 1970).

There are many reports of resistance to the abolition of segregation. A 1962 report submitted to the United States Commission on Civil Rights denounced the alarming rate of segregation within public institutions. The report highlighted the fact that education is a race in which poor families are handicapped, and that millions of children are not encouraged at home to do well at school (The Problem of Poverty in America, 1962). Another important document (Jencks et al., 1972) revealed the persistence of segregation, noting that "America spends far more money educating some children than others. These variations are largely explained by where a student happens to live and how much schooling he gets" (p. 29).

However, "the Brown decision was not really about schools. It was about first class citizens" (Ethridge, 1974, p. 27), for it established the basis for decisions about human rights, such as

> the right to equal educational opportunity; the right to sit at a public lunch counter and be served; the right to ride in the front as well as the back of a bus; the right to be treated at a hospital; the right to swim and play in a public park; the right to sleep in a public inn; the right to vote and have that vote counted; the right to equality in employment practices; the right to run for and to hold public office. (p. 27).

In fact, as stressed by Button and Provenzo (1983),

> changed schooling has changed society in the last quarter century or more: we know that those changes have been slight. The answer to George Count's question, "Dare the school build a new social order?" has been that it was dared, but that it was not done... The effort must and will continue, but having reflected upon the last quarter century of effort, we admit our disappointments. (p. 315)

The 1960s saw worrisome levels of social instability, perpetrated as much by the civil rights movement as by student and teacher revolts. The decade bore witness to the passing of legislation that defended human rights. Among the many notable events of the time, two assumed particular significance for the national and international memory: one occurred in Birmingham, where "commercial areas...still had segregated drinking fountains and public facilities"; the other occurred on August 28, 1963, when 200,000 people, led by Martin Luther King Jr., marched on Washington in a peaceful protest of the oppression of Blacks.[1] King shook the conscience of even the least attentive members of U.S. society with his famous "I Have a Dream" speech. After President Kennedy's assassination in November 1963, President Johnson, a "master of congressional strategy" (Spring, 1976, p. 175), put civil rights legislation on the congressional agenda on January 31, 1964. On June 19, Congress approved what would be known as the Civil Rights Act of 1964, "one of the most significant pieces of social legislation in the United States in the twentieth century" (p. 176).

Of the individuals who greatly distinguished themselves in the crusade against segregation, one of the most notable is Paul Robeson, who believed that the character of the nation should be determined not by the rich classes but by the common people, and that change was possible. Robeson became not only a force against McCarthyism, but a point of reference for the whole world. His public admiration for what was then the U.S.S.R, his connections with the Eastern Bloc, his explicit support for the liberation of African countries, and the fact that he increasingly represented a voice against segregation and exploitation in the United States led to his being under surveillance by the FBI.[2] Robeson's voice was directed at the more privileged, at the working class and, above all the American racial system: "I am a Negro. The house I live in is in Harlem—this city within a city, the Negro metropolis of America" (Robeson, 1971, p. 1).

The civil rights movement's struggle for a just society cannot be separated from the long tradition of social struggles in the United States—for example, against a eugenic society or a segregated education system—that were led by W. E. B. Du Bois, Sojourner Truth, Booker T. Washington, Frederick Douglass, and many others. Well before Kilpatrick's article "The Project Method" appeared, Washington was able "to build an entire school around a curriculum that was structured around projects of daily life at Tuskegee National and Industrial Institute" (Generals, 2000, p. 216). In contrast to Kilpatrick's "stimulated projects for classrooms activities, [Washington's] projects consisted of building the buildings for the institution" (p. 216). In many ways, Washington was a progressive *avant la lettre*. Six years before Dewey's *How We Think* (1910)—which debates, among other issues, the nexus of interest-curiosity—Washington (1904a, 1905) unfolded his pedagogical principle based on the interest, the knowledge, and the activity of the student. His entire educational idea was laboratory based. Moreover, the Tuskegee curriculum clearly demonstrates Washington's constant attempts to make education a politically relevant process. Tuskegee's curriculum platform not only highlighted "academic classrooms, and the industrial shops and fields, but also the theory [that] classes were directly connected to the industrial shops and fields" (Generals, 2000). Washington's philosophy prioritized learning by highlighting students' daily experiences; his contribution to curriculum was massive but also unjustifiably neglected (Washington, 1904b, 1905; also Tuskegee Catalogue, 1904).

The issues of curriculum relevance and schooling's social and political functions were pretty much at the center of Du Bois's (1932) educational philosophy as well. Although there was a complex "controversy concerning the type of education which American Negroes needed," Du Bois argued that "the Negro college has done a great work" (p. 60). The struggle for a relevant educational platform, Du Bois claimed, needed "first training as human beings in general knowledge and experience; then technical training to guide and to do a specific part of the world's work" (p. 71). A towering concern in Du Bois's theoretical approach was

the ideal of knowledge—not guess-work, not mere careless theory; not inherited religious dogma clung to because of fear and inertia and in spite of logic, but critically tested and laboriously gathered fact materialized under scientific law and feeding rather than choking the glorious world of fancy and imagination, of poetry and art, of beauty and deep culture. (p. 73)

Sojourner Truth, Du Bois, Washington, and too many others are vivid examples of the power of an autobiographical approach within the curriculum field, a crucial approach that was instigated, developed, refined, and complexified later on by Pinar (1994; cf. also 2004), Grumet (1981), and others. The need for curriculum relevance and a ferocious fight for social justice can be overtly identified in the civil rights movement as well. The civil rights crusade should not be dissociated from the student activist movement, which associated itself with the black cause, finding within the human rights movement the impetus for its own demands. Among other things, Noam Chomsky (1992) argues that the importance of the student movement must be understood as part of a wider social movement that included the women's movement and other social movements, which disturbed a

200-year-old lie and tried to destroy the historically established social apparatus.

This complex social picture greatly tarnished the U.S. foreign image, with the media in general and television in particular playing a crucial role. Television showed the nation (and the world) shocking images of the Vietnam War (Manchester, 1974), thus exercising its power to transform "the local into the national" (Spring, 1976, p. 161) and this in turn into the international, thereby transforming these social conflicts into a "battle of public images" (p. 161). The United States could not ignore the critical thinking and sentiment that the international community was beginning to express about the country's internal situation. However, the various presidential administrations, including Kennedy's, revealed dubious stances toward human rights. Thus, both education in general and curriculum in particular were not immune from this social turmoil. In a 1966 report, Goodlad, Von Stoephasius, and Klein argued that a different socially ethical curriculum approach was critical to the redevelopment of a more vigorous and vital curriculum field. They denounced the lack of balance in the curriculum subjects as one of the greatest challenges facing educators. Social dissatisfaction was spreading and critical voices were multiplying throughout the various social sectors, particularly through the music of Bob Dylan, Joan Baez, and Pete Seeger. A belief in the need for an "open education" was beginning to crystallize, a belief that broke free of the obsolete schemes of a traditional education and implied, among other things, strong interaction between students; curriculum activities that were centered on students; flexibility of the spaces, the scope, and the relevance of the topics dealt with; and, most important, a radical break from the status quo, which dictated that everything was to be conducted in perfect order to reach a previously determined objective. Educators, writers, and journalists were at the forefront of this movement for an open education, including Dennison, Friedenberg, Goodman, Henry, Holt, Illich, Kohl, Kozol, Leonard, McLuhan, Roszack, and Silberman, all of whom associated themselves with the struggle against the alienation of youth that was perpetuated by an irrelevant pedagogy. This group, labeled the romantic critics, the radical critics, the radical reform movement, or sometimes "counterculture intellectuals" (cf. Schubert, 2008, p. 405) was opposed to what was understood as the depersonalization of youth. They argued that teachers should place the emphasis of their work on children's individual interests and be able to mold the previously determined curriculum to those interests (Friedenberg, 1962; Holt, 1969), relying on various strategies to captivate students' interest (Holt, 1970).

On a smaller scale, Silberman (1970) performed a study on schools that was similar to the one Rice had done at the end of the nineteenth century, which noted the existence of a mindless pedagogy distanced from the interests of children. In the words of Van Til (1970), "Even young people from privileged backgrounds protest unreality in the curriculum" (p. 345). Antipathy toward the school was thus evident and, according to McLuhan and Leonard (1969), "the time is coming, if it is not already here, when children can learn far faster in the outside world than within school-house walls" (p. 106). The idea that "ideally, the polis itself is the educational environment" (Goodman, 1969, p. 103) was thus established, especially since "the monkish and academic methods which were civilizing for wild shepherds create robots in a period of high technology" (p. 100). The criticism against a compulsory educational system is still apparent in Illich (1971), who believed that education should be the responsibility of society and not schools, because schools are controlled by the government and serve the interests of a minority, and in Roszack (1969), who appealed to the need to eliminate the restrictions and conformism of the schooling institutions. Dennison (1969a) also called attention to an alternative program—"first street school"—for children of the less privileged classes and from families with reduced incomes who had been labeled as having learning and behavioral difficulties. This model was influenced above all by Neil, who argued for schooling that was "radical and experimental, [without] grades, graded report cards, [or] competitive examinations" (Dennison, 1969b, p. 228).

The school, Henry (1963, 1969) argued, was seen as an institution that made men and women more vulnerable and, further, that "the function of education has never been to free the mind and the spirit of man, but to bind them" (p. 77). Education, according to Henry (1963), inhibits creativity while stimulating competitiveness and hatred between children. He wrote that "what we see in the kindergarten and the early years of school is a pathetic surrender of babies" (p. 81), and referred to a hidden curriculum that had a profound power to (de)construct the culture transmitted in the schools.

Kohl (1988) also addressed the existence of a hidden curriculum in schools, arguing that the most important things taking place in schools did not occur during the lessons. He observed that "everything important in the classroom is happening between lessons" (p. 26). Kohl added that the "teacher must make mistakes" (p. 24); in other words, "when a teacher claims he knows exactly what will happen in his class, exactly how the children will behave and function, he is either lying or brutal" (p. 24).

Without minimizing the work of the previously mentioned authors, the fact is that Kozol (1967) played a pivotal role in advancing such Romantic Movement. Kozol believed that students were the victims of a profoundly oppressive and bureaucratic educational machine, and of the system's punitive pedagogy. He exposed the racial and social differences between teachers and students as the source of the divide that existed between them.

The romantic critics brought a breath of fresh air to society in general and to the education field in particular by exposing a combination of radical positions and solutions. However, their ideas also had a certain continuity with the projects and practices produced by Dewey and Horton. The romantic critics movement, however, was not a homogenous group. For some, the free schools were something pure, impartial, neutral, and impermeable to the political and social contexts. For others, the free school strategy went beyond the problems of pedagogy; in other words, it was to be understood as a political act that would help transform society, since the schools themselves did not have the means for such a radical revolution (cf. Graubard, 1972). Kozol (1972) maintained that the social meaning of school could not be looked for in the school itself, but in society.

Is impossible to understand the "period of the middle 1960s without reading Herb Kohl, Jonathan Kozol, Jules Henry, Paul Goodman—people known as the romantic critics" (Apple, 2000, pp. 81, 86; cf. Ayers, 1992). Moreover, it is impossible to fully grasp the political economy of U.S. education without a clear understanding of "slavery's contribution to the emergence of America's rise to world power" (Watkins, 2001, p. 12). It was in this era that people in the United States began to have more explicit contact with the work of authors like Marcuse, Habermas, and Ellul. Ellul (1964), influenced by Marx, denounced technology's influence on the economy and emphasized that the human dimension must not be eradicated from the technical apparatus. The culture of poverty was undeniably beginning to sharpen under the pressures of modern technology (Harrington, 1962), and it was increasingly clear that an effective freedom would only be possible for oppressed communities if there were a massive attack directed at the culture of poverty; in this, education was not an innocent bystander. Years later, Bowles and Gintis (1976) would argue that the capitalist system is not a simple technical process but also a social process. As discussed earlier, it was in the profound struggle against the status quo that Jackson published his work, *Life in Classrooms*. This leads us to disagree not only with the line of thought formulated by Kohlberg (1970) , for whom Jackson "invented the term 'hidden' or 'unstudied' curriculum to refer to 90 percent of what goes on in classrooms" (p. 104), but also with Eggleston's (1977) perspective, for whom "the 'hidden' curriculum was identified by Jackson" (p. 15).

Discussion of the hidden curriculum emerged not only in the works of the Romantic Critics, but also in research by Bellack, Kliebard, Hyman, and Smyth Jr. (1966), Huebner (1966), Macdonald (1966a, 1966b), and Shane (1968). The social instability expressed in the revolts by the civil rights movement and by students, and in the powerful criticism of the various sectors of U.S. society, led certain defenders of the disciplinary doctrine to reconsider some of their stances. Phenix and Schwab, great theorists of knowledge based in the subjects, significantly altered their positions in response to the student movement of the 1960s. Phenix (1969) saw that a curriculum approach fundamentally driven by the subjects could lead to a fragmentation of the curriculum that would be insensitive to certain social issues. Despite holding curriculum notions similar to those of Tyler (cf. Schwab, 1970), after considering the issues of the student movement, Schwab (1969) noted that "our students are man and woman without a country" (p. 41). He added that "our students are almost entirely deprived of proper curriculum occasions, especially sufficiently early occasions, for discovery, essay, and exercise of their competences with respect to form and structure, coherence and cogency, evidence and argument, recovery and formulation of meaning" (p. 40). The notion of change was gaining ground, and "the big mistake most schools have made is in showing reluctance to meet the child in his home territory" (Fantini & Weinstein, 1969, p. 6). In fact, education needed to become more appropriate for the disadvantaged, and "the educator's commitment is to produce thinking, well-informed, healthy, happy democratic American citizens" (Crary, 1969, p. 5; Metcalf & Hunt, 1970).

Although the 1960s enriched the curriculum field, it was not until the 1970s that the field would make a significant change (cf. Beauchamp, 1964; Brameld, 1961; Crosby, 1964; Inlow, 1966; Maccia, 1962, 1963; Neagley & Evans, 1967; Oliver, 1963; Passow, 1962). Although some, such as Reafferty (1970, p. 16), believed it was a mistake to continue to foster the right to equal opportunity from among the "mishmash known as 'social sciences,'" others felt there was real need for curriculum reform, in part due to the rapid transformations in society but above all due to the fact that the content taught in most classrooms was not relevant to the lives of the learners (Burns & Brooks, 1970). A profound transformation was essential; that is, there was no need for more of the same but precisely for more of the different (Frymier & Hawn, 1970), which comes from the knowledge that schooling "is not a unitary process from the beginning to end" (Dreeben, 1970, p. 86). This notion of the transformation of schools in general and the curriculum in particular was the main influence on Haubrich's (1971) ASCD yearbook.[3] The need for "the abandonment of the apolitical analyses of the past [and] to explain more effectively the forces at work in schools" was inevitable (Macdonald & Zaret, 1975, p. 16). Therefore, a theory of and investigation into the curriculum field were needed to provide answers for certain questions, such as "How can we conceptualize the process of instruction? What actually goes on during an instructional sequence?" (Macdonald, 1971b, p. 107). The attempt to construct an alternative curriculum approach—one that would challenge the hegemonic political conservatism dominating the field (cf. Popkewitz, 1979b)—was in its way, and it is in this context that we find the contributions, events, and movements of, among others, Goodlad and Klein (1970), Purpel and Belanger (1972), Ford (1973), Greene (1973), Bellack (1973), Haubrich and Apple (1975), Giroux (1981a, 1981b), and Popkewitz (1979a, 1979b), conferences such as the Rochester Conference (cf. Pinar, 1974) and the attempt (that created too many problematic fissures) to systematize a particular counterdominant curriculum tradition led by the reconceptualists, as we will reveal at length later on.

However, from among the varied attempts at transformation and the search for new approaches for the curriculum field that took place in the 1970s, we should highlight two books that, in our opinion, would come to serve as benchmarks for the field: the ASCD's *Schools in Search of Meaning* (Macdonald & Zaret, 1975) and *Schooling in Capitalist America* (Bowles & Gintis, 1976). In the latter, which took seven years to write, the authors carry on with some of the ideas of the romantic critics. In addition to restating that the genesis of social repression and inequality is clearly found in the structure and functioning of the capitalist economy, Bowles and Gintis stressed that "the educational system serves—through the correspondence of its social relations with those of economic life—to reproduce economic inequality and to distort personal development" (p. 48), a position that, as we discussed previously, would be challenged by Apple, Wexler, Giroux, and others.

The first, *Schools in Search of Meaning,* warned of something about to happen, which would later prove true in 1976 in Geneseo. Although a lack of equilibrium can be found between the introductory text and those of the contributing authors, it is obvious that all "were educators in search of meaning [and conscious that] the meaning of school in America society is the other side of the coin" (Macdonald & Zaret, 1975, p. 1). According to Macdonald and Zaret (1975), "Most of the curriculum talk is confused about modes of valuing and motives for talking" (p. 4). They claim that "moral and political modes must be emphasized" (p. 4), although the meaning of the school "cannot be totally reduced to political terms" (p. 5). They should see the school as a liberating force (Zaret, 1975) and teaching as a commitment to helping others to develop their possibilities, which could only be achieved if the children were not deprived of certain meanings, and of their memories, life experiences, and desires (Huebner, 1975). The "schools are a set of meanings, but only those meanings that preserve the status quo, perpetuating realities of the social order as perceived, structured, and defended by the dominant group" (Zaret, 1975, p. 38). From among these meanings, she added, there is a notable imbalance between woman and man. This notion is also reiterated by Mann (1975, p. 97), for whom the interest of the dominant class in the schools is verifiable in the "control of ideology, control of knowledge and control of training." He further noted that educators suffer from the myth of ideology reform, an ideology that conveys the fallacy that it is possible to cause profound social change in the structure of class without transforming that same structure. According to Mann, education was marked by contradictions: (1) "the fundamental problems in schools are best explained and acted upon in terms of an analysis of contradictions within schools; (2) the contradictions within schools are manifestations of the contradictions in society in general; (3) and the larger society constitutes the conditions for change within the schools" (p. 96). Such contradictions are also noted by MacDonald (1975) as "(a) work, (b) power and (c) language" (p. 98). He claimed that such contradictions originate from the attempts to find an answer to the question, "In whose interest is the activity of the school?" (p. 88). This problematic issue of power and language is also dealt with by Apple (1975), who links it to the ethical dimension that is intrinsic to the educational process. Apple argues that labels such as "slow learner, discipline problem, poor reader" (p. 129) are produced in the daily school practices. These labels, which ultimately should be interpreted as "rhetorical devices" (p. 130), are not neutral, but instead express specific class-oriented judgments of worth and stigmatize the students that are labeled.

The dice had been thrown, and the issue thus towered over several curriculum conferences. One of those conferences, entitled Curriculum Theorizing since 1947: Rhetoric or Progress?—which we think was quite emblematic—was held on October 7 and 8, 1977, at the State University College of Arts and Science in Geneseo. As the title suggests, three decades after the legendary conference Herrick and Tyler held at the University of Chicago in October 1947, it was necessary to analyze the progress—or stagnation or retrogression—in the field of curriculum theorization. Tyler (1977a) wrote that "the conference turned out to be little more than a concert—albeit a good one—in bugle playing" (p. 255), and that it lacked a broad, encompassing theory:

> Today we continue to build curricula without comprehensive theory. To shift the metaphor, we are carpenters, not architects. Can we not begin to build a sound architectural theory, one that is periodically reexamined, continually tested, and able to deal intelligently and comprehensively with changes in society and in knowledge? (p. 256)

Diamonti (1977a) too believed there was no such a thing as curriculum theory. Resuming this preoccupation, Kliebard (1977a), by means of a clear, careful, and analytical approach to the issues related to the development of a curriculum theory, highlighted the need to determine both the territory that would be covered by the curriculum theory and the type of theory that he regarded as adequate to do so, as well as something he called a "for instance." In other words, he thought we should try to see whether, in all those years, "anything has emerged that in the light of previous considerations could stand as an example of a curriculum theory" (Kliebard, 1977a, p. 260). "Since the central questions of curriculum are normative ones, in the sense that they involve choices among competing value options" (p. 263), adds Kliebard, "the question of empirical verification comes into play only in a peripheral sense" (p. 263)—in other words, "what is critically important is conceptual clarification" (p. 263). In fact, this perspective had already been proposed by Dewey. In Kliebard's words, "The central core of Dewey's curriculum theory is neither an empirically verifiable generalization nor an experimental finding, but a metaphor" (p. 263), and it is through the lens of this "metaphor that [he] was able to identify the crucial issues that define curriculum and so to clarify the concepts that arise from these problems"

(p. 263). Naturally, "the scope and the substance of a curriculum theory" bases itself not so much "in the domain of the distribution of knowledge as a kind of commodity, but in considering what effects would accrue from study...of a given domain" (p. 261). This problematic issue is taken up again by Apple and King (1977), along the lines of what Spencer initially had proposed, as did Apple later on.

The problematic of curriculum theorization is delved into further by Greene (1977), who focused "on the part the artistic-aesthetic might play in contemporary curriculum" (p. 283). Greene, referred to by Huebner (1977a) as "an ambassador," saw the curriculum "as a number of provinces of meaning, each one associated with the kinds of experiences available to young people of different biographies, different locations in the social world" (Greene, 1977, p. 287). Paralleling Kliebard's notions, Greene wrote that "aesthetic theory probably springs from the human necessity to make aesthetic choices" and that aesthetic experiences "involve us as existing beings in pursuit of meanings" (p. 293). In other words, "they involve us as historical beings born into social reality" and thus "they must be *lived* within the contexts of our own self-understanding, within the contexts of what we have constituted as our world" (p. 293). It is this human dimension to theorization, drafted by Greene, that led Kliebard to reiterate the normativity of the curriculum theory. Thus, although "we can come up with examples of applied fields, say engineering" (Kliebard, 1977b, p. 277), it is with great difficulty that one accepts "the fact that curriculum is an applied field of philosophy or any of the traditional foundations areas" (p. 277). Such a notion would later be contested by Diamonti (1977b), for whom curriculum theory is not theoretical but "purely applied theory" (p. 277). It is interesting that the position upheld by Tyler may still be identified here, a fact that confirms the complexity of his thought. On the one hand, he reiterated that "we may have to rely on some kind of systematized knowledge, modes of organizing experience, concepts that are useful, that can help to guide the practical enterprise of designing an educational program" (Tyler, 1977b, p. 278); on the other, he expressed a clear concern not only with curriculum relevance but also with the teachers' failure to understand what they taught (Tyler, 1977c). This and other positions adopted by Tyler, to which we have referred earlier, should make us reflect carefully on the Tyler rationale. Tyler was not a mere mechanic or a simple technician.

Distancing himself somewhat from this line of thought, Jackson (1977a) mentioned that we "must also look at the broader context of public opinion and social attitudes within which those writings achieve credibility. Nor must we be solely concerned with the truth of what is written, for what people believe to be true is a force of its own even though it later may be proven false" (p. 312). Justifying his position on the basis of his almost 25 years of experience, Jackson tried to maintain a neutral position—"I have witnessed sharp attacks from both extremes [left and right] of that ideological spectrum" (p. 313)—that would later prove difficult to maintain, as suggested by the light banter he exchanged, say, with Apple.[4]

In opposition to the technological legacy that dominated the field, Apple and King (1977) stress that "a number of sociologists and curriculum scholars, influenced strongly by the sociology of knowledge in both its Marxist (or neo-Marxist) and phenomenological variants, have begun to raise serious questions about the lack of attention to the relationship school knowledge and extra-school phenomena" (p. 341). The analysis of this issue, according to the authors, besides having to be sensitive to the relationship between school and cultural capital, to the power of the hidden curriculum, to the negotiated meanings, and to the practices of common sense in the school or in evaluation, must above all focus on three major issues: "a description of the historical process through which certain social meanings became *particularly* school meanings and thus have the weight of decades of acceptance behind them; empirical evidence, from a study of kindergarten experience, to document the potency and staying power of these particular social meanings; the questions of whether piecemeal reforms, be they oriented humanistically or in other directions, can succeed" (p. 343).

Ultimately, the 1977 conference decisively defined the field and incorporated the perspectives expressed at the conference held in 1947—a "turning point in a field" (Rosario & Demarte, 1977, p. 249) and the beginning of a more aesthetic and political approach to the curriculum field. The conference also uncovered deep divisions in the field, made obvious by the debates between Jackson, Huebner, and Apple. For Huebner (1977b), an understanding of the field implied not only having to "deal with Heidegger...with the Marxian orientation...with neo-Hegelianism [...and] with analytical philosophy" (p. 332), but also having to admit that Holt and Friedenberg—despite having decisively contributed to the field—would end up falling by the wayside and that their "criticisms lost their impact" (p. 334). But for Jackson, it was mandatory to know how to establish limits with the tools used in the approaches to the field, which many did not do in their desire to maintain a neutral position. Clearly denouncing problems that had their roots in the past—stating that he was "willing to go along with the Michael F. D. Young crowd to some extent" (p. 336) and getting personal even though he claimed he was not referring to Huebner—Jackson retorted:

> I do know enough about some of the people who are using this line, which in now called neo-Marxism, or what I'd prefer to call Marxoid, a Marxoid line of thought. I don't think they're testing the boundaries of the truth of that doctrine. They are indeed prisoners of a doctrine. Perhaps we all are. But maybe as prisoners it's our job to find out where the edge of the cave is and know that there is another perspective. (p. 335)[5]

Despite disagreeing with Jackson's position, Apple (1977a) not only reiterated that it is "unethical to criticize people from an elitist position" (p. 336) but also defended the neo-Marxist approach, which "is support for a certain way of looking at the world that is fruitful, that enables us to seek 'truth'...and it is the very search connections that makes it potent" (pp. 336–7). Drawing somewhat on Dewey's notion that schools create an artificial atmosphere, just as Huebner had previously proposed, Apple argued that schools "are not merely people sorting institutions" (p. 337). Defending the work of Bowles and Gintis as a good point of departure, although "sometimes historically inaccurate and overstated" (Apple, 1977b, p. 362), he distanced himself from the romantic position taken by Illich ("I am not an Illich supporter. I think he's incorrect. You don't do away with schools and then put the kids on a repressive labor market" [p. 363]) and from the dark period of Stalinist history, highlighting the neo-Marxist condition as a constant process.

Although the cynical note advanced by Jackson (1977c) "that the main function of educational research is to advance the careers of educational researchers" (p. 367) should be noted, the fact is that the Geneseo Conference effectively marked a significant turn in the curriculum field. It gave momentum to the change from an approach based in the "disciplinization" of knowledge to one that was more aesthetic and politically compromised.

On the one hand, participants at this conference clearly saw the consolidation of a neo-Marxist approach in the midst of the constant problematization of the legitimacy of the knowledge transmitted in schools—the very essence of the curriculum. On the other hand, they saw that the already fragile dogma of neutrality surrounding the approaches to the field was no longer tenable. In fact, it was Jackson himself who confirmed the impossibility of neutrality and the existence of partiality. In fact, the justification for Jackson's title compromises his theory. His confession speaks for itself:

> Originally, the title of the paper that you saw on your program was called "The hidden curriculum and criticism of schools," and I changed the title after a long deliberation…but I gave up the title "Hidden curriculum" because I've decided I'm not going to use that word anymore in my own writing. And the reason is that it's been used by people that I don't want to be associated with. (Jackson, 1977b, p. 336)

Beyond increasingly gaining strength, the problematic of the knowledge transmitted in schools, and the need to problematize the schools as vehicles of social transformation, political pedagogical events like the Geneseo Conference made even more visible a particular curriculum river within the progressive tradition, a non-monolithic wave with a conscience, and upgraded a particular research approach in the curriculum field, which rests on work from the previous century by Parker, Dewey, Bode, Counts, Rugg, and Horton, among others. The ideological path of some of the contemporary curriculum researchers must be understood as being a part of this line of thought.

In fact, during the 1970s and 1980s, the field would be swamped by a voluminous amount of work from a plurality of scholars exhibiting myriad distinct (fundamentally Western) epistemological perspectives (some of them severe) with tremendous repercussions, say, in several nations around the world, especially in European and Latin American nations. In fact, this was one of the golden moments for a particular set of critical progressive curriculists. In both the United States and the United Kingdom, the field was confronted with Apple's (1979, 1990), Giroux's (1981a), Pinar's (1980), Pinar and Grumet's (1976), Wexler's (1976), Willis's (1977), Whitty's (1985), Young's (1971), and Bernstein's (1977) powerful approaches, among too many others. It was, among other things, the sedimentation of a non-monolithic, powerfully heavyweight armada engaged in a critique of the field,[6] which they saw as trapped within dangerous ideological and cultural compromises and mortgaged to eugenic economic interests. Such tangles need to be put in perspective by returning to the general struggles that emerged in the field at the beginning of the nineteenth century. One thing was quite clear: the field would not be the same anymore. This group of scholars within the critical curriculum river dared to show everybody otherwise.

Drawing from common and uncommon (fundamentally Western) perspectives, scholars including Apple, Giroux, Mann, Wexler, and

McLaren were able to reframe the curriculum debate by bringing a new language to the field, if not precisely to introduce particular concepts. This progressive curriculum owes a great deal to the works of Huebner, Macdonald, Greene, Williams, Gramsci, and Freire, and later of Michel Foucault and others. The field now faced the need to debate and understand concepts such as hegemony, ideology, reproduction, resistance, transformative pedagogy, the hidden curriculum, conflict versus consensus. At a later stage, as critical theorists were blasting the field with this new, politically coded vocabulary, race, gender, and sexuality became entangled with class and identity. In the United States, such concepts were quite prevalent in the works of Apple, Giroux, Wexler, Aronowitz, McLaren, and many others, who reclaimed not necessarily the dictatorship of the political yet assuming the political as "the pillar" to interpret the curriculum and schools. To claim that we are before a nonmonolithic critical curriculum river within the progressive tradition that is hooked on a political approach towards schools and curriculum, seems not only inaccurate and reductive, but also minimizes important political approaches that one could identify in other progressive perspectives. No serious curriculist and/or curriculogus would deny the politicality advanced edified, say, by Greene, Pinar, and others. Arguably, Pinar's later work is much more politically coded than some of his earlier material[7]. *Gramscian* influences on Apple, Giroux, Wexler, Aronowitz, McLaren's approaches—through concepts such as hegemony, common sense, culture, the role of the (organic) intellectuals—gives credibility to our claim (cf. Gramsci, 1957, 1971; also Sassoon, 1982).

Armed with this new semantic artillery, these scholars, especially Apple and Giroux, pushed the field in a different direction. This "neo-Gramscian" stance had several main elements. The first was a basic understanding of individual relations as something organic rather than mechanical. A second was a view of culture as the foundation of new modes of labor, production, and distribution. Hence the belief that the working class should have agency in both the economic and political fields, and that specific cultural elements will lead to the construction of a working-class civilization. In other words, the aim is not only to achieve political and economic power, but also—and this is important—to gain intellectual power, since the ways we think are grounded in a complex mosaic of economic, political, and cultural issues.

The third element was the need to understand concepts such as hegemony and common sense and how they operate in society. Hegemony was perceived as a balance between coercion and consent, and it implied an intricate and complex set of compromises that played a key position within the framework of the state. The final and fourth element was the impossibility of disconnecting *homo faber* (the working man) from *homo sapiens*. This is one of the main concerns expressed by scholars both within and beyond the so-called critical progressive curriculum river. It actually fueled an endless and unfortunately irreparable fracture within the field, despite Pinar's (1979) several attempts to invite "disenchanted Marxists to participate in the process of definition of the reconceptualization" —attempts that probably deserved a different reaction from critical scholars. We will return to this issue later on.

By simultaneously amplifying and complexifying the way hegemony operates, neo-Gramscians such as Apple and Giroux promoted not only a vision that the cultural, political, religious, and economic beliefs of each individual are a point of both departure and arrival for a specific hegemonic articulation, but also a good way to seek a new common sense (cf. Eagleton, 1994, p. 199). Furthermore, this political perspective clashed irremediably with the reductive and atrophied Marxist dogma of the base/superstructure model, something that Gramsci (1985) saw "theoretically as primitive infantilism" (p. 43). For Gramsci and neo-Gramscians, education was a crucial path not to help the oppressed classes gain more cultural tools, but only, and this is important, to build a more powerful political and social consciousness.

As I stated elsewhere (Paraskeva, 2004), one shouldn't be naïve in thinking that critical hermeneutics such as *Ideology and Curriculum* (the towering piece that I dubbed "Apple's Trilogy"; see Paraskeva, 2004) and *Ideology, Culture and the Process of Schooling* emphasize a concept such as hegemony for no particular reason. In examining Apple's chapter called "On Analyzing Hegemony," one not only sees that Apple takes a huge step beyond issues raised in McLure and Fisher's (1969) research but also gains a clearer understanding that he presents a new key to secular problems, thus giving researchers and scholars access to new windows of opportunity. This towering political concept was also unveiled in Giroux's (1981a) initial material. He claimed that "hegemony is rooted in both the meanings and symbols that legitimate dominant interests as well as in the practices that structure daily experience" (1981a, p. 94; 1980). According to Giroux (1981a), one can perfectly perceive how hegemony functions in the school system by paying attention to "(1) the selection of culture that is deemed as socially legitimate; (2) the categories that are used to *classify* certain cultural content and forms as superior and inferior; (3) the selection and legitimation of school and classroom relationships; and (4) the distribution of and access to different types of culture and knowledge" (p. 94). Thus it is crucial, Giroux maintains, to understand that "as the dominant ideology, hegemony functions to define the meaning and limits of common-sense as well as the forms and content of discourse in society" (p. 94).

This concept plays a major role in McLaren's (1986) *School as a Ritual Performance* as well. In trying to understand schooling from the perspectives of cultural and performance, McLaren relies on the concept of hegemony and how particular rituals "reinforce or reproduce the political and economic dominance of one social class over another" (p. 86), and in so doing attempts to examine "who benefits most from the [hegemonic] ritual structures and who is marginalized" (p. 83). As Wright (1994) pointed out, the arguments of Apple, Giroux, Aronowitz, Wexler, McLaren, and many others were based on the urgent need to completely change the "game board"—that is, the curriculum platform—to dramatically transform the very idea of schooling and curriculum, and to initiate a new platform for the field of curriculum theory, one with the potential for making schools more relevant in a society that proclaims itself to be democratic. Watkins (2001) states sharply that ideology really plays a key role in the nexus of the education and industrial order, since it is "the currency of those dominating the culture, [is] imparted subtly and made to appear as though its partisan views are part of the 'natural order.' The dominant ideology is a product of dominant power" (p. 9).

Although Pinar, Reynolds, Slattery, and Taubman (1995) claim that Wexler "emerged [in the seventies as] the most sophisticated critic on the Left of Apple and Giroux, and quite possibly the most sophisticated theoretician on the Left in contemporary field" (p. 44), it is impossible to ignore the dominance of Apple and Giroux. As Pinar et al. argued vividly:

> The effort to understand curriculum as a political text shifted from an exclusive focus upon reproduction of the status quo, resistance to it, then again, to resistance /reproduction as a dialectical process, then again—in the mid-1980's—to a focus upon daily educational practice, especially, pedagogical and political issues of race, class, and gender. The major players in this effort continued to be Apple and Giroux, Apple through his voluminous scholarship and that of his many students, and Giroux through his prodigious scholarly production. (p. 265)

Such prominent leadership would face severe criticism, not only from the dominant tradition but from the very marrow of the progressive tradition. Liston and Zeichner (1987) expressed the urgent need to accurately perceive the very meaning of radical or critical pedagogy within the critical education platform. Nor was Wexler (1987) shy in expressing his frustrations, not necessarily with the political approach per se but with the path that the approach had taken. In mercilessly criticizing the emphasis on reproduction and resistance, which made "the new sociology of education historically backward-looking and ideologically reactionary" (p. 127), Wexler claimed there was a need to incorporate poststructural and postmodern tools to better understand schools and curriculum, a juicy epistemological avenue that scholars like Giroux and McLaren did not ignore. Wexler's claim should not be seen as a detour but as an upgrade of the political.

Liston (1988) too is quite clear about the puzzling and unacceptable silences within the critical progressive curriculum river. He argued that the works of a particular radical Marxist tradition within this river (including the works of Apple and Wexler) exhibit a "functionalist approach and have neglected crucial empirical investigations" (p. 15). Such criticism is undeniably severe and probably deserves much more attention that it has gotten from the field. Oddly, Liston's claims that particular radical critical Marxist approaches were criticizing functionalist dominant and contradominant traditions relied precisely on a functionalist approach.

The reactionary impulse of the political was, in a way, implicit in Ellsworth's (1989) interesting critique as well. Before the nationwide eruption of racist violence in communities and on campuses in 1987 to 1988, including the University of Wisconsin–Madison, Ellsworth took the opportunity to discuss this kind of turmoil in the course, Curriculum and Instruction 608: Media and Anti-Racist Pedagogies. According to Ellsworth, particular concepts of critical pedagogy such as empowerment, student voice, dialogue, and even the term "critical" are representative myths that perpetuate relations of domination. In claiming the need to fight for a pedagogy of the unknowable, Ellsworth was acknowledging the prominence of the poststructural and postmodern approaches.

Such claims and counter claims deserved a properly deep and detailed analysis. As some of us are claiming, perhaps a composite approach that incorporates critical and poststructural perspectives, or, as I will describe later on, a deterritorialized approach is needed and possible, and I think that needs to be done in a near future. These scholars not only showed how the field maintained its tradition within a place and time of intense struggles and heated conflicts, but also unveiled the tensions, clashes, and ruptures within a particular critical curriculum river, one in which particular scholars swim and whose source needed to be contextualized back at the turn of the nineteenth century—which we will do in the next chapter. Like Gore (1993), we don't want "to claim or imply a monopoly on pedagogical discourse for the disciplinary field of education. There has been some 'crossfertilization of ideas on pedagogy among disciplines, especially among Woman Studies, Literary Studies and Education" (pp. xiii–xiv). In fact, the days of an epistemological monopoly on education are over. As we will see, without laying out any prescription, the future of critical pedagogy relies on this assumption. Any successful strategy needs to be seen as a possible solution to the deaf dialogues, which are fueled by egos that have been permeating the field and forcing it into what might be called its second moribund stage. In the next chapter, we will flash back as we trace the roots of this critical progressive river by digging around in the so-called socio-reconstructionist movement.

CHAPTER 7

THE EMERGENCE AND VITALITY OF
A SPECIFIC CRITICAL CURRICULUM
RIVER

Early in the year 1919, approximately one hundred people gathered at the Washington (D.C.) Public Library to attend a meeting of what would come to be known as the Progressive Education Association (initially the Association for the Advancement of Progressive Schools), which was organized by Tyrus Cobb (Graham, 1967). Marietta Louise Pierce Johnson had been insisting for some time that Cobb create "a national association to support [her] principles" (p. 18). However, this task would prove to be very complex, given that Cobb "doubted the wisdom of a national organization committed to a single educational philosophy" (p. 18).

Johnson (1974), who in the summer of 1907 had accepted the invitation of Mr. and Mrs. Comings to open a free school that was "based strictly on developmentalist principles" (Kliebard, 1995, p. 163), set up her own project. She was profoundly influenced by Nathan Oppenheim (1898), who argued that "the present methods *teach* too much and allow too little opportunity for development" (p. 112). Johnson was also influenced by Charles Hanford Henderson (1902), who stated that "education is a practical process, and it must act through the channels of the inner life, and must reach the mainspring of human action, the very source of power" (p. 69).

Johnson (1974) questioned "the system of grading and rewards that develops and emphasizes self-consciousness—definitely undermining human power" (p. 4). She continued: "[We] want growth, we want the finest physical development, the keenest mental activity, the most sincere and self-conscious emotional life...[This] does not require tests or measurements, examinations or quizzes or records" (pp. 274, 303). Johnson felt strongly that education "is life[,] and the school program, to be educational, must be life-giving" (p. 10). However, despite this noteworthy project and a philosophy that challenged the status quo,[1] Cobb saw no reason to create an association based on Johnson's work. It was not until the winter of 1919 that Cobb, pressured and persuaded by Smith and Johnson, agreed to create an association. Thus the Association for the Advancement of Experimental Schools was formed, changing its name to the Progressive Education Association after the 1920 convention.[2] For Johnson, it was the realization of a dream.

Hence, as Kliebard (1995) states, "The Progressive Education Association was probably born in the mind of…Johnson" (p. 163). It had Morgan as its president, and Eliot served as honorary president. However, according to Cobb (1928), "The pioneer of this progressive movement in education in this century was Francis Parker" (p. 10). As director of the Cook County Normal School of Chicago, Parker put into practice a combination of educational theories in which the influences of Pestalozzi and Froebel were remarkably evident. Parker (1894b) wrote that "the working out of the design of a human being into character is education,…the realization of all the possibilities of human growth and development is education" (p. 25), and, finally, "education is the generation of power" (p. 303). Given the dismal state of education, the Progressive Education Movement was able to obtain great support from "the progressive educative parents" (Cobb, 1928, p. 9).

The "progressive education has a rich pre-history" (Lawson & Peterson, 1972, p. 25), having been significantly influenced by the works of Rousseau, Pestalozzi, Froebel, Fourier, Comenius, Rousseau, Herbart, Mann, Barnard, and Parker (cf. Brameld, 1950). One could say that Parker's works contributed to the genesis of the progressive philosophy, although it was only later that it became a movement.

The progressive movement extinguished itself in the mid-twentieth century, but the struggle for control of the field would go on. We are thus confronted by a movement that is unable (and never will be able) to find a consensual, monolithic definition, especially because "throughout its history, progressive education meant different things to different people" (Cremin, 1964, p. x). Kliebard (1995) aptly described the complexity of the movement:

> I was frankly puzzled by what was meant by the innumerable references I had seen to progressive education. The more I studied this the more it seemed to me that the term encompassed such a broad range, not just of different, but of contradictory, ideas on education as to be

meaningless. In the end, I came to believe that the term was not only vacuous but mischievous. It was not just the word "progressive" that I thought was inappropriate but the implication that something deserving a single name existed and that something could be identified and defined if we only tried. My initial puzzlement turned to skepticism, my skepticism to indignation and finally to bemusement. (p. xv)

Although Kliebard's position is understandable—we too have observed contradictions and variations in the movement's research—we still are able to identify a practical and theoretical movement in the curriculum field. This movement is opposed to the determinism and dehumanization present in an education system that was modeled on the social efficiency doctrine; it is also dedicated to building a society that is more just and equal in the political, economical, and social spheres. Those most prominent in this movement were Dewey, Kilpatrick, Du Bois, Bode, Rugg, and Counts, as well as Horton, who was unjustly hidden and silenced by the majority of curriculum research. Nevertheless, the complexity inherent in a movement of this dimension creates some difficulties when attempting to provide an all-encompassing description of the work of its main thinkers.

Dewey was a profoundly complex figure, with a reach much broader than any label one could affix. Thus, trying to identify him with any particular movement raises problems. His ideas sometimes seem to be those of a social democrat; at other times they seem more identifiable with liberal postulates; and there are times he seems most closely identified with radical positions (cf. Berube, 2000; Davidson, 1901; Lawson & Peterson, 1972; Meyer, 1961; Rorty, 1979). For the purposes of this work, we will identify him as someone who had an enormous impact on the social reconstructionist tradition, not as an icon but as a "conceptual persona" (cf. Popkewitz, 2005, p. 6).

Dewey (1929c) saw that education as a "mode of life, of action [and] an act...is wider than science; education is by its very nature an endless circle or spiral. It is an activity which *includes* science within itself" (p. 75). Evoking a Rousseauian notion, Dewey (1915) argued that education "should be based upon native capacities of those to be taught and upon the need of studying children in order to discover what these native powers are" (p. 1). He believed that education is a "continuous reconstruction of experience" (Dewey, 1930, p. 93) and that the human mind did not learn in a social vacuum (cf. Ratner, 1940).

One sacred value of Dewey's philosophy is democracy. In fact, his whole intellectual life was built around democracy, with the school being the practical workshop of this social ideal and the individual its guarantor. Democracy needed to be understood as a totalizing, practical concept; that is, as "more than a form of government; it is primarily a mode of associated living, of conjoint communicated experience" (Dewey, 1930, p. 101).

Thus, for Dewey (1946), schools were par excellence "an element of the democratic credo" (p. 60). In essence, rather than proposing the school as the basis of democracy, rather than a democracy with a powerful social and political significance, rather than a democracy born out of freedom of mind, Dewey defended democracy as the method and the means by which the school proceeds with the transformation of society. Schools, he claimed, "have power to modify the social order" (Dewey, 1909, p. v; cf. also Campbell, 1996).

For the school to perform this function, however, a transformation of its very core had to be undertaken. Dewey (1899) criticized the educational concept that was "dominated almost entirely by the medieval conception of learning" (p. 37), adding that the concept impeded the development of an educational process based on natural development (Dewey & Dewey, 1943). It is within this context that Dewey (1910) defends the perspective of learning by doing and stresses that "learning, in a proper sense, is not learning things, but the meanings of things, and this process involves the uses of signs, or language in its generic sense" (p. 176). Dewey (1946) also maintained that the "absence of democratic methods [was] the greatest single cause of educational waste" (p. 65) and that "from the standpoint of the child, the great waste in school comes from his inability to utilize experiences he gets outside the school in any complete and free way within the school itself...he is unable to apply in daily life what he is learning in school" (Dewey, 1899, p. 85).

The need for a transformation also meant changing the consciousness of habits. Dewey (1935–1937) believed that force of habit is a "stronger and deeper part of human nature than is desire for change" (pp. 133–4), especially since habits should be seen as the active means that project themselves as vigorous and powerful forms of acting. In fact, Dewey (1887) stresses that habits, whether "intellectual or volitional[, mean] the connection of ideas or acts" (p. 100), a rather dynamic state that should not be dissociated from human interest.

His association with Herbartianism enabled Dewey to involve himself more seriously in educational issues and to develop his curriculum theory, although he had some reservations about the Herbartian movement.

Dewey (1897) was not opposed to the scientific study of the child, a practice defended by the developmentalists. However, he did think it should be conducted with great prudence and was critical of any direct application of scientific study to the demands of the classroom. Moreover, the child study movement sometimes seemed to Dewey to be atheoretical, deprived of speculation, and removed from reality. Dewey further criticized the segregationism of Hall, who believed that the education of a child should prepare them for what society would become.

On the other hand, Dewey believed that Harris's proposal revealed a lack of cohesion (cf. Archambault, 1966). Because Dewey (1902, 1930) considered education an expansion of life experiences, he felt that the fragmentation of knowledge that was at the heart of Harris's proposal impeded the recognition of organized knowledge as something related to human experiences and needs. It is fundamentally on the basis of this conflict between humanists and developmentalists that Dewey formulated his curriculum theory, which was put into practice when he founded his Laboratory School in Chicago in 1896 (Kliebard, 1995).

The curriculum theory proposed by Dewey essentially stems from the Herbartian concepts of correlation, concentration, culture epochs, and, above all, recapitulation theory (Kliebard, 1992), all of which we discussed previously. Dewey (1929a) maintained that "the social life of the child is the basis of concentration, or correlation, in all his training or growth...[and] that the true center of correlation on the school subjects is not science, nor literature, nor history, nor geography, but the child's own social activities" (p. 293). Another concept central to Dewey's curriculum theory was the so-called theory of the occupations, which allowed for a bridge and for harmony between individual and social ends. In Dewey's opinion, this constituted the central problem of curriculum theory (Kliebard, 1995).

What was being "reconstructed in the curriculum was not the stages in the development of human history as the Herbartians advocated, but stages in the way human beings gained control of their world through the use of intelligence—stages in the development of knowledge" (Kliebard, 1995, p. 72). The capitalist society, according to Dewey, could be altered without a civil war, as had recently occurred in Russia (Gonzalez, 1982).

According to Dewey (1902), "all that society has accomplished for itself is put through the agency of the school, at the disposal of its future members...all its better thoughts of itself it hopes to realize through the new possibilities thus opened to its future self. Here individualism and socialism are at one" (p. 7). However, as Kliebard

(1995) notes, "What Dewey did not anticipate...was the rise of standardized achievement tests in the twentieth century" (p. 68), which rapidly, and completely, subverted his theory by placing great value on the dynamics of learning based on the three Rs.

In Dewey we are, in fact, confronted by a figure who is extremely difficult to analyze, and any estimate of his value should be made prudently, especially if we aim to fully comprehend his thinking (cf. Boydstom & Poulos, 1978). He was a complex intellectual who adopted controversial positions, including his strange support of America's involvement in World War I (cf. Zerby, 1975); the report he prepared on a Polish community and his identification of U.S. military and commercial interests (cf. Feinberg, 1975); his perspective on Russia's education system (cf. Dewey, 1929b); and his involvement in Leon Trotsky's trial (Dewey, 1937).

Nevertheless, Dewey "was a staunch opponent of communism" (Gonzalez, 1982, p. 103). He renounced the Russian Revolution as a political methodology of social transformation—"A revolution effected solely or chiefly by violence can in a modernized society like our own result only in chaos" (Dewey, 1934a, p. 90)—and instead initiated a "curriculum revolution" in his Laboratory School in Chicago. Because Dewey (1966) was categorically opposed to the dialectic materialism concept by which "the end justifies the means" (p. 55), his Laboratory School became a project that relied on the notions of people like Eliot, Small, Harris, and Hall. According to Dewey, the school was one of the viable and safe avenues for a divorce between the psychological and the social. Education needed to relate to students' current life, not just to prepare them for a future life (Dewey, 1895). By understanding theory as the best practice for all things, Dewey (1929c) exposed a curriculum theory that upheld education as a process of living (Dewey, 1929a) and the school as a field for the democratic theory and practice supported by experience (1916, 1930).

The divorce between the education system and society increased rapidly, forcing the school into a crisis that required urgent curriculum reform. In response to this need, Kilpatrick formulated his Project Method in 1918. This new curriculum concept considered education "as life itself and not as a mere preparation for later living" (Kilpatrick, 1918, p. 320). For Kilpatrick (1926), the changes being brought about by science were leading to "a growing social integration with [a] correlative increase in interdependence [that] is one of the most obvious effects of our growing industrialization" (p. 21). This interdependence was further strengthened "by the growing division of labor" (p. 22).

The advent of industrialization and its consequent demands (specialization, aggregation, and integration) required open-minded people who would "prepare the rising generation to think that they can and will think for themselves, even ultimately, if they so decide, to the point of revising or rejecting what we now think" (Kilpatrick, 1926, p. 60). Technological progress put pressure on the schools (Kilpatrick, 1933), which in turn led to a segregationist tendency in the determination of aims or objectives. Kilpatrick (1951) criticized the old curriculum concept that assumed "that education consists precisely of the acquisition of pre-formulated knowledge presented to the learner in textbooks or orally by teachers (or parents)" (p. 312), adding that such a conception "limits man and his educated life predominantly if not solely to intellect and counts memory as the primary means to intellect building" (p. 313).

Believing that the major objective of education "is to continue and enrich [the] life process by better thought and act" (Kilpatrick, 1926, p. 134), Kilpatrick defended a new curriculum concept that was based on a "continuous reconstruction of experience" (p. 123). He argued that culture and language are essential platforms of democracy, which he understood as a way of life that should be based on six fundamental aspects: "sovereignty of the individual...the principal of equality...rights implies duties...cooperative effort for the common good...faith in free play of intelligence...freedom of discussion" (Kilpatrick, 1951, pp. 139–40).

As Kliebard (1995) notes, "The project method became the major alternative to scientific curriculum-making" (p. 141). Kilpatrick's proposal was opposed to "the 'cold storage' view of knowledge, in which facts and skills were stored up for future use" (p. 143). He recommended instead a curriculum project "that de-emphasized the acquisition of knowledge in favor of a curriculum that was synonymous with purposeful activity" (p. 143).

Due to its enormous following, Kilpatrick's Project Method had drastically changed the terms of the curriculum debate (Kliebard, 1995), and critics were not in short supply. Faced by the obvious euphoria about the Project Method, Charters (1922) counseled prudence, especially because he saw many shortcomings in Kilpatrick's proposal, including the fact that it was not a curriculum that prepared students for what they would need to know in the future. Charters encouraged a renewed emphasis on subject matter. In essence, Kilpatrick's Project Method polarized even further the two groups most prominent at that time in the struggle to dominate the field: the social efficiency movement and the child centered movement.

However, a new vision was soon to emerge, with the 1927 publication of Bode's *Modern Educational Theories.*

Bode's approach tended to be more "cautious and reasoned if not more politically sophisticated in its persistent attention to the social implications of the various proposed reforms of the curriculum" (Kliebard, 1995, p. 150). The progressive education, Bode (1938) argued, "is confronted with the choice of becoming the avowed exponent of democracy or else of becoming a set of ingenious devices for tempering the wind to the shorn lamb" (p. 26). Bode believed that the definition of democracy included an education system "which centers on the cultivation of intelligence, rather than submission to authority[, which implies that] our educational theory thus inevitably becomes a theory of social relationships, or a theory of democracy" (p. 60). He argued further that "if democracy is to have a deep and inclusive human meaning, it must have also a distinctive educational system" (p. 26). By perceiving progressive schools not so much as places of learning but rather as "a way of life" (p. 9), Bode (1929) resorted to Thorndike's notion that learning is analysis and defended learning as "a process of selecting both the stimulus and the response; [a process] of substituting the part for the whole" (p. 267). He continued: "The supreme task of education...is to organize its various resources and agencies in such a way that the development of civilization may be seen as a progressive liberation of intelligence" (p. 295).

Bode launched further criticism at the postulates formulated by Bobbitt, whose concept of curriculum impeded a progressive social transformation; by Charters, who argued that it is impossible to apply the industry model to the school; by Snedden, whose reductive notion that the educational objectives were sociologically determined; and even by Kilpatrick, who, according to Bode, had presented a limited curriculum model and a fundamentalist position, based on which "the key question of what to teach lay in the unfolding of natural forces within the child" (Kliebard, 1995, p. 52) was upheld (cf. also Bode, 1938, 1940). Bode objected to "Kilpatrick's emphasis on the latter at the expense of the former" (cf. Chambliss, 1963, p. 25); he believed the emphasis should be on the political, cultural, and economic. Bode felt it was important to act quickly, stating that "a new social order is in the making, which makes it necessary to develop a new system of education" (p. 26).

Hence, despite their differences, the works of Dewey, Kilpatrick, and Bode should be understood as an integral part of a specific curriculum river within the bosom of the Progressive Education Movement, which opposed the status quo. Nonetheless, criticism of Dewey's positions—to which we could very well add those of Kilpatrick and Bode— was "mild compared to that showered on his followers who accepted the viewpoint of social reconstruction, particularly on Rugg, whose textbooks were accused of 'twitting the Founding Fathers,' and on George Counts, who was referred to as the 'Red Russia Apostle' " (Lawson & Peterson, 1972, p. 36) in some newspapers in the 1930s.

In fact, the publication of Rugg's (1926a, 1926b) two volumes of the National Society for the Study of Education's *Twenty-Sixth Yearbook*, a sign of the drastic changes the curriculum field needed, marked the (re)emergence and the consolidation of yet another movement within the bosom of the progressive education movement, the social reconstructionists, represented by Rugg and Counts. They readdressed some of the issues Ward had raised at the end of the nineteenth century, which were described previously.

Rugg (1952) believed that the design of education "must start with a theory of man living in society, and molded by his culture. Hence it starts with the great concepts which are the keys to the life of that culture" (p. 152). Rugg (1933) wrote that the economic crisis that began at the end of the 1920s brought about dramatic social changes, and that the apparatus of the nation was impotent to deal with it. He determined that the changes society so badly needed could not be achieved with the existing school model: "It is no longer conceivable that memorizing and reciting the facts of encyclopedic text-books...will produce informed critical students of our industrial civilization...that writing 'themes' to order, dissecting European classics, reciting the lines of standard drama...will teach you to portray the meaning of life appreciatively and creatively" (pp. 257–258). Furthermore, he continued, the school completely neglected five important areas: "real work, [a] personally and socially useful sex and home life [environment],...inferiority and the intimate problems of personal living,...the insistent controversial issues of the social system—property and the struggle for power, race conflict and control of public opinion...religion" (Rugg, 1943, p. 674). He believed that education should, among other things, "promote the assimilation of minority groups and a belief in justice to minorities [, and] foster vigorous and abiding interest in the discussion of public affairs" (Rugg & Withers, 1955, p. 144).

According to Rugg (1933), it was imperative to initiate a new reconstructionist philosophy of education based on three axioms: "school as including all of the educative activities of community life,...school age [as] the entire life of men, from infancy to old age,

[and] . . . education for a whole life" (p. 261). Given this new approach to education, Rugg continued, the curriculum would no longer represent a reductive space but would construct itself around six major platforms: "the life of the school as a whole, . . . introduction to changing civilizations and cultures, . . . introduction to creative and appreciative arts, . . . body education, . . . introduction to the physical and natural world, [and] to human behavior" (pp. 266–267). Obviously, all this would require the "reconstruction of our teachers' colleges in which future teachers will be trained" (p. 278; cf. also Rugg, 1936, 1939). Teachers, he said, should act primarily as guides and only incidentally as monitor and judge (Rugg & Brooks, 1950).

In a "truly democratic society," Rugg (1936) stated, "government is education, and education on the social side is the practice of government" (p. 15). The curriculum—"the great intermediary between the child and society, . . . an ugly, awkward, academic word, but fastened upon us by technical custom" (pp. 17–18)—is really the entire program of school's work. Faced by this scenario, the curriculum assumed a new significance to Rugg: "Much more than an outline of reading and writing assignments, [the curriculum] becomes The Life and Program of School [and] the school does, indeed, become a School of Living" (pp. 333–4). To Rugg, therefore, the fundamental curriculum issue was not based on Spencer's old maxim of "what knowledge is of most worth" but on "what experience can be used most educatively" (p. 334), and he (Rugg, 1943) argued that the curriculum should be constructed with the participation of "parents, children and the youths, the teachers, and the director and administration" (p. 659).

Rugg (1931) held that the first "task of social reconstruction is essentially educational reconstruction [and that] the school must become an agency of social regeneration" (p. 256). In keeping with Dewey's thinking, Rugg stressed "experience" as the keyword of the new education (cf. Rugg & Shumaker, 1969).

Rugg separated himself from the positions defended by the child-centered curriculum movement because he felt they did not satisfy the needs of society. He also felt, however, that the "scientific approach to curriculum development advocated by the social efficiency educators was [also] clearly out of question" (Kliebard, 1955, p. 174), since it helped maintain the status quo. As a faithful expression of his sociopolitical project, Rugg and his team of researchers produced a series of social studies textbooks, which fundamentally bear witness to the importance he conferred on social studies. Rugg felt strongly that the curriculum had to have social value, and he created a magnificent project for which he collected data on three thousand problems by mining the education field. His project was based on what he called the frontier thinkers—Dewey was among them—who were "a few clear-minded individuals in France, England, Germany, America, and other countries, [who] began to apply their minds to the solution of the difficult social problems" (Rugg, 1932, p. 187).

However, the revolutionary anticapitalist approach adopted by such textbooks led to many attacks by more conservative groups. At the forefront of these critics was Armstrong (1940), who felt that the textbooks placed at risk the purest social values of the nation, and the textbooks were banned in many states in the early 1940s.

Nevertheless, Rugg had shaken some of the pillars of institutional power. Then, in 1932, Counts "troubled the waters of education [even more] with the publication . . . of his manifesto 'Dare the school build a new social order?'" (Lawson & Peterson, 1972, p. 41), thus reinforcing the positions and perspectives of social reconstructionism. Counts, Kimmel, and Kelly (1934), for whom "the highest and most characteristic ethical expression of the genius of the American people is the ideal of democracy" (p. 9), argued that "the perpetuation of any human society is dependent on the process of education" (p. 252).

Counts and his colleagues described the curriculum as a field of struggles. By understanding society as "divided into sects, parties, classes, and special interests, each of which, in proportion to its strength, strives to incorporate its viewpoint into the curriculum" (p. 272), they defined the curriculum as "a resultant of the play of these battling forces upon the school" (p. 272; cf. also Counts, 1928).

Counts (1962) claimed that "all human experience demonstrates that education in any living society is never neutral[, so] it is not enough . . . to say we need more and more education as if it were an autonomous process governed by its own laws and dedicated to human freedom" (pp. 53–4). School was "the American road to culture," he stated (Counts, 1930, p. 17), and a good or bad process of learning does not depend on the laws of learning, but on the "conception of life and civilization which gives it substance and direction" (Counts, 1962, p. 54). In essence, he saw education as the means of a certain human commitment: "Education is always a function of some particular civilization at some particular time in history; . . . it can never be an autonomous process, independent of time and place and conducted according to its own laws" (Counts, 1953, p. 23). Counts (1922, 1926, 1962) criticized the stigma of social inequality, remarking that U.S. society had millions of citizens who "by reason of race, economic condition, or cultural deprivation, remain 'second class' citizens in this land of liberty and plenty" (1962, p. 61).

Every educational program should, according to Counts (1945), "endeavor to rear the young in the spirit and practice of equality" (p. 124). He (Counts, 1930) thus criticized the "intolerance of cultural and racial diversity" (p. 104). Such a socially lethal approach turned the schools into "an instrument for the perpetuation of the existing social order rather than a creative force in society" (p. 126). Counts (1929) believed that "if education...is to be effective in modifying practice, it must keep close to society;...school cannot build a utopia...and cannot become socially progressive by mere resolve" (pp. 67–8).

Profoundly influenced by the Soviet model (cf. Lawson & Peterson, 1972), Counts, like Rugg, believed that the U.S. education system could lead a social transformation. On the basis of this crucial principle, Counts directed violent criticism at the progressive education movement. He felt that "the weakness of Progressive education...lies in the fact that it has elaborated no theory of social welfare[, and that] progressive education could not place its trust in a child-centered school" (Counts, 1932, p. 9). Counts clearly believed that education was surrounded by fallacies:

> The fallacy that man is born free,...the fallacy that the child is good by nature,...the fallacy that the child lives in a separate world of his own,...the fallacy that education is some pure and mystical essence that remains unchanged from everlasting to everlasting,...the fallacy that the school should be impartial in its emphasis, that no bias should be given instruction,...the fallacy that the great object of education is to produce the college professor. (pp. 13–21)

Either education would be transformed, said Counts, or democracy would surely die, as it is not possible to transform society without transforming the school (Counts, 1931). Counts still professed with certainty that social transformation entailed a revolution, particularly because the rich classes would never peacefully surrender their privileges. However, the school would have to play a prominent role in this revolutionary process because "the failure of revolutions is a record of the failure to bring education into the service of the revolutionary cause" (p. 66).

Counts (1931) understood capitalism as a wasteful, inhuman, cruel model that led to the exploitation of natural resources without taking into account the future social needs, that made technology into a weapon for the most privileged, and that constantly multiplied social inequality. Consequently, Counts denounced the benefits of indus-trialization, stating that "if the machine is to serve all, and serve all equally, it cannot be the property of the few" (p. 44).

Counts will forever be associated with the emergence of *The Social Frontier* in 1934. This publication represented an explicit reinforce-ment of the social reconstructionist position on the child centered movement and social efficiency. *The Social Frontier* upheld the idea that "the age of individualism in economy is closing and that an aged market by close integration of social life and by collective planning and control is opening" (Counts, 1934, p. 4). It stressed that, as a political project, it "acknowledges allegiance to no narrow concep-tion of education; while recognizing the school as society's central educational agency, it refuses to limit itself to a consideration of the work of this institution" (p. 4), which is a position similarly expressed by Dewey (1934).

Through the body of work by Rugg and Counts, the work of another figure would become prominent in the social reconstructionist move-ment, namely, Brameld. Brameld (1950a) wrote that although "pres-sure groups, some of them classified by official sources as pro-fascist, litter the desks of principals and schools boards with 'proofs' that the Deweys and Ruggs of education are Bolsheviks disguised," the fact was that "no other theory was so brilliant [as progressive education or so] convincingly expounded in the schools" (p. 32). Brameld (1950a, 1950b) argued that the hate for and opposition to the progressive movement was supported not only for economic reasons, but also by the "widespread confusion and sheer ignorance, which confront any departure from routinized practices" (1950a, p. 35). To confront this challenge, he argued, the progressive education movement should not only construct a theoretical framework that would stress "new goals for American and world democracy," but also be "encouraging the kind of free self-expression which alone guarantees that the new America can be built out of the experiences and wants of the peoples themselves" (Brameld, 1950a, p. 38; 1957).

By understanding culture as a social reality and the school as a cultural agent, Brameld (1965) viewed the curriculum "in relation to cultural order, teaching-learning in terms of cultural process, and the control of education in view of cultural goals" (p. 75), adding that "we need to think of the curriculum of general education not only in terms of the present relationships of people, but in terms both of their roots in the past and their directions toward the future" (p. 77). To Brameld (1970), the major imperative of education was "to engage in a radical shift away from both traditional investigations of the rich history of the past and exclusive concentration upon contemporary experience. The shift that is now required is, above all, toward the *future*" (p. 23).

However, we cannot understand this radical critical tradition within the curriculum field specifically and education in general unless we understand the counter-hegemonic traditions both within and outside curriculum in informal struggles related to unions, civil rights, etc. Thus, the works of Dewey, Bode, Rugg, Counts, and Brameld should also be contextualized within the deeply influential and powerful tradition of counterhegemonic educational work outside of education.

In fact, there is a history of an indigenous, radical education community in the United States and powerful internal traditions linking education to larger struggles over civil rights, exploitation, and domination. These struggles were found not only within the curriculum field or in the formal sphere of education, but also, and just as importantly, in informal social movements that established their own schools. In fact, the work of a critical progressive curriculum river—one that includes, for example, the work of Apple, Giroux, Wexler, Aronowitz, McLaren, and others—must be seen as emerging not only out of the internal political history of curriculum but out of such experiments as the Highlander Folk School, the early Mechanics Institutes (the early worker's college), and the Rand School. Moreover, we must mention important figures such as Du Bois, Robeson, and King, who, while in the midst of the African-American struggle, were prominent in the leadership of these counterhegemonic movements and helped to politicize the field of education.

The Highlander Folk School is associated with the name of Myles Horton. In fact, "in large part, the Highlander Folk School was the product of a personal and intellectual odyssey by its cofounder, Myles Fall Horton" (Glen, 1988, p. 6), a person whom, according to MacLean (1966), "American education needs to know...better, for he is perhaps America's best creative and effective adult educator" (p. 487). He was profoundly influenced by the works of Marx, Ward, Dewey, and Counts, among others (Adams & Horton, 1975; Parker & Parker, s/d). On November 1, 1932, Horton founded his school "in one of the eleven poorest counties in the United States" (Adams & Horton, 1975, p. 30), giving it the slogan, "Learn from the people; start their education where they are" (p. 206).

In the summer of 1932, as a consequence of the Depression, a coal miners' strike erupted at nearby Wilder Mine, and the social impact of Highlander was soon felt. In fact, by adopting the objective of actively participating in the transformation of U.S. society, the Highlander Folk School would forever be remembered for the role it played in eastern Tennessee helping unionize southern textile workers, and even helping "some 100,000 blacks become literate and thus qualified to vote" (Parker & Parker, s/d). Horton quickly saw the strike as an instrument for learning; besides confirming "the power structure's determination in the 1930s and 1940s to cripple labor unions" (pp. 5–6), the strike permitted Horton to develop the Highlander Labor Program.

Toward the end of the 1950s and the early 1960s, the Highlander Folk School developed an educational program in the black community that "significantly increased black voter registration, black political awareness and involvement, [and] helped elect black mayors, sheriffs and other officials in the 1970s and 1980s" (Parker and Parker, s/d, pp. 5–6) The impact of Horton's efforts were immortalized in the words of Rosa Parks: "The only reason I don't hate every white man alive is Highlander and Myles Horton. He's the only white man the Negroes fully trust" (Parks, Apud, & MacLean, 1966, pp. 487–91). Horton perceived social activism as being intimately connected to education and as the platform for the transformation of society (cf. MacLean, 1966; Kennedy, 1981, Bell, Gaventa, & Peters, 1990).

As its political power developed, especially relative to the civil rights movement, the Highlander Folk School "became the target of a series of attacks spearheaded by Southern segregationists" (Glen, 1988, p. 173). Horton and the idea of Highlander demonstrated above all the potential and the effectiveness of education as an instrument of social transformation.

Macdonald, Huebner, and others did not minimize the importance of this perspective. Macdonald (1966a) thought that the "schools must have both a pedagogically packaged cultural heritage and the means for bringing it to life and for understanding the deeper meanings of individual and cultural existence which pervade learning in the experiences of persons" (pp. 3–4). He considered this task extremely difficult, not only because the "curriculum, all dressed up in its new suit, may well appear to the child much like the emperor's clothes" (p. 3), but also because of the "apparent lack of comprehension by the scholars of the history of curriculum in the twentieth century" (p. 3). He understood that there was something "terribly wrong about schooling" (Macdonald, 1969–1970, p. 45), which was not exactly its "irrelevance per se [but] simply that living in school is an essentially inferior, vulgar, imitative, second-rate experience" (p. 45).

In a field that was dominated by the powerful Tylerian model, Macdonald (1966a, p. 17; cf. also Macdonald, Wolfson, & Zaret, 1973) criticized the behaviorist objectives model and put forward an alternative model of schooling based on three dimensions—sociocultural, psychological, and transactional—which was profoundly articulated by an "increasing thrust for liberation, participation and pluralism of all participants" (1966a, p. 17). Clearly, Macdonald believed that "the curriculum is the cultural environment which has been selected as a set of possibilities for learning transactions" (p. 17). His major concerns were the defense of the school "as an environment for living, the nature of this environment, what this environment communicates to youngsters, and the role verbal communication may have in this environment" (Macdonald, 1969–1970, p. 46). This is a Deweyan position that made Macdonald recognize the importance of understanding a theory as a potential creation of reality, as a process that should be seen as an act of creation and not merely as an act of presentation. To Macdonald (1982), then, theorization was much more than a rational process or a validation of practice; it was a religious act, an act of faith.

It is in this context, with a clear distancing from Tyler and Schwab and a denunciation of reductionism in the field of critical theory, that Macdonald advanced the mythopoetic approach. He (1982, p. 60) argued that "the focus of curriculum is not simply a context where a curriculum is a metaphor operation," a reality that is completely neglected by the technical approach and that the critical approach, as the core of the emancipatory political approach, failed to fully explain. In this way, according to his perspective it would be essential to challenge the debate based on four fundamental questions: (1) What brackets surround curriculum talk? (2) Is curriculum theory only talk about talk, or is it also talk about work and power? (3) Is curriculum talk essentially descriptive or is it talk about change? and (4) What kinds of cultural tools are most appropriate for curriculum talk? (Macdonald, 1977, pp. 13–15).

Huebner (1966) did not distance himself from such concerns.[3] In one of his more brilliant works, he insisted that curriculum language is immersed in two tyrannical myths: "one is that of learning—the other that of purpose,... almost magical elements the curriculum worker is afraid to ignore, let alone question" (p. 10). He argues that "learning is merely a postulated concept, not a reality and objectives are not always needed for educational planning" (p. 10). For Huebner, the major problem in the world of education, "which has been short-circuited by behavioral objectives, sciences, and learning theory, was the fact that we were not dealing with the autobiography, we were not dealing with life and inspiration" (Huebner, 2002, Tape 1).

The language of education is full of "dangerous and non-recognized [and unchallenged] myths" (Huebner, 1966, p. 9), which makes it impossible to question whether the "technologists maybe were going in the wrong direction" (Huebner, 2002, Tape 1). This becomes much more complex and alarming in a society that is facing the fact that "the problem is no longer one of explaining change, but of explaining nonchange" (Huebner, 1967, p. 174), and that a human being, by his transcendent condition, "has the capacity to transcend what he is to become, something that he is not" (p. 174):

> For centuries the poet has sung of his near infinitudes; the theologian has preached of his depravity and hinted of his participation in the divine; the philosopher has struggled to encompass him in his systems, only to have him repeatedly escape; the novelist and dramatist have captured his fleeting moments of pain and purity in never-to-be-forgotten aesthetic forms; and the [man] engaged in the curriculum has the temerity to reduce this being to a single term—learner. (Huebner, 1966, p. 10)

As a reaction to this reductionism, Huebner (1966) proposed five value systems that contain "forms of rationality which may be used to talk about classroom activity" (p. 20). These value systems include the technical, which is expressed almost completely in the "current curriculum ideology"; the political, in which "all educational activity is valued politically;... [and] the teacher or other educator has a position of power and control"; the scientific, where "educational activity may be valued for the knowledge that it produces about that activity"; the aesthetic, in which "educational activity would be viewed as having symbolic and esthetic meanings"; and the ethical, which sees "educational activity as an encounter between man and man" (pp. 14–18). For Huebner, in fact, there is a difference between curriculum languages, which model the thought of the curriculum specialist, and the need to understand the theorized educational act as a prayerful act, as proposed by Macdonald, Wolfson, and Zaret (1973). Notwithstanding the fact that "curriculum as a guidance strategy demands that educational activity be valued primarily in terms of moral categories," Huebner (1964) saw learning as "the guiding concept in educational thought,...a major cornerstone in the [educational] ideology" (pp. 1–15). Based on this, Huebner (1968) later divided the actual use of curriculum language into six categories: "descriptive, explanatory, controlling, legitimating, prescriptive, and the language of affiliation" (pp. 5–7).

Huebner (2002) explained that his idea "was not to transform the world. What I was trying to transform was the language by which we speak of education which then leads to the transformation of the world" (Tape 2). He believed that "the crucial problem was and still is the way everyday people talk about education. They are not aware of how that is limiting them in their view and their actions, or their control" (Tape 2).

On the basis of Dewey's (1902) belief that the function of the educator is to determine the environment of the child, Huebner (1966) proposed a broad and humane concept for the curriculum process in which the "educator participates in the paradoxical structure of the universe" (p. 8). In fact, Huebner (1968) argued that "man and his language form a paradoxical relationship" (p. 4) that places him in a constant dialectical relation with the world (Huebner, 1967). The curriculum, therefore, must be perceived as an environment "which would embody the dialectical forms valued by society" (p. 177). Such an environment "must include components which will call forth responses from the students [that must] be reactive [and] must provide opportunities for the student to become aware of his temporality, to participate in a history which is one horizon of his present" (p. 177). We are thus confronted with a curriculum concept, the roots of which had, in fact, already emerged in Huebner's doctoral thesis (Huebner, 1959; cf. also 1974a). It is in this conceptualization that Huebner (1968, 1974a) defends education as a political act that transmits strong dynamics of power. According to Huebner (1974b), "schooling is inherently political, it always has been, [and] it always will be [because it] implies that someone or some social group has use of power...to intervene in the life of others" (p. 1). Thus, the use of power "to intervene in the life of others is a political act" (p. 1). Naturally, and given the political essence of education, Huebner (1962a, 1979) defended the need to "destroy the prevailing myth that education can be conflict free, [a myth] that is reinforced by the so called objective methods of evaluation and the movement towards accountability in the USA" (1979, p. 2).

Huebner (1977c), in what for us is his best work, proposes "dialectical materialism as the method of doing education...[Although] current methods of education impede the development of dialectical consciousness or dialectical method, and deprive students and teachers of his power to live temporally, to live educationally" (p. 4), Huebner defends the need for a dialectical method. As he points out, "the materialist base of the method of doing education is the acceptance of Marx's claim that it is not consciousness of men that determines existence, but their social existence determines consciousness" (p. 5). In this way, Huebner (1967) argues, educators should understand that the dialectical materialistic foundation extensive to all human life "is not futural...nor is it past, but, rather, a present made up of a past and future brought into the moment...in other words, man is temporal...[a] historical [being]" (p. 176).

Huebner (1961) does not uphold schooling exactly as an art but as a "creative art," in which students and teachers interact "as in a jazz quartet, each one find[ing] his own way of adding beauty to the Jazz form" (p. 10). Thus, the classroom "is a busy place but not an unruly place" (p. 10). Just as "the poet cannot write without controlling words, the artist cannot paint without knowing symbols" (p. 11), so it goes in the "classroom studio, [where] part of the time is devoted to learning about the tools of the art and their limitation" (p. 11; cf. also Alexander, 2003).

Clearly, the approach Huebner defended interfered a good deal with the power instituted in the field. The ideas that he defended would lead him into some heated and unpleasant confrontations with his peers during his final moments at Teachers College. In fact, tensions had been building from the beginning. There were his deep differences with Passow, because Huebner (2002) "kept arguing against the tightening up of the standards" (Tape 1), and with Foshay and Goldberg because Huebner opposed the excessive dependency on the learning theory that both defended. However, the crisis became more acute toward the end of the 1970s, when "Cremin was president and brought Noah...an economist, to be his dean" (Tape 1). Huebner could not agree in any way with Cremin's political strategy for transforming Teachers College into "a world leader in the development of human resources" (Tape 1). For Huebner, it was totally incomprehensible and unacceptable that a historian of education "talked about human beings as human resources" (Tape 1), and from that moment he felt that he "no longer was a part of that institution" (Tape 1).

Huebner (1975b) felt that the field had surrendered to a dangerous demagogy ("don't talk psychological individualism to me. Don't preach Kant's moral imperatives tinged with a religious doctrine of salvation. That is put-down language" [p. 276]), which explained the field's accentuated and alarming theoretical frailty. Teaching is submerged in severe complexities (Huebner, 1962b). Aware of Johnson's (1968) and Mann's (1968) approaches, Huebner (1968) stressed "the lack of organization of the ideas and efforts related to theorizing about curriculum and to the problem curriculists have with their own history of theorizing" (p. 2). The curriculum field, he warned, was following a dangerous course at various levels:

> The major problem seems to me that both at a local school level and also at the school of education level there is no real understanding of what the real educational problem is. They are so busy solving problems...that they are not able to take a long stance in order to invite people in to talk with them about what may be happening at their own level, or to teachers and students. The problem of school basically is a lack of respect for the individuality of the teachers and the student. When you build a system that ignores the human dimension of the interactions, that becomes the source of the problems. The school is not run for the benefit of the kids. The alienation that goes on in school is the source of the problems. It is the alienation of kids from themselves, kids from teachers, kids from their society.
>
> Part of the difficulty is that investment in education has occurred at universities at the research level. And the money that has gone into building the superstructure of the study of education with thousands of people involved means that there is less money to put in local schools. Schoolteachers have problems; they don't have time to solve them, and the university people take these problems from the teachers into their rarefied atmosphere and use their empirical techniques to try to solve them. Clearly you have a theory-practice problem. The theory-practice problem is a political problem, in terms of who studies the problems of teaching. Teachers do not study their problems, and that's the problem. Underneath this the continued attack on teachers, partially justified because the quality of teacher education is another major problem, and the assumption that you can improve teaching by undercutting the stamina and enthusiasm of teachers is a profound mistake. The use of Henry Ford's production line in school [is] a complete nonsense ideology. (Huebner, 2002, Tape 2)

Expressing disbelief at the course of events, Huebner lashed out and provided incisive criticism of the institutions that had strong responsibilities in the field, such as ASCD. Huebner (2002) already considered ASCD a caricature of the initial 1940s project (Tape 2). By renouncing the vision of the school as "a manifestation of public life" (Huebner, 1975b, p. 280) and thus not perceiving educators as "political activists who seek a more just public world" (p. 280), ASCD was an institution without a future. Huebner (1976) recognized that the field was in a chaotic state:

> If *The Curriculum* (1918) marked the early maturity of the curriculum field, then the past ten to fifteen years were its golden years. Now the

end is here. Many individuals and groups with various intentions have gathered together around this now aged enterprise, "curriculum." Let us acknowledge its demise, gather at the wake, celebrate joyously what our forebears made possible—and then disperse to do our work, because we are no longer members of one household. (pp. 154–5)

Looking at the state of the field at the beginning of this century, we have to concur that Huebner was, in fact, an *avant la lettre* curricularist. Incisive, Cicerian (meaning "cutting," as in Cicero's oratorical style) Huebner "was writing in an idiom and using a language that [the status quo of the field] was not familiar with, because [he] was bringing under question the predominant structure, namely, behavioral sciences" (Huebner, 2002, Tape 1).

After denouncing the absence of a critical and historical dynamic—something that Schwab had also denounced but in a somewhat simplistic fashion—Huebner gradually moved away from the field of secular education to that of religious education (Huebner, 2002, Tape 1). Greatly influenced by Tillich's Protestant principle, among others, Huebner was able to implement a much more critical project within religious education. Such project "becomes one of the major vehicles for liberation, or recreation or creativity" (Tape 1), a language "that secular education didn't like to hear" (Tape 1).

It is within the intricate context of the work of scholars like Mann, Apple, Giroux, and others that a particular tradition of a radical critical progressive curriculum must be understood. The voluminous amount of work identified with this tradition gains intellectual momentum and historical and political significance when inserted into the progressive curriculum river that we have addressed. This understanding is palpable in the works of Apple, Huebner, and Kliebard, and made them react furiously against the term "reconceptualization" that was advanced by the reconceptualists, as expressed by Apple (2000a; 2000b; cf. also Marshall, Sears & Schubert, 2000):

I totally reject any language that talks about curriculum reconceptualists: I have never been one; I don't think there ever have been any in the field; and I think it's a total misreading of history. Certainly,...Kliebard, myself, and many others who were included in that tradition never saw ourselves as reconceptualizing anything. We are simply standing on the shoulders of a very, very long tradition that has its roots in the very beginning of the curriculum field. (2000b, pp. 103, 242)

Vehement reaction to this term was not limited to a particular critical progressive curriculum river of scholars. In fact, Tanner and Tanner

(1979), Jackson (1980), Wraga and Hlebowitsh (2003a, 2003b), and others were also profoundly nervous about such (re)definition of the field. According to Tanner and Tanner (1979), the reconceptualist movement would not add anything new to the field. The reconceptualists, they argued, were a group of people who needed to be seen as the "new alchemists and concierges of a counter cultural ideology" (p. 12) that was attempting to create changes in the field. Tanner and Tanner did not measure their aggressive semantic arguments, claiming that "just as paranoid phraseology characterized the rhetoric of student demagogues and radical critiques of the 1960's, so paranoid phraseology suffuses much of reconceptualists 'theoretical' writing" (p. 8).

Jackson's critique took on a different tone. Among other issues, Jackson's impatience with reconceptualism was driven by the fact that curriculum theory and workers were running away from the daily problems of the practice and hence were useless to real teachers. Reconceptualism, Jackson argued, offered a way of thinking and talking about schools that was quite detached from the complexity that determined daily school practices. Reconceptualization, Wraga (1999) argued, not only "praises a sort of hopelessness for reforming public school curriculum" (p. 16) but also, oddly as it might be, claims to be an absolute historical truth.

Sears and Marshall (2000) argue that "several of the field's prominent members, including Maxine Greene, Apple, Eisner, distanced themselves from any association with 'reconceptualization' while welcoming the larger zeitgeist of openness and change" (p. 207). However, I believe that the reconceptualists' turmoil was much more complex than a simple clash between the "University of Wisconsin–Madison—Teachers College and Ohio State University—University of Rochester" (p. 204). This claim is actually quite clear in Greene's (1979) critique, which deserves to be quoted in length:

> Although I have participated in a number of "reconceptualist" conferences and my work has appeared in various "reconceptualist" publications, at no point did I think of "reconceptualism" as a movement with which I was becoming allied... My critique of Pinar began with an approving comment on the explicitness of his vantage point, something missing in the Tanners' piece, and I objected to what I conceived to be a self-serving use of some of Jurgen Harbermas' ideas from a secondary source by Pinar... I also objected to Pinar's interpretation of twentieth century curriculum history, his arbitrary use of categories, and his "slotting" of people like Tyler, Beauchamps and Schwab. It was clear to me that he was inventing a new theological history with

all the developments over the past half-century reaching a grand con-summation in what Pinar choose to call an "emancipatory discipline of curriculum"...My major criticism of William Pinar's work derived from the conviction that the schools function the way they do because of the demands of the American industrial system, the moralistic and political traditions of public education, the omnipresence of bureau-cracies, the dominance of behaviorisms and the exclusions and humili-ations due to sexism and racism...I would not, however, go so far as William Pinar and describe the school as an agency committed to a mind of murder (and embalming) or, alternatively, to driving people mad. (p. 25)

Green's perspective reveals how problematic the concept "reconcep-tualist" is. In an attempt to systematize the mixed feelings expressed by scholars within and outside of the so-called critical progressive curriculum tradition, we can highlight seven claims. The first is that reconceptualism appears to propose a new curriculum concept, fun-damentally based only on the thinking of authors who may be found in a book (cf. Pinar, 1975), which confers a profound fragility on the concept. The work of scholars such as Greene, Macdonald, Mann, Apple, Giroux, Aronowitz, McLaren, Pinar, and others needs to be directly or indirectly, consciously or unconsciously, related to certain historical and political perspectives in the heart of the field.

Second, by silencing the significance of a historical curriculum, reconceptualism furthermore seems to neglect the important rela-tions of complicity that the curriculum field had developed with society, both influencing it and being influenced by it. This, paradox-ically, was a sentient alert, as expressed by Pinar (1975, p. 396): "The curriculum theory field has forgotten what existence is [and] it will remain moribund until it remembers." The struggle against models (and what models really represent) epitomized by Bobbitt and later by Tyler did not start with the reconceptualists or reconceptualism—a point we think the reconceptualists would readily agree with. Such struggle has a long tradition in the field, since the end of nineteenth century. It is within that context that the *Journal of Negro Education* (1932), for example, emerged. As the editorial of the 1932 volume claims, "It can be truthfully said that proposals affecting the educa-tion of Negroes have not been subjected to an abundance of critical investigation and thinking" (p. 2).

Third, some critics argue that the concept of reconceptualism needs more explanation. Pinar (1994) explained that the term "reconceptu-alization derives from...Macdonald and his much quoted 1971 piece on research in curriculum" (p. 63), adding that it only "contributed to its popularization by using the idea to sketch a picture of where the field had been, where it is now, and where it might be going" (p. 63). However, if we examine Macdonald's (1971a) text, nowhere does he make the claim in such a way; in fact, the opposite is true. Pinar (1994, cf. also 1988) admitted to his confusing use of the term: "It is appropriate to note a confusion illustrated by the frequent use of the term 'reconceptualism' rather than 'reconceptualization.' I suppose I contribute to this misunderstanding by subtitling the 1975 book of essays *Curriculum Theorizing: The Reconceptualists*" (1994, p. 70). Were "the reconceptualists" addressing the call put forward by Bruner, as was overtly expressed by Macdonald (1971a)?

Fourth, the reconceptualist notion of "currere" needs clarification. According to critics, reconceptualism not only contributed to "the danger of borrowing concepts and methods from other traditions" (Pinar, 1975, p. 401) but, by ignoring the history of the field, has also created a concept that is disconnected "from their historical and intellectual contexts and placed [it] in alien ambiences" (p. 401).

Fifth, the dimension of currere or of the curriculum "as experience in educational contexts" (Pinar, 1975, p. 413) sounds more like Parker, Dewey, or even Johnson. And there is still another question: to reconceptualize what? What should the referent of reconceptualization be?

Sixth, some critics react harshly to the very structure that presents the reconceptualist movement as greatly polemical. By dividing the book *Curriculum Theorizing: The Reconceptualists* into four parts, critics claim that reconceptualists sunk their theory in an enormous contradiction. This division not only lacks a good explanation, it gives legitimacy to some doubts. For example, while discussing Cremin in the section on the state of the field, Pinar's explanation renders the choice fragile by claiming that "he cannot be called a reconceptualist" (p. xii). Their critics find it hard to understand and justify the inclusion of Mann and Apple in a group said to represent "political and methodological criticism" while relegating Huebner or Greene to the margins, placing them in a postcritical dimension. As far as we are concerned, the politicization of the field led by Mann and Apple can also be found in the works of Huebner and Macdonald. Moreover, how can reconceptualists explain the inclusion of Phenix in this group of postcritics? Could the article by Phenix, "Transcendence and the Curriculum," define his position in the field? Arguably not. What logic emerges from both the 1973 Rochester Conference, and the 1975 book, *Curriculum Theorizing: The Reconceptualists*?

It is impossible, furthermore, not to notice how white this interesting movement is. What about the many African-American intellectuals and educators such as Du Bois, Parks, and others, who understood educational curriculum theory "as an intellectual task of creating better ways to conceptualize" (Macdonald, 1971a, p. 195)?[3] If the issue is "to reconceptualize," such a struggle needs to pay attention to an interesting historical tradition in the field. In fact, according to Macdonald, "curriculum theory is much in need of historical study, with a goal of untangling what Huebner referred to as the different uses of curriculum language" (p. 197).

Finally, it is quite problematic to engage in a debate about post-reconceptualism, even about its very meaning, when the concept of reconceptualism is not that clear and has so many problems. If the term "reconceptualization—not reconceptualism—accurately describes what is underway in the curriculum in 1970s" (Pinar, 1994, p. 71), then, there is all the more reason not to dissociate the work of Huebner, Greene, Mann, Macdonald, Apple, Giroux, Pinar, Grumet, and others from its historical context. In a way, Pinar, by including himself in the group of the reconceptualists *avant la lettre,* annuls the historical significance of his own interesting work in which the contributions of Johnson, for example, must not be forgotten.

Despite such severe criticism, the reconceptualists tried to overcome natural tensions and fissures. While not overtly admitting the turmoil created by the movement, Pinar (1980) did not hesitate to respond to some of its most bitter critics. One such response deserves to be quoted in length:

> Conversation cannot occur unless the participants are willing to maintain a minimal civility, a pedagogic orientation, and a willingness to be changed by the other. With such conditions present, a vital conversation, indicative of a vital field can occur. I, for one, am open to being influenced by my critics. And so I invite Daniel Tanner, Laurel Tanner, and Philip Jackson to critique my writing once again, or other reconceptualist writing, but with one stipulation: that they cast their critiques in terms that I and others can use. This openness, it seems to me, is a prerequisite for not only individual development but—writ large—the advancement of the field itself as well. Those of us who care for the field will cultivate it. (pp. 397–8)

This posture undeniably deserved a different reaction that never did occur. There are without question elements of good sense and bad sense in this wrangle that one cannot minimize. However, incidents like the one overtly denounced by Wraga and Hlebowitsh (2003b) did not help any attempt to construct a serious and fruitful local conversation, let alone an international one. In fact, precisely the opposite occurred:

> We originally prepared our manuscript in response to an open invitation to continue the conversation about the state of the U.S. curriculum field that appeared in the *Journal of Curriculum Theorizing* (*JCT*), which had also published several comments about our work. *JCT* informed us that our submission was rejected on the grounds that "*JCT* is committed to nourishing the work that Bill Pinar started over 20 years ago with the reconceptualization of the field" and our "attacks" do not "nourish but attempt, rather, to destroy" that work. We then revised the manuscript by adding the section revisiting Schwab's signs of crisis and leaving the section on imperative issues intact. We were pleased when *JCS* (*Journal of Curriculum Studies*) informed us that the piece would appear along with responses solicited from other scholars—and grateful that *JCS* has no ideological litmus test for manuscript submissions. (p. 425)

These tensions certainly deserve further discussion. In any case, Eric Malewski (2010) attempted an interesting move (I know some will say, why more ashes to an eternal fire) to clarify the waters. I see some very positive, as well as problematic issues with Malewski's claims. I concur with him that there will be some unmeasured exaggeration in Wraga and Hlebowitsh's claims. For instance, since its social insemination the field has always lived in crisis and has developed through crisis. As we claimed previously, the crisis is its very DNA of the field. There is no known historical generation in the field which has not lived, and has not itself been both producers and victims of successive and successful crises. It is also undeniable that it is dangerous to claim a vacuity between knowledge and power relations. Another crucial aspect is that every non-ideological claim is in itself and ideological claim. As I was able to claim in another context one can only 'kill' ideology ideologically (Paraskeva, 2011b). Therefore Wraga and Hlebowitsh's claim that the curriculum field and power need to be ideologically sterilized is in itself an ideological claim. My sense is that Wraga and Hlebowitsh know quite well that "the very attempt to stepping out of ideology is the very form of our enslavement to it" (Žižek, 1994, p. 6). History—or histories—really matters (Mahoney, 2000; Goody, 2010), and curriculists and curricologos, as I was able to claim elsewhere (Paraskeva, 2005) really have, as Malewski (2010) stresses, a "racial and ethnic background, Nationality, gender, sexual orientation, and position in the academy." The curriculum field needs to be understood within the dynamics of ideological production. After all who denies that 'reconceptualization' is an ideological claim? Who denies that counter reconceptualists claims have an ideological pillar? The very reconceptualization ideology cannot be understood without a counter-reconceptualization ideology as well. In fact, who denies, as Žižek (1994, p. 8) would put it that "they know very well what they are doing, yet they are doing it."

However, I think that Wraga and Hlebowitsh's claims are much more powerful, complex and interesting and go well beyond over who/what is 'in' and 'out' in the field and who determines those cartographies. Wraga and Hlebowitsh's "Tylerian/Schwab bent" have a political and ideological context that cannot be minimized since Tyler, for example, was able to edify a particular rationale capable of speaking to several traditions simultaneously. Ignoring the success of Tyler in outreaching to so many traditions is precisely a contribution to the perpetuity of some theoretical dead blocks.

I am also not certain, as Malewski (2010, p. x) claims, that "studies in curriculum become less about traditionalism's obsessive focus." Are we claiming that the 'counter-dominant is dominant'? Within the internationalization momentum this needs further analysis since dominant traditions cannot be understood outside the dynamics of the local contexts. Despite the debris that naturally arises from any theoretical clash one needs to welcome and foster the democratic debate.

In a way, sometimes, one feels that we are actually not facing a field in perpetual disarray and crises. Sometimes when we look at the field, we don't actually know if we are before a field of knowledge in perpetual crises, a field of knowledge which its very existence relies overwhelmingly in its capacity to perpetuate crisis and chaos; crises is the very *core* of the field; or quite contrary we are before a tragedy, in which a tragic mass choir laudably worships, sings, and dances quite a few curriculum Dionysus. I prefer the crisis. It is the crises that allow inclusively the silences of the debates, however it cannot allow silencing the conversation. That is a tragedy.

In an attempt to understand the field more fully and engage in an open conversation as we lay out the last sentences of this chapter, we will summarize the various stances taken by scholars within and outside the critical progressive curriculum tradition vis-à-vis reconceptualism-reconceptualists-reconceptualization. Thus far, we have gradually unfolded our arguments regarding the general tensions within the field of curriculum and the impact of a progressive curriculum tradition. We demonstrated how that impact constrained and promoted new ways of thinking within a field deeply affected by tensions, struggles, and clashes.

Page's 2003 address at the American Educational Research Association conference held in Chicago offered one of the clearest pictures of the current moribund state of the field and reminded us of the positions taken by Schwab and Huebner more than three decades ago. Page noted that AERA Division B had lost more than 30 percent of its members, who had joined other Special Interest Groups (SIGs) dealing with class, gender, race, and critical education. While this should not be minimized, we do not believe the field should be seen as suffering from a terminal illness. After all, a quick look at the history of the field shows that it has experienced one crisis after another. These crises seem to be in its very DNA: permanent conflict, permanent crisis, a permanent search for meaning, permanent contradictions—in essence, a permanently unstable condition. Practical and theoretical diversity "is one of the field most notable features" (Connelly, Fang He, Phillion and Schlein, 2008, p. xi) Thus, the explosion of SIGs could arguably be seen as a sign not of the failure of the curriculum field but of the permanent conflict and contradiction that are its very marrow. The explosion could also be seen as expressing a change in the commonsense view of the field's identity and limits; in other words, the field went in too many directions, and there is now a need to rethink how we define it.

Trueit, Doll, Wang, and Pinar (2000), Pinar (2003), and many others already have made a positive move that we should congratulate. However, while that move should be applauded, it also raises serious concerns, given its view of curriculum as a "complicated conversation," a position that Pinar, Reynolds, Slattery, and Taubman (1995, p. 848) put forward a couple of years ago. It is our task to complexify this challenge and to ask such questions as, Who is part of the conversation and why? Who is not part of the conversation and why not? What kinds of issues are at the core of the conversation? Where are the voices of real teachers and real students? What is the impact of the conversation on classroom practices? Who benefits from that "complicated" conversation? In which language(s) will this conversation occur? If the major purpose is to internationalize the "complicated conservation" (and I think this is not the case), we should point out that for curriculum scholars in Brazil, Spain, Portugal, Argentina, and many other nations, internationalization occurred many decades ago. Thus we must ask if this international conversation is challenging what Sousa Santos (2007) denounced as epistemicides. Is it engaged in opening up the canon of knowledge? Or, as we fear—and we hope we are wrong—is it an attempt to edify a new canon? If so, it would be a disaster.

CHAPTER 8

CHALLENGING EPISTEMICIDES:
TOWARD AN ITINERANT
CURRICULUM THEORY

CRITICAL APPROACHES: LIMITS
AND POSSIBILITIES

Despite the severe criticism faced by many critical theorists and critical theory itself, one cannot deny that early in their intellectual development, many critical scholars struggled with both the limits and possibilities of their critical theoretical approaches as a way to analyze social formations. This is visible, for instance, in both Giroux's and Apple's organic intellectualism. As I claim elsewhere (Paraskeva, 2004), in his early intellectual growth, Apple (1990) struggled with both the limits and the possibilities of critical approaches. I argued that although *Ideology and Curriculum* showed a deep intellectual concern for class analysis and sympathy toward the reproductive approach, one couldn't ignore the fact that Apple's analysis is keenly sensitive to the fact that "reproduction" alone cannot explain the intricate dynamics of schooling. In fact, *Ideology and Curriculum* opens the door for both *Education and Power* (Apple, 1995; I maintain that the two books could be published in a single volume) and *Teachers and Texts* (Apple, 1986), as well as the rest of his vast intellectual work. So, for Apple, the "traditional" critical theoretical tools were clearly insufficient to allow an acute interpretation of social formation and its consequential transformation. Later on, Apple, together with Weis and McCarthy, claims the need to move beyond a reductive platform. While Apple and Weis (1983) called for the need to perceive the structure of school's ideological formation, thus arguing that the cultural sphere was relatively autonomous, McCarthy and Apple (1988) introduced the non-synchronous parallelist position to promote better understanding of race, class, and gender issues in education. As McCarthy and Crichlow (1993, p. xiv) argue a new pan-ethic-cultural framework of racial origins and identity overlaps the reductive Marxist and neo-Marxist perspectives. Later on, Apple and Carlson (1998) defended the need for a combined critical-poststructural platform, adding that "Gramscian discourse has highlighted the roles that economic and technological forces as well as ideological struggles played in reshaping the post-Fordist cultural landscape. Foucault's work focuses our attention on the role of the State and expert knowledge in constructing normalized citizens and subjectivity" (p. 6). More recently, Hypolito (2001) complexified McCarthy and Apple's (1998) approach by calling for a spiral nonparallelist, nonsynchronous position to better understand class, race, and gender issues in education.

Giroux was also responsive to the silences and possibilities of critical theory. In *Ideology, Culture and the Process of Schooling*, Giroux (1981a) claims that "the task of radical educational theory is to identify and move beyond those classroom structures which maintain an oppressive hidden curriculum" (p. 82). The radical core of any pedagogy, Giroux argues, "will be found not in its insistence on a doctrinal truth as much as in its ability to provide the theoretical and structural conditions necessary to help students search for and act upon the truth" (p. 86). Moreover, Giroux was quite aware that "the perception of hegemony redefines class rule, and also reveals a relationship between ideology and power, which is viewed not simply as one of imposition, but as Foucault points out, a "network of relations, constantly in tension, in activity, rather than a privilege one might possess...power is exercised rather than possessed" (p. 25). Giroux later crystallizes the need to pay attention to postmodern and poststructural insights and argues that the reinvigoration of critical theory depends on such a move. For example, in *Towards a Postmodern Pedagogy* (Giroux, 1996), he summarizes the need to overcome the towering vacuums within the very marrow of the critical epistemological armada. It is worth quoting at length:

> Critical theory needs a language that allows for competing solidarities and political vocabularies that do not reduce the issues of power, justice, struggle, and inequality to a single script, a master narrative that suppresses the contingent, historical, and the everyday as a serious object of study. Critical pedagogy needs to create new forms of knowledge through its emphasis on breaking down disciplinary boundaries and creating new spaces where knowledge can be produced. It is not an epistemological issue, but one of power, ethics, and politics. The Enlightenment notion of reason needs to be reformulated within a

critical pedagogy. Critical pedagogy needs to regain a sense of alternatives by combining a language of critique and possibility. Postmodern feminism exemplifies this in both its critique of patriarchy and its search to construct new forms of identity and social relations. Critical pedagogy needs to develop a theory of teachers as transformative intellectuals who occupy specifiable political and social locations—rather than defining teacher work through the narrow language of professionalism. Central to the notion of critical pedagogy is a politics of voice that combines a postmodern notion of difference with a feminist emphasis on the primacy of the political. (pp. 691–695)

As Darder, Baltodano, and Torres (2002) stress in the introduction of their *Critical Pedagogical Reader,* "Giroux's work is credited with repositioning the education debates of the 'New Left' beyond the boundaries of reproduction theories and the hidden curriculum" (p. 24).

In a way, Apple's and Giroux's positions demonstrate a credibility check of the accuracy of some of the criticism thrown at critical theory. However, it seems that Giroux was more willing than Apple to pioneer a full engagement with a vast and complex postmodern and poststructural literature. Despite this, both Apple and Giroux allow one to trace a series of discontinuities in their intellectual journey; that is, their voyage did not remain fixed in the reproductive approach toward the educational process. Instead, the reproductive approach served as a launching point that allowed them to go beyond reproduction. Arguably, they are more neo-Gramscian than neo-Marxist.

Wexler (1976) too was not shy in unveiling some of the puzzling limits of the critical theoretical framework.[1] He argued that too much emphasis had been put on the social effects of schooling and not enough on the study of the nature of school knowledge. It seems that to Wexler, the study of school content or knowledge was somehow dangerous for sociologists. Despite the fact that a number sociologists have studied school knowledge, their approach, according to Wexler, is bounded by social images and outdated paradigms. The lack of consensus about what should be taught in the schools highlights the need for a serious debate about school content. Simply put, critical theory was facing severe charges from deep within its ranks. There is no doubt that the reinvigoration of critical theory depends on its ability to go beyond its own silences, although this is not an easy task. Recent works by Gore (1993), Pedroni (2002), Paraskeva (2006a, 2006b, 2007), Macedo and Frangella (2007), Lopes (2007), Baker (2009), and others can help a great deal here.

These works posit the need to overcome some of the loose ends of the critical theoretical platform by advancing an inclusive approach that incorporates critical and poststructural dynamics. Pedroni (2002), in a deeper and more detailed analysis, unveiled not only the need to address some puzzling blockages within critical theory but also the possibilities for a collaborative framework, meanwhile noting the importance of paying attention to positive elements of both epistemological spaces. He argued that not only was "neo-Marxism in a need of a post-structural reworking [but also that] post-structural educational research would also benefit from a neo-Marxist reworking" (pp. 2, 6). The task was not simplistic in any sense of the word. Relying on Fraser and Fiske, Pedroni argued that the task at hand was neither a function of juxtaposing the critical with the poststructural nor an effort to "Gramscianize Foucault while Foucaultianizing Gramsci," but, rather, to precisely and "simultaneously Gramscianize and Foucaultianize our own analyzes" (p. 7). The task, Baker (2007) accurately claims, is to master a new wave of research, thus making visible the eloquent silences that were petrified (and sometimes ossified) by secular occlusions.

In *The Struggle for Pedagogies,* Gore (1993) denies any attempt to formulate "a prescriptive guidance." According to Gore, the best way to deal with the ongoing debates within radical pedagogies (specifically between critical and feminists theories) is to avoid any attempt to map out the entire field of radical pedagogy, as "such aims would be impractical" (p. xiii). Instead, one should "capture the dangers and gaps in the ongoing struggles for radical pedagogies" (p. xiii). An attempt to do just this appears in some interesting and powerful curriculum research platforms emerging in Brazil (cf. Alves, Sgarbi, Passos, & Caputo, 2007; Amorim, 2007; Bellini & Anastácio, 2007; Eyng & Chiquito, 2007; Ferraco, 2007; Garcia & Cinelli, 2007; Lopes, 2007; Macedo & Frangella, 2007; Pessanha & Silva, 2007; Rosa, 2007; Veiga Neto et al., 2007; Vieira, Hypolito, Klein, & Garcia, 2007). These scholars argue that the issue clearly is not about claiming a particular fixed critical or poststructural posture or assuming a kind of mixed position, but about a move from the critical to the postcritical or the poststructural perspectives. It detours from those platforms without denying them, sliding constantly within those approaches while in the midst of a friendly crossfire. In a way, it goes beyond a compositive approach. It is instable in that very position and it assumes a idiosyncrasy that is sentient of the intricate dynamics of issues such as hegemony, articulation, emancipation, identity, image, sounds, space*less*, time*less*, the (multiplicity of the) biosocial (multitude) self. In fact, the point is to be aware of assuming any position that is more complex than a hybrid position, one that cannot be atrophied by any claim of hybridity. It is not a hybrid position. Bhabha (1995) helps a great deal here:

> Hybridity is the sign of the productivity of colonial power, its shifting forces and fixities; it is the name for the strategic reversal of the process of domination through disavowal (that is, the production of discriminatory identities that secure the "pure" and original identity and authority). Hybridity is the revaluation of the assumption of colonial identity through the recitation of discriminatory identity effects. It displays the necessary deformation and displacement of all sites of discrimination and domination. It unsettles the mimetic or narcissistic demands of colonial power but reimplicates its identifications in strategies of subversion that turn the gaze of the discriminated back upon the eye of power. (pp. 38–9)

The point is to assume a posture that slides constantly among several epistemological frameworks, thus giving one better tools to interpret schools as social formations. Such a theoretical posture might be called a "deterritorialized" rather than a compositive device, as I will argue later. Conceptualizing it in this way can profoundly help one to grasp the towering concepts, such as hegemony, ideology, social emancipation, and power, more fully. Before the nightmare of the present, as Pinar (2004) puts it, assuming this posture is quite valuable and it needs to be done.

Taking this posture is a powerful way not only to challenge the hegemonic way of thinking that gave to the word a privileged position in scientific writing (Alves, Sgarbi, Passos, & Caputo, 2007), but also—and this is crucial—to challenge and overcome what Gore (1993) accurately denounces as U.S.–centric discourses—or, as Autio (2007) put it, "curriculum superdiscourses."

Popkewitz (2001, p. 245) did not minimize the strategies used in the production of reason and social progress, stating that "modern empirical methods in the social and educational sciences are largely predicated on the *eye* as giving truth." He maintained that

> qualitative studies, also, make the discipline of the *eye* a central repository of truth. Methodological discussions in education, for example, often discuss ethnographies as "naturalistic" studies. Such discussions pose the observation of "natural" events as directly visible through the *eye* and therefore more truthful than the vicarious methods of surveys. (p. 245)

Gore (1993) argues further: "Since the U.S. is the location of much of the critical and feminist pedagogical discourses, one needs to question if that reflects an ethnocentrism or U.S.-centrism that ignores important pedagogical work going on elsewhere" (p. 45). I claim that the critical progressive curriculum river needs to be responsive and yet to go beyond such clashes, vacuums, screaming silences, and cacophonous debates within and among the critical and poststructural platforms. The task is to fight for cognitive diversity.

While it is undeniable that curriculum knowledge was (and still is) a major concern not only in Apple's and Giroux's political projects but in those of Carnoy (1972), Young (1971), Dale, Esland, and MacDonald (1982), Young and Whitty (1977), Whitty (1985), Bernstein (1977), and Bourdieu (1971), it is also undeniable that little attention was paid to what Wexler (1976) coined as "cognitive pluralism" (p. 50). "The epistemological diversity of the world is [undeniably] potentially infinite" (Sousa Santos, 2005, p. xix) and we are thus facing a huge task. As Pinar (2004) argues, "*What* we teach is at least as important, if not more important, than *how* we teach" (p. 175). The point is to move beyond questions such as "what/whose knowledge is of most worth" despite not having figured out a correct answer, and to fight for (an)other knowledge outside the Western epistemological harbor. Therefore, we need to engage in the struggle against epistemicides. One needs first to assume consciously that (an)other knowledge is possible and then to go beyond the Western epistemological platform, paying attention to other forms of knowledge and respecting indigenous knowledge within and beyond the Western space. Needless to say, this fight is only possible precisely because of the advancements, developments, gains, and frustrations experienced by the particular critical approaches edified by Apple, Giroux, and many others both within and outside the critical progressive curriculum river, yet within the complex progressive tradition. In fact, the struggle for (an)other knowledge needs to be contextualized in the struggle for curriculum relevance. This is the next big struggle, which in reality is a struggle for social justice. Both Sousa Santos and Connell teach us a great deal in this regard.

CHALLENGING EPISTEMICIDES: (AN)OTHER KNOWLEDGE IS POSSIBLE

As we have examined in great detail elsewhere (Paraskeva, 2011a; forthcoming), the best way for schools to fight for a just and equal society—especially when facing the impact of neo-radical centrist policies and strategies —is to engage in a struggle for what Sousa Santos,

Nunes, and Meneses (2007) call epistemological diversity. These authors argue that there is no such thing as "global social justice without cognitive justice" (p. ix). In fact, by identifying as "official" particular forms of knowledge, schooling participates in what Sousa Santos (1997) called epistemicides—a lethal tool that fosters the commitment to imperialism and White supremacy (hooks, 1994).

Sousa Santos et al. (2007) astutely claim that the "suppression of knowledge [of indigenous peoples of the Americas and of African slaves] was the other side of genocide" (p. ix). Their argument is worth quoting at length here:

> Many non-Western (indigenous, rural, etc.) populations of the world conceive of the community and the relationship with nature, knowledge, historical experience, memory, time, and space as configuring ways of life cannot be reduced to Eurocentric conceptions and cultures...The adoption of allegedly universal valid, Eurocentric legal and political models, such as the neoliberal economic order, representative democracy, individualism, or the equation between state and law often rests...on forms of domination based on class, ethnic, territorial, racial, or sexual differences and on the denial of collective identities and rights considered incompatible with Eurocentric definitions of the modern social order. (pp. xx–xxi)

Thus, one cannot deny that "there is an epistemological foundation to the capitalist and imperial order that the global North has been imposing on the global South" (p. ix). What we need, Sousa Santos (2004) argues, is to engage in a battle against "the monoculture of scientific knowledge [and fight for an] ecology of knowledges" (p. xx), which is

> an invitation to the promotion of non-relativistic dialogues among knowledges, granting equality of opportunities to the different kinds of knowledge engaged in a ever broader epistemological disputes aimed both at maximizing their respective contributions to build a more democratic and just society and at decolonizing knowledge and power. (p. xx)

The fight, therefore, should be against the coloniality of power and knowledge. In fighting this battle, one will end up challenging particular notions, concepts, and practices relative to multiculturalism that are profoundly

> Eurocentric, [that] create and describe cultural diversity within the framework of the nation-states of the Northern hemisphere...the

prime expression of the cultural logic of multinational or global capitalism, a capitalism without homeland at last, and a new form of racism, tend[ing] to be quite descriptive and apolitical thus suppressing
the problem of power relations, exploitation, inequality, and exclusion.
(pp. xx–xxi)

We actually need a multicultural approach that adopts an emancipatory content and direction aimed mainly at the multiple articulations
of difference. Thus, we will be allowing for the fruitful conditions of
what Sousa Santos (2004) calls the sociology of absences. In other
words, what we have is a call for the democratization of knowledges
that is a commitment to an emancipatory, non-relativistic, cosmopoli-
tan ecology of knowledges, a

bringing together and staging [of] dialogues and alliances between
diverse forms of knowledge, cultures, and cosmopologies in response
to different forms of oppression that enact the coloniality of knowledge and power. [We need actually] to learn from the South (since) the
aim to reinvent social emancipation goes beyond the critical theory
produced in the North and the social and political praxis to which it
has subscribed. (Sousa Santos et al., 2007, p. xiv)

In fact, it would be a mistake to dissociate Western hegemonic epistemologies from the dehumanizing imperialist and colonialist ideological platforms. As Smith (1999) notes,

Imperialism and colonialism are the specific formations through
which the West came to "see," to "name," and to "know" indigenous
communities. The cultural archive with its systems of representation,
codes for unlocking systems of classification, and fragmented artifacts
of knowledge enabled travelers and observers to make sense of what
they saw and to represent their new-found knowledge back to the
West through the authorship and authority of their representations.
(p. 60)

The preponderance of non-Western forms of knowledge is also highlighted by Connell's (2007) approach. By claiming Western sociology
as a classed, raced, and gendered science of the new industrial society
(cf. Smith, 1999), Connell emphasized the need to pay close attention
to indigenous forms of knowledge developed in Africa and within the
Islamic sphere. According to Connell (2007), "sociology developed
in a specific social location: among men of the metropolitan liberal
bourgeoisie. Those who wrote sociology were a mixture of engineers

and doctors, academics, journalists, clerics and a few could live on their family capital" (p. 14). She continues:

> At the very time Durkheim and his colleagues were building the impe-
> rial gaze into their sociology, other French social scientists engaged
> intellectuals of the Islamic world in dialogue about modernity, colo-
> nialism, and culture. In the same generation, Du Bois moved from a
> focus on race relations within the United States to a strongly interna-
> tionalist perspective, with particular attention to Africa. In the first
> half of the twentieth century, black African intellectuals such as Sol
> Plaatje and Jomo Kenyatta dialogued with metropole through social
> science as well as political struggle. The mainstream of metropolitan
> sociology made little use of such contacts; but this other history is also
> real, and we need to build on it today. (p. 25)

First, North Atlantic metropolitan epistemologies arrogantly neglected the importance of a well-established indigenous sociology edified by intellectuals, like Akiwowo, who persistently attempted to "reorient the discipline to the African reality through an integrated system of conceptual schemes, theories, and methodological techniques drawn up in relation to both African and European thought-ways and social practices" (Connell, 2007, p. 90; cf. also Akiwowo, 1980). Having the ritual oral poetry of the community as a major source, Akiwowo fought for the need to develop an African sociological platform deeply based on African concepts and import those concepts to Europe, instead of submitting African sociology to the colonization of North Atlantic concepts completely detached from African *sui generis* reali-ties. Second, North Atlantic metropolitan epistemologies minimized and silenced the important struggles, debates, tensions, and clashes within the very marrow of African epistemologies. Actually, hege-monic science has shown "either a passive inability or an active hos-tility to recognizing scientific work autonomously produced" (Sousa Santos, 2005, p. xxiii) by non-Western countries. Let us briefly pay attention to some of the most towering tensions within the very mar-row of a particular African epistemological vein. In doing so, we will flag other interesting epistemological developments in the Arab world and in Asia. One will perceive implicitly how dead wrong the Western epistemological paradigm is in minimizing, silencing, and ignoring such interesting epistemological clashes.

In his *Contributions to the Sociology of Knowledge from African Oral Poetry*, Akiwowo (1986) emphasized the need to understand oral poetry as a major source of knowledge in African cultural social formations. Akiwowo points to the African *Asuwada* principle as the way to edify meanings, and to understand the person and reality. The Asuwada principle is well summarized here by Connell (2007):

> The unit of social life is the individual's life, being, existence, or character; the corporeal individual, essentially, cannot continue-in-being without a community; since the social life of a group of individual beings is sustained by a spirit of sodality, any form of self-alienation for the purpose of pursuing a purely selfish aim, is morally speaking, an error or sin; and a genuine social being is one who works daily, and sacrifices willingly, in varying ways, his or her cherished freedom and material acquisitions for self-improvement as well as for the common good. For without one, the other cannot be achieved. (p. 91)

This was ferociously challenged by Lawuyi and Taiwo (1990, cited in Connell, 2007, p. 91), who argued that Akiwowo was trying to base African sociology Anglo–North American concepts and was not developing any kind of sociological theory in *Yoruba* terms. Actually, this is not a minor issue. As Gyekye (1987) argues, "Language, as a vehicle of concepts, not only embodies a philosophical point of view, but also influences philosophical thought" (p. 29); in fact, language "does not merely suggest, but may also embody philosophical perspectives, every language implies or suggests a vision of the world" (p. 31).

Tempels complained that European colonizers never paid attention to the fact that African people had a well-grounded philosophy "that equates being with a vital force of life" (Connell, 2007, p. 98; cf. also Tempels, 1945). The idea of a well-established African philosophy is made crystal clear in Hountondji (1976):

> When I speak of African philosophy I mean literature, and I try to understand why it has so far made such strenuous efforts to hide behind the screen, all the more opaque for being imaginary, of an implicit "philosophy" conceived as an unthinking, spontaneous, collective system of thought, common to all Africans or at least to all members severally past, present and future, of such-and-such an African ethnic group. (p. 55)

Challenging ethno-philosophical approaches, Hountondji argues that the idea of African philosophy is based in customs, chants, and myths. Again, we have a hot-button issue here. Gyekye (1987, p. 25) claims that one "cannot deny that philosophy is a product of culture" and that "African philosophical thought is expressed both in the oral literature and in the thoughts and actions of people"

(p. 13). The same sort of claim is overtly denounced by Hamminga (2005):

> In classical African culture, knowledge is not produced, but it comes, it is given to you by tradition, the ancestors, as heritage. So knowledge acquisition is purely social matter, a matter of teaching, of being told, "uploaded" (by living, dead, or spiritual powers) only. Like the Greek language, knowledge, has nothing to do with sweating or working. (p. 76)

Kaphagawani (1998, p. 241) claims that Chewa's people have a conception of knowledge that is profoundly flooded with proverbs, such as *Akuluakulu ndi m'dambo mozimila moto* (The elders are rivers where fire is extinguished); such messages stem from the cultural concept that "the elders have most, if not all, the solutions to any kind of problem; they are live encyclopedias to which reference can be made for the answers to troublesome questions." Machel (1985), the Mozambican independence leader, consciously assumes such a perspective, arguing that "we must be aware that the new generations are growing up in contact with the old generations who are passing on the vices of the past. Our practical experience shows how children and young people in our own centres can be contaminated by decadent ideas, habits and tastes" (p. 28). He continues:

> No book by Marx ever arrived in my home town, nor any other book that spoke against colonialism. Our books were these elders. It was they who taught us what colonialism is, the evils of colonialism and what the colonialists did when they came here. They were our source of inspiration. (p. x)

As Hountondji (1983) accurately counterargues, such ethno-philosophical approaches assume that the African way of thought is something static, something immune to change, to transformation, and something that is unacceptable for performing and leading social changes. He concludes that ethno-philosophy is fundamentally a conservative pastoral.

Hountondji's rejection of both Tempels's and Mbiti's arguments was based on his belief that it was a profound scientific mistake to build any kind of homogeneity into African thought. In this context, the very concept of African philosophy is an oxymoron. Although Mbiti (1969), in *African Religion and Philosophy,* criticized Tempels's (1945) *Bantu Philosophy* for generalizing the African way of reading the wor(l)d (as Freire would put it), the fact is that he falls into the same conceptual trap. It is impossible, Hountondji (1983) argues, to claim any kind of uniformity in the logic and perception of African people. Appiah (1992) also challenges any attempt to claim African philosophical homogeneity. As he argues, it is culture, not just race, that shapes and works on people's identities. Essentially, any proposed homogeneity needs to be seen as a form of cultural politics perpetrated by Western dominance. It reflects the way that the Western scientific dominant discursive views science.

Clearly, for Hountondji (1983), Mudimbe (1988), Gyekye (1987), and others, African philosophical thought needs to be seen on a continuum with severe fractures. On the one hand there are those who surrendered their philosophical thought to Western epistemological frameworks, and on the other are those who struggled to edify non-monolithic philosophical thought based on African concepts and multiple ways of reading the wor(l)d. In fact, one of the heated debates among African intellectuals is the tension of differentiating between the individual and the personal. Appiah (1992) is one of the African intellectuals struggling to clarify such tensions. While in a Western plant,

> 50 identical individual machines [are] operated by 50 individual workers—from the management point of view neither are treated as personal, in Africa even machines quickly acquire their own personal features, as repairs are not usually made in a standard way. In Africa a machine (car, bus, etc.) can usually be operated only by persons knowing this particular machine personally. (Hamminga, 2005, p. 79: cf. also Appiah, 1992)

As Appiah (1992) articulates, the tension between the beliefs that "everything is individual versus every force is personal" is a crucial issue that connects epistemological apparatuses with daily life.

Western epistemological hegemonic dominance has played a significant role in the construction of an Anglo–North American metropolitan global culture. This intentionally silences the existence of a secular solid African epistemological vein, which originated with Panafricanism and Negritude intellectual movements, and continued through contemporary Mbeki's Renaissance, which was based on "cultural change, emancipation of African woman, mobilization of youth, the promotion of democracy; and sustainable economic development" (Connell, 2007, p. 106). This particular renaissance has been profoundly damaged by genocidal events in Rwanda, Congo, and, quite recently, Zimbabwe. As Kebede (2004) argues, "Native rulers starting to think and acting like former colonizers make up the substance of African elitism" (p. 157).

However, this African renaissance is profoundly related to the struggle against what Connell (2007) felicitously called "epistemological disenfranchisement" (p. 109). It is a point of departure for the deracialization of intellectual production, a cultural scream from the "nothing people" (cf. Aidoo, 1997). Dehumanization has reached a point where the African people "have chosen to live near the rebuilt walls of [their] memory" (Senghor, 1998, p. 3).

To be fully aware of a well-developed African sociology and philosophy, one must pay attention not only to Kenyatta, Nyerere, Senghor, and Cesaire, but also to Cabral, Andrade, Mondlane, and others. As Oruka (1975) and Hallen (2002) note, Cabral, together with Mondlane, Machel, Kaunda, Nyerere, Sekou Toure, Nkrumah, Senghor, Rodney, Cesaire, Amin, and many others, represent the leading figures of what might be called the nationalist-ideological philosophy. Some of them are clearly working within a Marxist ideology, which, as Mudimbe (1994) argues, "seems to be the exemplary weapon and idea with which to go beyond what colonialism incarnated and ordained in the name of capital" (p. 42).

Cabral (1980), Guinea Bissau's leading intellectual, whom Freire (2009) epitomized as a pedagogue of the revolution, argues that African people "believe that the material and human wealth of their countries are part of the patrimony of humanity and should be made to serve the progress and happiness of their own peoples in all countries" (p. 27). Moreover, Cabral argues, national liberation is an act of culture:

> A people who free themselves from foreign domination will not be culturally free unless, without underestimating the importance of positive contributions from the oppressor's and other cultures, they return to the upwards paths of their own culture. The latter is nourished by the living reality of the environment and rejects harmful influences as much as any kind of subjection to foreign cultures. We see therefore that, if imperialist domination has the vital need to practice cultural oppression, national liberation is necessarily an *act* of culture. (p. 143)

In *The Weapon of Theory,* Cabral (1969) dares to answer the question, "Does history begin only with the development of the phenomenon of 'class' and consequently of class struggle?" (p. 95). Cabral argues that to answer "yes" would be to consider that various groups in Africa, Asia, and Latin America "were living without history, or outside history, at the time when they were subject to the yoke of imperialism—something that we refuse to accept" (p. 95). Moreover,

Cabral claims, the toughest battle was "against our own weakness" (p. 91). Cabral (1980) was actually on the very front line, struggling for what he called independence of thought and action:

> Although independence is always relative,…we always acted on the basis of independence of thought and action. We have been capable, and must constantly be more so of thinking deeply about our problems so as to be able to act correctly, to act strongly so as to be able to think more correctly. We must be able to bring these two basic elements together: thought and action, and action and thought. This independence in our thought is relative. It is relative because in our thought we are also influenced by the thought of others. (p. 80)

Lumumba (1963), the Congolese independence leader, takes the same line of political argument: "Africans are…simply Africans, and our policy is positive neutralism." The perspicacity of his radical Africanization deserves to be quoted at length:

> History never takes a step backward. We are not communists and we never will be, despite the campaign of destruction and obstruction that enemies of our independence have waged throughout the country. We are simply Africans. We do not want to subject ourselves to any foreign influence. We want nothing to do with any imported doctrines, either from the West, from Russia, or from America. The Congo remains the Congo. We are Africans. We want to make the Congo a great free nation. We do not want to escape one dictatorship only to fall in beneath another. We are not what people think we are, because we are a decent people…That Africa is not opposed to the West, to the United States, to the Soviet Union, or to any other nation, that Africa has asked only one thing, to be liberated completely so that we may collaborate with the West in total freedom. I am going to be even more specific about my intention in this regard, because there is so much talk about two blocs (the West and the East). The question of these two blocs doesn't interest us either. What interests us is the human element; we are African and we shall remain Africans. We have our philosophy and our code of ethics and we are proud of them. Africa will tell the West that it wants the rehabilitation of Africa now, a return to the sources, the reinstitution of moral values; the African personality must express itself; that is what our policy of positive neutralism means. Africa will not be divided into blocs, as Europe has been, on the contrary, there will be active African solidarity. We are going to carry out a psychological decolonialization, because the people have been subject to false indoctrination for eighty years. False ideas have been put in people's heads; they have been told that in order to have money, in order to have enough to eat, they have to work

for Europeans. We are going to tell the people that this is not true, that in order to live happy lives, they must get to work and plow the land. That is how things really are. We are aware of the facts. We are going to develop the country ourselves, we have no technical skills, we are going to develop the Congo with our brains, with our hands. (pp. 283–325)

It is, however, undeniable that during the 1960s, as Mudimbe (1994) argues,

> the vocabulary of criticism of colonial ratio was Marxist, that of the African independences as well as of the nonalignment programs was Marxist. The regimes, the progressive movements, and their leaders were Marxist. Similarly, *interlocuteurs valuables* ("authorized representatives") in Africa were Marxist, or, at least, wielded a syntax that have a Marxist aspect; the Africanists who were respected and accepted, both by Africa and by the West, were, more often than not, Marxists, or, at the very least Marxists sympathizers. The discipline of the future that attracted or terrorized political economy was Marxist. (p. 44)

However, as Mudimbe (1994) argues, the notable Marxist metaphors of "an egalitarian society organized on the basis of economic registers in the service of the betterment of people, of all people, (although) formally brilliant, over the years revealed themselves to be nothing other than deviations of the Marxists projects they were claiming to establish" (pp. 42–3). Obviously, Mudimbe adds, such failures, "contrary to the racist clamor, does not seem to be solely a failure of African intelligence; indeed one can link this failure to that of Marxist Africanism and its epistemological incoherencies" (pp. 42–3). As I was able to examine in detail elsewhere (Paraskeva, 2004), such failures were also due to exogenous conditions, namely, particular predatory foreign policies instituted by Western nations.

As Onyewuenyi (1991) argues, "knowledge and wisdom for the African consists in how deeply he understands the nature of forces and their interaction" (p. 41). Moreover, "the African thought holds that created beings preserve a bond of one with another, an intimate ontological relationship. There is interaction of being with being, that is to say, of force with force. This is more so among rational beings known as *Muntu,* a term which includes the living and the dead, Orishas, and God" (p. 41).

The struggle against epistemicides will allow us to highlight and learn how science was powerful in what is considered pre-colonial

India. As Baber (1995) documents—and in contrast to hegemonic historian pastorals—medicine, technology, and mathematics were quite developed in precolonial India and heavily based on the Indian way of reading the word and the world. This struggle forces one to pay attention, not only to multifarious ancient epistemological platforms in Africa, Asia, and Latin America, but also to understand the challenges edified by some non-Western intellectuals to Western epistemological frameworks. This is the case, not only of Amo,[2] a Ghanaian philosopher who in his second doctoral dissertation edified a severe critique of the modern French philosopher Descartes (Hallen, 2002), but also of Khoza (1994), who challenged the Western concept formulated by Protagoras that man is the measure of all things. Admitting the validity of such a claim, Khoza (1994; cf. also Prinsloo, 1998 argues, admits to the absence of the possibility of the supranatural in codetermining social events as something peaceful, and also silences such tragedies as slavery, holocausts, racism, nuclear, and biological wars. It is perhaps not necessary to mention that African philosophers (and, in a way, philosophy) were profoundly important during the Greco-Roman period. As Masolo (2004) reveals, Origen, Tertullian, Plotonius, and Hypatia were "the earliest Western female philosophers on record" (p. 51).[3] There is, Bernal (1987, 2001) argues, a clear imposition of Semitic and Egyptian culture on the Greek (an issue conveniently neglected by mainstream academic discourse), thus raising the question of who can most legitimately write Greek history.

As Smith (1999) declares, "Some scholars have argued that key tenets of what is now seen as Western civilization are based on black experiences and black traditions of scholarship, and have simply been appropriated by Western philosophy and redefined as Western epistemology" (p. 44). As odd as it might be, "indigenous Asian, American, Pacific, and African forms of knowledge, systems of classification, technologies and codes of social life, which began to be recorded in some detail by the seventeenth century, were regarded as 'new discoveries' by Western science" (p. 61). The fact is, as Sousa Santos (2005) notes, "in the name of modern science, many alternative knowledges and sciences have been destroyed, and the social groups that used these systems to support their own autonomous paths of development have been humiliated" (p. xviii). To summarize, in the name of science, "epistemicide(s) have been committed, and the imperial powers have resorted to it to disarm any resistance of the conquered peoples and social groups" (p. xviii).

There is scientific validity in cognitive spheres other than the West. As Hallen (2002) stresses,

> a number of philosophers in and of Africa contend that there are elements to African cognition that are sufficiently unique or distinctive to somehow set it apart. Their major complaints against the so-called universalists is that by placing undue emphasis upon the supposedly common or universal elements of African cognition, these uncommon features are underrated and fail to receive the recognition they deserve and the credibility they merit as alternative pathways to understanding. (p. 35)

As Mudimbe (1988) argues, it is quite problematic to frame African gnosis in a Western semantic yarn. One needs to question whether "African reality is not distorted in the expression of African modalities in non-African languages" (p. 186) and whether African reality has not been "inverted and modified by anthropological and philosophical categories used by specialists of dominant discourses" (p. 186). It is time, Mudimbe straightforwardly argues, to question if we are not in a need of an "epistemological shift" (p. 186). Moreover, it might be possible "to consider this shift outside of the very epistemological field which makes [Mudimbe's] question both possible and thinkable" (p. 186). As Appiah (1992) argues, traditional African cognition bluntly reflects critical, reflexive, and rational indigenous African intellect. As in any other philosophical sphere, Oruka (1990) stresses, a philosophical sagacity is well-developed in Africa, a sagacity that produces a particular idiosyncrasy.

According to Oruka (1990), one can identify four currents in African philosophy: ethno-philosophy, the work that attempts to describe the worldview of a specific African community as a whole; philosophical sagacity, the thought—and action—of rigorous indigenous thinkers (sages) who did not benefit from modern education; nationalistic-ideological philosophy, African intellectuals attempting to create a sui generis new socialist order; and professional philosophy developed and conducted by African philosophical scholars. Having said this, we can now recognize Oseghare's (1990) position about what African philosophy is and is not. He explains that African philosophy is not "the writings of some black Americans; the negritude movement literature, and ethnological and anthropological works" (p. 252).

The struggle against epistemicides will open several paths to grasp (an)other knowledge; to master, for example, how crucial the African philosophy *Ubuntu* is in terms of an "African view of life and world view, a collective consciousness of African people deeply ingrained in Africans' own religions, Africans' own ethical views, Africans' own political ideologies" (Prinsloo, 1998, p. 41). More than a theoretical framework, Ubuntu is a way of living and "it takes seriously the view that man is basically a social being" (p.41). From an Ubuntuan plat-form, "a person is a person through other persons" (Prinsloo, 1998, p. 43; Maphisa, 1994). Unlike Western humanism, which is intel-lectual, individualistic, and aesthetic, Ubuntu is religious, expansive, transcendental, centrifugal, dynamic, and holistic (Prinsloo, 1998, p. 46). It is hardly necessary to mention the role education plays in such way of living. In fact, education was a social sphere quite empha-sized by non-Western intellectuals, while precisely in the midst of the struggle against colonialism. Cabral was attentive to the importance of education in the emergence and consolidation of African thought. In fact, creating schools was one of the very first steps that inde-pendence movements, like PAIGC in Guinea Bissau and Cape Verde and FRELIMO in Mozambique, created in liberated areas. More than a space to improve knowledge, schools were seen as a base for the masses to seize power and teachers and students were militants (Machel, 1979). Moreover, knowledge was the base of comradeship (Machel, 1979). The importance of schools is quite clear in Cabral's (1980) argument:

> Set up schools and develop teaching in all the liberated areas. Constantly strengthen the political training of teachers. Persuade parents of the absolute necessity for their sons and daughters to attend school, but organize activity for the pupils in such a way that they can also be useful at home in helping their family. Set up courses to teach the adults to read and write. Combat among the youth, notably among the more mature, the obsession with leaving the country to go and study, the blind ambition to be *doctor,* the inferiority complex and the mistaken notion that those who study the courses will have privileges tomorrow in our land. Protect and develop manifestations of our people's culture, respect and ensure for the usages, customs and traditions of our land. Combat all par-ticularisms prejudicial to the unity of the people. Teach ourselves, and teach others to combat fear and ignorance. Learn from life, learn with our people, learn in books and from the experience of other. Constantly learn. (pp. 242–3)

In fact, Rukare (1971, p. 286) claims that "the cry to revolution-ize education does not imply that the African educationalist has to adopt everything that is contained in the surviving African culture(s)...[This] is not an end in itself, it is but a necessary means in the process of rediscovering our identity" (p. 286).

The struggle against Western hegemonic epistemological paradigms will also bring to the fore the importance to study the Islamic nahda, or as Kassir (2006, p. 49) unveils, Arab renaissance, and how Nahdawis (the men of the renaissance) "reconstructs [themselves] on the basis of the discovery of the Other, the European Other." It was during Nahda, as Kassir reveals, that the world saw an impressive cultural interplay between the West and Arab cultures. Profoundly connected with the mammoth Ottoman Empire, Nahda shaped humanism, a significant cultural and epistemological revolution, a "colossal metamorphosis" that created space for "the most extensive and varied debates: on scientific discoveries, the virtues of commerce, the struggle against superstition, women's education, historical analyzes, rationalism" (p. 51). Nahda included both Muslim and Christian nahdawis. If it is important to understand why and how realities such as Orientalism (cf. Said, 1978) and Eurocentrism (cf. Amin, 1989) have been edified and scientifically perpetuated by Western hegemonic scientific paradigms, it is no less important to perceive, study, and understand deeply what kind of debates are permeating non-Western societies. We need to challenge what Abu-Lughod (2001) calls the politics of negation portrayed by Zionists in the Middle East, which denies an identity to the Palestinian people and their culture. The issue is to understand the Western social construction of the so-called Arabic malaise (Kassir, 2006), and to perceive why, as Boroujerdi (2001) argues, the intellectual and political landscape of Iran often has been labeled "anachronistic, bewildering, enigmatic, incongruent, intricate, ironic, multidimensional, paradoxical, permutable, recondite, serendipitous, and unpredictable" (p. 13). Within the Islamic plethora, one needs to pay attention to overly specific complex issues, including democracy, epistemology, and the interpretation of Islam, the interplay between Islam and ideology, the relationship between religion and science/technology, and rights and freedom. These issues and others cannot not be understood (just) with Western ontological and epistemological tools. Thus, it is crucial to understand Western epistemological supremacy beyond its "internal inventiveness and the virtues of its unique entrepreneurial spirit" (Abu-Lughod, 1989, p. 18). Unfortunately, as Goody (1996) arrogantly argues, "The rise of the West has often been associated, by Westerners, with the possession of a rationality not available to others" (p. 11). Western dominant discourse dangerously denies medieval Islam's great achievements in areas such as philosophy, mathematics, astronomy, medicine, and poetry (cf. Jahanbegloo, 2007; Torres Santomé, 2011). The task, therefore, is to replace the Western and Eurocentric bias of the curriculum with non-Western literature (McCarthy, 1998).

As I argue frequently, something is quite wrong within Western society that keeps it from understanding the hatred non-Western society exhibits toward the West. Meanwhile, the vast majority of individuals in the West know virtually nothing about non-Western social formations. Hate is not developed overnight, nor is it something that you can explain away with flamboyant concepts, such as underdevelopment and barbarianism.

Summing up, the struggle against epistemicides not only reveals multiple ways to pursue other forms of knowledge, besides those under the Western scientific epistemological umbrella, but also confirms that the dominant stream of modern science is a reductive, functional paradigm project edified by white males. Shiva's (1993a) argument deserves to be quoted in length:

> The dominant stream of modern science, the reductionist or mechanical paradigm, is a specific projection of Western man that originated during the fifteenth and seventeenth centuries as the much acclaimed scientific revolution. Central to this domination and subjugation is an arbitrary barrier [between] "knowledge" (the specialist) and "ignorance" (the non-specialist). This barrier operates effectively to exclude from the scientific domain consideration of certain vital questions relating to the subject matter of science, or certain forms of non-specialist knowledge. (p. 21)

According to Shiva (1993a), modern Western patriarchy's special epistemological tradition is reductionist, since it not only "reduces the capacity of humans to know nature both by excluding other knowers and other ways of knowing, but also because it manipulates science as inert and fragmented matter" (p. 22). In a way, such a mechanism and reductionism are "protected not merely by its own mythology, but it is also protected by the interests it serves. Far from being an epistemological accident, reductionism is a response to the needs of a particular form of economic and political organization" (p. 23). The mechanical reductionist Western scientific paradigm, Shiva argues, together with "the industrial revolution and the capitalist economy are the philosophical, technological and economic components of the same process" (p. 24). It is needless to mention that the challenge against epistemicides is a collective one that needs to consolidate inside and outside Western cartography. As Shiva argues, Third

World and feminist scholarship have began to recognize that such dominant systems "emerge as a liberating force not for humanity as a whole (though it legitimizes itself in terms of universal benefit for all), but as a Western male-oriented and patriarchal projection which necessarily entailed the subjugation of both nature and woman" (p. 21). The task is to decolonize science as well. The struggle against epistemicides implies, as Shiva claims, the decolonization of the North as well. Shiva (1993b) notes:

> The White Man's Burden is becoming increasingly heavy for the earth and especially for the South. The past 500 years of history reveal that each time a relationship of colonization has been established between the North and the nature and people outside the North, the colonizing men and society have assumed a position of superiority, and thus of responsibility for the future of the earth and for other peoples and cultures. Out of the assumption of superiority flows the notion of the White Man's Burden. Out of the *idea* of the White Man's Burden flows the *reality* of the burdens imposed by the White Man on nature, women, and others. Therefore, colonizing the South is intimately linked to the issue of colonizing the North. Decolonization is therefore as relevant in the context of the colonizer as in that of the colonized. Decolonization in the North is also essential because process of wealth creation simultaneously create poverty process of knowledge creation simultaneously generates ignorance and process for the creation of freedom simultaneously generate unfreedom. (p. 264)

According to Shiva (1993b, p. 265), "decolonization in the North becomes essential if what is called the environment and development crisis in the South is to be overcome. The North's prescription for the South's salvation has always created new burdens and new bondages, and the salvation of the environment cannot be achieved through the old colonial order based on the White Man's Burden, the two are ethically, economically and epistemologically incongruent." This decolonization process will help interrupt, to use Beck's (2009) lens, Africa being seen as a "transnational idea and the staging of that idea[, which is] a counter Africa, an imagined community" (p. 27) fabricated by the oppressor, consumed by a self-depreciated oppressed (Freire, 1990), and ignorant of the fact that "for the slave there is nothing at the center but worse slavery" (Achebe, 2000, p. 95).

This is precisely the same political sentiment that one sees in Appiah's claims. According to Appiah (1998), "neither of us [Westerns and Africans] will understand what modernity is until we understand each other" (p. 245). After all, colonization needs to be seen as a shared culture "for those who have been colonized and for those who have colonized" (Smith, 1999, p. 45). However, any decolonizing struggle needs to be understood in what one might called a Mphahlelean framework, as South African writer Ezekiel Mphahlele (1965) explains:

> The blacks have reconciled the Western and African in them, while the whites refuse to surrender to their influence. This is symbolic of the South Africa situation. The only cultural vitality there is to be seen among the Africans: they have not been uplifted by a Western culture but rather they have reconciled the two in themselves. (p. 22)

This sentiment was already palpable in Kenyatta's (1960) argument that people in Kenya "are not worried that other races are here with us in our country, but we insist that we are the leaders here, and what we want we insist we get" (p. 301). Moreover, the struggle against epistemicides is not simultaneously a naïve romanticization of indigenous cultures that is quite fluent in some elements of the negritude movement. It is precisely the opposite. The struggle against epistemicides is indeed a struggle against what we might call "indigenoustude"—a mystification of indigenous cultures and knowledges. Mphahlele's (1965) position, again, is crystal clear:

> Now to *negritude* itself. Who is so stupid as to deny the historical fact of negritude as both a protest and a positive assertion of African cultural values? All this is valid. What I do not accept is the way in which too much of the poetry inspired by it romanticizes Africa—as a symbol of innocence, purity and artless primitiveness. I feel insulted when some people imply that Africa is not also a violent Continent...Sheer romanticism that fails to see the large landscape of the personality of the African makes bad poetry. The synthesis of Europe and Africa does not necessarily reject the negro-ness of the African...I refuse to be put in a Negro file—for sociologists to come and examine me...I refuse to be put in a dossier. (pp. 23–25)

The complexity or consequences involving negritude as a movement—quite explicit in Mphahlele's (1965) words—might be a good metaphorical signal to help us avoid some of the dangerous abysses that the curriculum field currently is facing:

> We are told that negritude is less a matter of theme than style. We must strive to visualize the whole man, not merely the things that are meant to flatter the Negro's ego. Let it not be forgotten, too, that negritude

has an overlap of 19th century European protest against machines and cannons. In the place of the cuckoo, the nightingale, the daffodil, Africa has dragged to the altar of Europe. Negritude men should not pretend that this is an entirely African concept. (p. 25)

Nkrumah (2006, p. 25) is overtly corrosive with regards negritude labelling it as a "pseudo-intellectual theory serving as a bridge between African foreign-dominated middle class and the French cultural establishment. It was irrational, racist, and non-revolutionary." Soyinka (1988) was also not shy in his criticism of the dynamics of the Western ideological formation at the very root of negritude. As he claims, negritude proponents were incapable of a clear rupture with Western indigenous rationality, thus mortgaging quasi perennially the emergence of a real new nonromanticized African voice.

Undeniably, the struggle against epistemicides (those that have been edified by Western male hegemonic epistemologies) is a Herculean task, but one that we cannot deny if we are truly committed to a real and just society. Actually, as Cox (2002) reminds us, "globalization is [also] a struggle over knowledge of world affairs" (p. 76). The struggle against the Western eugenic coloniality of knowledges is the best way to transform the school and its social agents into real leaders in their struggle to democratize democracy. As Sen (1999) claims, the emergence of democracy was *the* event of the twentieth century. The real issue, he says, is to perceive how a particular community prepares itself through democracy, not trying to scrutinize whether or not it is ready for a democratic society. This is a paradoxical time, Sousa Santos (2005) argues; on the one hand, "our current time is marked by huge developments and thespian changes, an era that is referred to as the electronic revolution of communications, information, genetics and the biotechnological" (p. vii). On the other hand,

It is a time of disquieting regressions, a return of the social evils that appeared to have been or about to be overcome. The return of slavery and slavish work; the return of high vulnerability to old sicknesses that seemed to have been eradicated and appear now linked to new pandemics like HIV/AIDS: the return of the revolting social inequalities that gave their name to the social question at the end of the nineteenth century; in sum, the return of the specter of war, perhaps now more than ever a world war, although whether cold or not is as yet undecidable. (p. vii)

As Andrew (2009) explained in "Leaner and Meaner? The Perils of McDonaldizing the Academy and Kinesiology," the Alan G. Ingham

Memorial Lecture he gave at Miami University, one needs to engage and foster the critique of knowledge production within the academy and kinesiology. The task, Andrew stresses, is to challenge the accelerated process of McDonaldization—the accelerated rationalization of society associated with late capitalism that has led to an epistemological McDonaldization. Such an imperial pastoral marginalizes particular kinds of knowledge related to critical, sociological, historical, and qualitative analyses. Andrew challenges the way the corporate academic jungle surrendered to such a dangerous pastoral, which is a real obstacle to better understanding the human movement.

It is the role of teachers as public intellectuals, Giroux (1994) argues, to position the curriculum in a way that decenters it from its Westernizing forms and content. The real issue, according to Giroux, is "how to democratize the schools so as to enable those groups who in large measure are divorced from or simply not represented in the curriculum to be able to produce their own representations, narrate their own stories, and engage in respectful dialogue with others" (p. 18). He argues further that one good way to do it is to be conscious of the difference between political and politicizing education:

> [While the former,] which is central to critical pedagogy, would encourage students to become better citizens to challenge those with political and cultural power as well as to honor the critical traditions within the dominant culture that make such a critique possible and intelligible [meaning] decentering power in the classroom and other pedagogical sites so the dynamics of those institutional and cultural inequalities that marginalize some groups, repress particular types of knowledge, and suppress critical dialogue can be addressed, [the latter] is a form of pedagogical terrorism in which the issue of what is taught, by whom, and under what conditions is determined by a doctrinaire political agenda that refuses to examine its own values, beliefs, and ideological construction. (p. 18)

Schooling has to play a leading role in addressing one of most challenging issues we have before us—democratizing democracy. Vavi (2004) argues that democracy is bypassing the poor, giving credence to Sousa Santos's (2005) claim that we are living in an era with modern problems but without modern solutions. In order to democratize democracy, Sousa Santos suggests, we need to reinvent social emancipation, since its traditional modern form was pushed into a kind of dead end by neo-liberal globalization.

However, an insurgent cosmopolitanism or counter-hegemonic globalization has propelled a myriad of social movements and transformations, challenging the hegemonic neoliberal perspective (Paraskeva, 2011b). It is within the very marrow of such counter-hegemonic forms of globalization—and in its clashes with the neo-liberal hegemonic agenda—that new itineraries for social emancipation are developing (Sousa Santos, 2008). Such economic, political, and cultural quarrels were metaphorically coined by Sousa Santos (2005) as a clash between North and South, which would bring to the fore the struggle between representative and participatory democracy. Despite appearing hegemonic, globalization has been promoting a low-density democracy, one that is anchored in arguments about privatization, which is creating more social inequality.

Thus, the struggle for democracy "is primarily a political struggle on the form of governance, thus involving the reconstitution of the state and creating conditions for the emancipatory project" (Shivji, 2003, p. 1). This is especially important to emphasize in light of the hegemony of neoliberal discourse, "which tends to emasculate democracy of its social and historical dimensions and present it as an ultimate nirvana" (p. 1).

Somehow, we are clearly before what Sousa Santos (1998, 2007) calls a State that should be seen as a spotless new social movement[4]; in other words,

> a more vast political organization in which the democratic forces will struggle for a distributive democracy, thus transforming the state in a new—yet powerful—social and political entity. Such a State is even much more directly involved in redistribution criteria, and profoundly committed with economic and cultural inclusive policies. (Sousa Santos, 2007, p. 60)

It is actually this State as a spotless new social movement "that will reawaken the tension between capitalism and [real] democracy, and this can only be achieved if democracy is conceived and plasticized as redistributive democracy" (Sousa Santos, 2007, p. 41). The struggle for a redistributive democracy is the first crucial step in reinforcing the state's role in a more just society, a claim addressed by Kenyatta (1960):

> If we unite now, each and every one of us, and each tribe to another, we will cause the implementation in this country of that which the European calls democracy. True democracy has no colour distinction. It does not choose between black and white. We want to prosper as a nation, and as a nation we demand equality, that is equal pay for equal work. We will never get our freedom unless we succeed in this issue.

> We do not want equal pay for equal work tomorrow—we want it right
> now. It has never been known in history that a country prospers with-
> out equality. (pp. 306–8)

The task, therefore, is to determine how to reinvent a democratized
democracy in an era where globalization and localization are "the
driving forces and expressions of a new polarization and stratification of the world population into globalized rich and localized
poor" (Beck, 2009, p. 55). In fact, globalization needs to be understood as a process of globalizing particular localities (Sousa Santos,
2008). What we need, according to Nussbaum (1997), is "to foster a democracy...that genuinely [considerers] the common good"
(p. 19). It is not good for democracy "when people vote on the basis
of the sentiments they have absorbed from talk radio and never questioned" (p. 19). Most likely, an entirely new struggle has to begin.
Mozambican writer Couto (2005) claims that this is the best way
to move forward in order to challenge a past that was portrayed in a
deformed way, a present dressed with borrowed clothes, and a future
already ordered by foreign interests. As Nyerere (1998) wisely claims,
it will be judicious to not choose money as our weapon, since "the
development of a country is brought about by people, not by money"
(p. 129), which is something that marketers seem to neglect. Public
education does have a key role in claiming that (an)other knowledge
is possible and explaining how that is crucial for the transformative
processes of democratizing democracy. As Aronowitz (2001), who
is on Horowitz's list of the 100 most dangerous professors in the
United States, accurately reminds us, "We need to fight for a politics
of direct democracy and direct action. The reinvigoration of the Left
depends upon this" (p. 149).

Such tasks imply a different theoretical curriculum wave, one that
I have tagged elsewhere (Paraskeva, 2007) as an itinerant curriculum
theory (ICT) which is the future path of the critical curriculum river.

DETERRITORIALIZING CURRICULUM THEORY; WORKING TOWARD AN ITINERANT CURRICULUM THEORY

As discussed previously, Huebner (1966) warned us of the importance
of fighting for new ways to talk about curriculum, just as Deleuze's
approach allows us to perceive curriculum theory as (a) a way of deterritorialization, (b) as an act of becoming, and (c) as a simulacrum. In fact,
Deleuze helps us fully understand the need to think and feel differently.

Reading Deleuze (1990a, 1990b, 1994) and reading about Deleuze (cf. Agamben, 1999; Khalfa, 1999; Roy, 2003) allows us to understand how crucial it is to shape our own image of thinking, which has been dominant in the course of history. The issue, Deleuze (1994) argues, is to subvert the world by questioning the dominant tradition within the very marrow of human thinking—this is representationalism. According to Deleuze, we need to challenge the representationalist thought that has subjugated our very thinking and is an obstacle we must overcome to be able to act more freely. Representationalism, Deleuze stresses, does not capture the global scale of difference.

In framing Deleuze's approach to theoretical and practical fields of education and curriculum, it can be argued that this approach is crucial to understanding teacher education. The overwhelming majority of teacher-education programs are deeply insensitive to fostering different ways of thinking. Teachers are already exhausted by the attempt to produce "similarities" in the midst of an increasingly diverse and intricate multiplicity (Roy, 2003). We need, according to the Deleuzean approach, to understand teacher education free from a representationalistic framework, which will allow young teachers to think in new ways and understand the productive and relational power of difference (Roy, 2003; cf. also Paraskeva, 2007). Indeed, it is difference rather than similarity that drives the whole process of changing. The challenge is to work within critical curriculum theory and practice to find mechanisms that incorporate teachers' and students' understanding of difference in positive ways (Roy, 2003; cf. also Paraskeva, 2007). What is at stake is the interface of identity and difference, and the need to challenge false assumptions like the existence of stable identities.

Basically, drawing from Deleuze's (1994) analyses, we need to fight for a curriculum theory and practice that departs from areas governed by the dominant systems of meaning that keep us confined within certain frameworks, but without neglecting or diminishing them. In a word, we need to deterritorialize curriculum theory. If we are able to do so, we also prove that every crack in the dominant platform produces differentiation that expands our powers of action and commitment, and our emotions (Paraskeva, 2007). In other words, curriculum theory should be read as an "act of becoming," as something that seeks to produce difference and thus articulates new wor(l)ds (Roy, 2003; cf. also Paraskeva, 2008).

Relying on Hartley (1977), I argue that curriculum theory needs to reflect the understanding that education should take us from the space and time in which we find ourselves, and that its effects can imprison us in a techno-rational meaning as a unique way of thinking. In short, education ignores ontological knowledge and unarticulated thought that speaks the language of the unpredictable, the imagination, and the passions—none of which can be reduced, discretely or objectively, to analyzable entities. Taking the example of teacher education, deterritorialized curriculum theory is exploring new ways of thinking and feeling and finding ways to produce new and different purposes of mind (Roy, 2003; cf. also Paraskeva, 2006a, 2006b, 2007, 2008). In essence, curriculum theory should give voice to an engineering of differences by deterritorializing itself and looking for new ways of thinking and feeling about education. It is important that curriculum theory cover other spaces and times, which is something quite valuable in both Huebner's and Deleuze's approaches. Indeed, both perspectives challenge us to recognize that educational practices must move from traditional common sense to creating new values and new directions. In fact, Deleuzian concepts such as "encounters" and "simulacrums" are very important in this context. As Deleuze (1994) argues, there is something in the world that pushes us to think, and that something is not a subject of recognition but a crucial encounter. Curriculum theory needs an encounter with the very practices and the reality that surround it.

In essence, and to rely on Deleuze's (1990a) framework, curriculum theory should contribute to subverting and reversing the Platonic position, which sees the world as a reproduction of a particular original model and perceives it as a simulacrum or a copy without an original (Roy, 2003; Paraskeva, 2006a, 2006, 2007, 2008). As Roy (2003) argues, rather than approaching 'things' as ideal states, we need to find advantages in their own variations and dynamics.

To fight for a deterritorialized curriculum theory and practices that privilege the cult of difference implies the need to understand education as a set of relationships in which the personal plays a leading role. Moreover, and drawing from Deleuze and Guattari (1987), fighting for a deterritorialized curriculum theory and practice means being aware that growth and development do not occur through "the acquisition of systems, parts or components, but precisely for their loss(es)" (p. 48). In fact, whereas learning emerges in the modernist state "in terms of acquisition," in the Deleuzean and Huebnerean approaches it becomes more a production of difference(s). As revealed previously, Huebner was profoundly critical of approaches that tended to reduce students to a pale category of learners. Both Deleuze and Huebner opened the door to deterritorialized curriculum theory and practices, and in so doing allow for the building of a new language, one in which we think of education as a critical source for edifying a more just society and leading to the transformation of the world, a world fuelled by a culturally and economically just democracy.

The great challenge facing curriculum theory is, in essence, to figure out how "to operate a new order, a new system anchored in new and powerful non-state ways of articulation, which imposes new geographies of centrality" (Sassen, 2004, p. 126). Therefore, we need a curriculum theory and practice that reescalate their very own territorialities, which reflects an awareness that the new order and counterorder must be seen within the framework of power relations. As Foucault (1994) argues, one does not have the discourses of power on one side and on the other the discourses that oppose the discourses of power. Discourses are, rather, elements or tactical blocks in the field of power relations. The current dominant forces of education and curriculum have shown an unprecedented absence of responsibility by systematically refusing to think about schooling as being impeded by certain taboos. Schooling issues such as assessment, subject matter, hours of attendance, textbooks, and the knowledge being transmitted are wrongly accepted as dogma. Such a limited vision makes it almost impossible to have an education and a curriculum outside a particular framework that is bounded by issues related to standards, classification, objectives, disciplinary orthodoxy, and competences—in other words, the official curriculum language. It is a dangerous fact that you cannot have schooling without meeting such conditions. In this regard, Bourdieu's (2001) analysis is helpful. He argues that the official language has been imposed on the whole population as the only legitimate language, and that it is produced and maintained not only by the authors who claim the authority to write, but by the dominant curriculum forces that codify it and the teachers whose task is to teach based on that language.

The task, therefore, is to think of education in general and curriculum in particular from a diametric perspective because, as Latour (2006) highlights, there is no greater crime than facing current intellectual challenges with the equipment of the past. We must deal with issues of interest rather than with issues of fact, because reality is not just defined by issues of fact. Moreover, Latour argues, questions of fact should be seen as controversial and political versions of issues of interest. Defending a disciplined school that is bent to the rhythms of classification and compartmentalization, headed by spurious dynamics, and rendered to segregated outcomes, is to rely on Latour (2006), as matter of curriculum fact.

Basically, one big Latourian question is whether or not one can seek another powerful descriptive tool that addresses the issues of interest, issues that will allow the production of new languages, new words of order (Deleuze & Guattari, 1987). Thus, relying on Deleuze and Guattari's (1987) approach, deterritorialization is the new word of order of contemporary curriculum theory—something we have been consistently claiming (Paraskeva, 2006a, 2006b, 2007, 2008, 2011a). Such a task is not utopian; the stability, the overcodification of such a concept is deeply related to an approach that understands curriculum theory and practices according to what Latour (2006), drawing from Tarde, called the sociology of mobility. That is, it is important to understand curriculum policies and practices while taking into account the fact that the social is not locked in a static conception of society but emerges from the mobile associations among "things." In essence, deterritorialized curriculum theory implies a commitment to fight for a different research platform, one that pushes research to a "level of instability, not stability, generating concepts also, in itself, unstable" (O'Brien & Penna, 1999, p. 106). In doing so, a deterritorialized curriculum theory increasingly becomes an itinerant theory, a theory of non-spaces (Auge, 2003). In essence, as Gough (2011) claims, one needs to assume a rhizomatous approach that sees reality beyond dichotomies, beyond beginnings and ends, one that breeds from the multiplicity of immanent platforms, and from its centerless and peripheryless position, and that defies clean knowledge territories (cf. also, DeLeuze & Guattari, 1987; Eco, 1984).

Said's (2005) arguments are quite significant in this regard. He claims that when human experience is recorded for the first time and is then given a theoretical formulation, its strength comes from the fact that it is directly linked to actual historical circumstances and is an organic result of these circumstances. The subsequent versions of such a theory cannot reproduce its original power, since the situation has calmed down and changed, the theory has been degraded and deteriorated, has been domesticated, and has been transformed into a substitute for the same thing. Its initial purpose (political change) has been subverted. In essence, Said (2005) challenges the way that theories travel to distinct situations, losing in this process part of their original power and rebellion. We need a myriad of ways to build a deterritorialized curriculum theoretical posture that will force curriculum research to deal with multiple, not fixed, frameworks within ample and intricate epistemological waves.

While it is true that we are in the presence of an itinerant theoretical edification that tries to overcome previous theoretical formulations, it is also a fact that this itinerant position should be seen as transgressive (cf. Bataille, 1986). Along with Said (2005, p. 41), one might say that "the purpose of curriculum theory[ists], is to travel, to go beyond the limits, to move, and stay in a kind of permanent exile." A theory of non-places and non-times is, in essence, a theory of all places and all times. The curriculum theorist is, as Jin (2008) put it, a constant migrant who experiences "a series of [epistemological] events" (cf. Khalfa, 1999). We are claiming an atypical epistemological approach that will be able to deconstruct the images of thought. The task is actually to complexify Doll's (1993, p. 3) megaparadigmatic claim, into a ultraparadigmatical framework that will foster and grasp the "new sense of the educational order." Such an approach will unfold naturally, as Merlau-Ponty (1973) put it, into voluntary and involuntary creations. Furthermore, the curriculum worker needs to be seen as "an *auctor*, which is *qui auget,* or the person who augments, increases, or perfects the act (in fact), since every creation is always a co-creation, just as every author is a co-author" (Agamben, 2005, p. 76). The educational and curriculum theorist needs to be seen as an epistemological pariah who is challenging and challenged by a theoretical path that is inexact yet rigorous (Deleuze, 1990b). Such itinerant theory(ist) provokes (and exists in a midst of) a set of crises, and produces laudable silences. It provokes an abstinence of theoretical uniformity and stabilization. The theory(ist) is a volcanic chain, who shows a constant lack of equilibrium, is always a stranger in his/her own language. He/she is an itinerant theory(ist) profoundly sentient of the multiplicities of lines, spaces, and dynamic becomings (Deleuze, 1990b). Such a theoretical course is defined by a cutting edge, a "Malangatanian"[5] and "Pollockian"[6] set of processes, not because it is abstract but because oppressive in its freedom. It is not a sole act, however; it is a populated solitude. This itinerant theoretical path, claims a multifaceted curriculum compromise, and "runs away" from any unfortunate "canonology." It is actually an invitation to "get involved with alternative readings that have been hidden, erased, or marginalized within the curriculum field" (Malewski, 2010). Such itinerant curriculum theory (ICT) is an anthem against the indignity of speaking for the other (Deleuze, 1990b).

    This itinerary theory(ist) is much more than an eclectic approach; it is actually a profoundly theoretical discipline that, "challenges one of the most pejorative judgments of educational research [which claims such research as] decontextualized, that it has failed to consider the context, that it is out of context, or even that it has been miscontextalized" (Luke, 2010, p. 145). After all, as Popkewitz (2001) claims, "the challenges about knowledge are not only about academic knowledge, but about cultural norms of progress and social change that are part of the politics of contemporary life" (p. 241).

This itinerant posture provides powerful space in which to engage in a global conversation that is attentive of the globalisms (Sousa Santos, 2008); profoundly aware of the multiplicities of public spheres and subaltern counter publics (Fraser, 1997); deeply attentive to the production of localities (Hardt & Negri, 2000) and militant particularism (Harvey, 1998), and to the (de)construction of new, insurgent cosmopolitanism (Popkewitz, 2007; Sousa Santos, 2008); conscious of the wrangle between the globalized few and the localized rest (Bauman, 2004); and yet profoundly alert to the dangerous hegemony of the English language (Macedo, 2003).

Such a conversation needs to occur in languages other than English. As I have mentioned before, it is a rude fact that the vast majority of counterdominant Western epistemological views seemed to neglect other linguistic forms and other forms of knowledge. It is no surprise that the majority of bibliographical references used by Western scholars, even those whose lives are dedicated to the struggle for a just society, are by English-speaking scholars and in the English language. The overwhelming majority "does not know (and if they do know, they do not value) the scientific knowledge produced in the semiperiphery or periphery; it is considered inferior in everything; and it is easily cannibalized and converted into a resource or raw material by core science" (Sousa Santos, 2005). In some cases, it has become common to "use" indigenous realities, and scientists have co-opted and wrapped such realities in Western concepts, what Sousa Santos calls "the proletarization of semiperipheral and peripheral scientists" (p. xxiv). Spivak (1995), in her notable book *Can the Subaltern Speak?* challenges the ability of particular intellectuals to edify credible narratives based on the daily experiences of individuals "among the illiterate peasantry, the tribals, the lowest strata of urban subproletariat who have been visited by the epistemic violence of the colonial encounter" (p. 28). One should not forget, Guha (1983) argues, that subalternity is "materialized by the structure of property, institutionalized by law, sanctified by religion and made tolerable—and even desirable—[thus] by tradition, to rebel [is] indeed to destroy such signs" (p. 1). As Altbach (2008, p. 55) argues "the products of knowledge are distributed unequally." That is, countries like the United States, the United Kingdom, France, Germany, and Russia, "dominate the systems which distribute knowledge, they control publishing houses and produce scholarly journals, magazines, films, and television programs which the rest of the world consumes" (Altbach, 2008, p. 55).

These facts open the door for us to make the claim that Western epistemological views need to pay attention and learn from other non-Western epistemological views in and beyond the West, and inside and outside the English language. Otherwise, claims against the English-only movement are just rhetorical. As Macedo (2000) insightfully reveals, we are experiencing the colonialism of the English language. Neglecting this struggle is to be complicit with cultural and linguistic genocide. Western hegemonic epistemologies were raised and sustained themselves by the imperialism of particular signifiers or, more accurately, by the imperialism of the signifier, thus only specific "official meanings" were validated. We are actually confronting a despotic overcodification, to use DeLeuze's (1990b) term, that legitimates peculiar political channels in the struggle between "*langue and parole*." Moreover, as Kawagely (2009) stresses, literacy is not just about words; it is, rather, a holistic complex process and a journey of joy and pleasure. Making this journey, we will be able to teach what it means to be humans, thus fighting one of the biggest dangers resulting from technology: loneliness.

One must not forget, as Wa Thiong'o (1986) notes, that "language was the most important vehicle which power fascinated and held the soul prisoner. The bullet was the means for physical subjugation. Language was the means of the spiritual subjugation" (p. 9). Linguistic genocide is actually at the very core of the colonial and neo-colonial project. Wa Thiong'o's position is well worth noting:

> The real aim of colonialism was to control the people's wealth; what they produced, how they produced it, and how it was distributed; to control, in other words, the entire realm of the language of real life. Colonialism imposed its control of the social production of wealth through military conquest and subsequent political dictatorship. But its most important area of domination was the mental universe of the colonized, the control through culture, of how people perceived themselves and their relationships to the world. Economic and political control can never be complete or effective without mental control. To control a people's culture is to control their tools of self-definition in relation to others. For colonialism this involved two aspects of the same process; the destruction or the deliberate undervaluing of a people's culture, their art, dances, religions, history, geography, education, orature and literature, and the conscious elevation of the language of the colonizer. The domination of a people's language by

the languages of the colonizing nations was crucial to domination of the mental universe of the colonized. (p. 16)

And yet, as Achebe (1977) argues, "the only place where culture is static, and exists independently of people, is the museum, and this is not an African institution" (p. 29). The museum, Visvanathan (2009) writes, "is a quasi rationality of piracy" (p. 488). In other words, the museum, as a Western political creation, "represents the paradox of West and East encounters that create a hierarchy of cultures legitimizing violence as legitimate tactic against those labeled as primitives, underdeveloped" (p. 489; cf. also Coomaraswamy, 1947). Hence, Coomaraswamy claims, more than being a cultural encounter, the museum incorporates the arrogant objectivity of Western modern science and its profound smell of death. The museum was and is the extension of a eugenic laboratory.

However, as Wa Thiong'o (1986) remarks, "African languages refused to die" (p. 23). This too is a crucial part of the deterritorialized posture. This is not a minor issue, especially since, as Popkewitz (1978) argues, theoretical frameworks need to be seen as political tools. Educational theory, he claims, is a form of political affirmation it is potent because its language has prescriptive qualities. A theory guides individuals "to reconsider their personal world in light of more abstract concepts, generalizations and principles. These more abstract categories are not neutral" (p. 28). Fighting for a conversation that is sentient of the globalism in languages other than English is to struggle with a feasible ideal that has a secular tradition on the African continent. At the beginning of the twentieth century, the Reverend Agbebi (1903), an African engineer and spiritual leader, led a struggle to abolish English hymns and English books, as well as European names and clothes, in the African church. He called for "Christianity without its non-essentials"; despite his violent criticism of Christianity and its bloody association with European imperialism, he felt this would create a natural space for an African spirituality and religiosity based on "original songs" and discursivity (Agbebi, 1903; cf. Falola, 2003).

Therefore, as Gough (2000, p. 334) insightfully stresses, curriculum inquiry needs to be seen as a process that focuses on the pertinence of location as well as on "one form of contemporary cultural production through which a transnational imaginary may be expressed and negotiated" (p. 334). After all, "the globalization of knowledge and Western culture constantly reaffirms the West's view of itself as the centre of legitimate knowledge, the arbiter of what counts as knowledge and the source of 'civilized' knowledge" (Smith, 1999, p. 63). Faced by such persistent efforts to maintain positional superiority, as Said would put it, one needs to be cautious of any attempt to claim the defeat of Western-Eurocentric patriarchal epistemological hegemony within the field of education in general, and in the curriculum in particular. Although I understand the context in which some curriculum theorists claim such victorious momentum—Pinar (2004), for example, declares that "the patriarchal and Eurocentric concept is no longer in fashion" (p. 224)—I prefer to point out that Western scientific hegemonic dominance is facing a profound crisis of epistemological confidence, as Sousa Santos (2005) would put it, which was instigated by a myriad of counter-hegemonic Western and non-Western epistemological forms. Needless to say, although such loss of epistemological confidence "is opening spaces for innovation, the critique of epistemology will be for a long time much more advanced than the epistemology of criticism" (p. xix). Such curriculum labor is, Wraga (2002) claims, a "kaleidoscope of actions" (p. 17), and as Applebee (1996) argues, it raises complex questions about who should orchestrate such conversations. However, this is not the only crucial issue. Spivak's (1990) political position helps a great deal here:

> For me the question "Who should speak?" is less crucial than "Who will listen?" "I will speak for myself as a Third World person" is an important position for political mobilization today. But the real demand is that, when I speak from that position, I should be listened to seriously; not with that kind of benevolent imperialism. (pp. 59–60)

Gough (2000) accurately describes how tough our task is, yet it needs to be done:

> The internationalization of curriculum studies might then be understood not so much in terms of translating local representations of curriculum into a universalized discourse, but, rather, as a process of creating transnational spaces in which local knowledge traditions in curriculum inquiry can be performed together. Indeed, the need for vigorously and rigorously recuperating local knowledge systems, in both their performative and representational idioms, has been amplified for me by some recent experiences of doing curriculum work in southern Africa. Here, many local knowledge traditions have been rendered invisible by the effects of universalizing imperialist discourses and practices. In countries such as Zimbabwe and Malawi, for example, the concept of "good education" for the vast majority of

> African students, most of whom live in rural subsistence settlements, is equated with failing Cambridge University O-level examinations in English. (p. 339)

In essence, these perspectives consolidate a kind of new curriculum revisionism that challenges frameworks, claiming that the authority of particular discourses and hierarchies need identity, rights, subjectivities, and experiences. This new kind of curriculum revisionism not only reinforces the need to complexify, clarify, and overcome (or not) particular tensions within a particular critical progressive curriculum river, it also offers juicy arguments for a truthful relational analysis of schools and curriculum, which allows us to have the most current tools to fight what Pinar (2004) claims is the contemporary curriculum nightmare—presentism. In fact, presentism has been fostered by representationalist approaches. A new epistemological discipline will allow us to understand more accurately our own struggles for pedagogies (Gore, 1993) that can solve the repressive and (un)finished myths (Ellsworth, 1989) and overcome functionalist traps (Liston, 1988), while recognizing that the task "is not to celebrate the challengers, but to read across disciplinary literatures" (Popkewitz, 2001, p. 241).

Deterritorializing curriculum theory would pay attention to, as Smith (1999) would put it, solid political engagement in decolonizing methodological frameworks. As Kaomea (2004) argues, "The process of decolonization requires our continual efforts toward questioning and revealing hidden colonial influences in past and current beliefs and practices, those of the *haole* (or foreigner) as well as those of our own *kanakaa maoli* (indigenous people), including our *kupuna* (elders), our ancestors, and ourselves" (p. 32). However, as Smith (1999) claims, decolonizing research does not imply a complete rejection of Western theories and research approaches. Conversely, it implies the deconstruction of dominant Western views of science, challenges the Western totalitarian view of science and what counts as science, and above all implies a profound collaborative work among native and non-native researchers that is sentient of the complexities examined by Espinosa-Dulanto (2004) over "who gets to be native/indigenous vs. foreigner / outsider" (p. 45). In a way, as Mutua and Swadener (2004) insightfully claim, decolonizing research creates conditions to question, among other issues, "who defines and legitimizes what counts as scholarship, who has the power to name? How does naming reify existing power relations? Are the tools for decolonization only available to indigenous researchers or can this be a shared process? How has the discourse on decolonizing research been colonized or appropriated?" (p. 2). These are tough questions, since we all know quite well that "the structure of the university is an impediment to the decolonization of research" (Blauner & Wellman, 1973, p. 324). Such difficulties are connected not only with administrative bureaucratic problems, but also with the Paleolithic habitude of the sovereignty of the disciplinary knowledge. Western hegemonic scientific pastoral(s) were able to instigate and foster the cult of a paradigm anchored in "its strict and narrow divisions among disciplines, its positivist methodologies, that do not distinguished objectivity from neutrality, its bureaucratic and discriminatory organization of knowledge into departments, laboratories, and faculties that reduce the advance of knowledge to a matter of corporatist privilege" (Sousa Santos, 2005, p. xix).

A severe critique of disciplinary knowledge comes from Smith (1999), who claims that

> the ethnographic "gaze" of anthropology has collected, classified and represented other cultures to the extent that anthropologists are often the academics popularly perceived by the indigenous world as the epitome of all that it is bad with academics. Hanuni Kay Trask accuses anthropologists of being "takers and users" who "exploit the hospitality" and generosity of native people. Livingstone refers to this discipline as the "science of imperialism par excellence." (1999, p. 67)

The issue is how we engage in such a task. Žižek's (2006) example is quite apt:

> This is an old joke that circulated in the defunct East Germany. It is about a German worker who found work in Siberia. Aware that all of his letters will be read by censors, he explains to his friends: "We will establish a code. If you receive a letter from me written in blue ink it means that I am telling the truth. If the letter is written in red ink, it means that I am lying." A month later his friends received the first letter written in blue ink: Here everything is beautiful, the shops are full of goods, the food is plentiful, the rooms spacious and well heated, the cinemas show Western movies, there are many girls available. The only thing missing here is the red ink." (p. 17)

Žižek shows us how you lie about the lie, thus insinuating the truth. The real issue is to decide in which color we will write the itinerant curriculum theory (ICT). As Kliebard (1995) argues, the task of the curriculum field in the next 50 years is to develop alternatives to the way of thinking that clearly dominated the early years of the field, before the lethal impact of neoradical policies; this is the better way for the field to have developed but it is not ideal. Actually, it is the best interplay between theory and practice that one cannot dichotomize. I believe that it is not accurate to prioritize one over the other. Understanding curriculum in such a way shows how we are caught in a nonstable terrain that has been determined by the myriad experiences of students, teachers, and the community. These experiences reveal a relevant pedagogic environment through dialogue and negotiation, knowing, as I claim elsewhere (Paraskeva, 2010a, 2011a; forthcoming), that there is no social justice without cognitive justice. Such a curriculum posture also encourages what I called the curriculum indigenous (students and teachers) to engage in a nonstop confrontation with real problems, thus establishing a connection within daily life, which, one must say, is nondeterministic.

I am not claiming a way out that will please everybody. In fact, "a coherent theory is an imposed theory which falsely mythologizes a pseudo-scientific process that has no more to do with real science than astrology does" (Quantz, in press). An itinerant theoretical approach dares to violate the methodological canon and attempts to go beyond some interesting (counter-)dominant clashes to overcome some dead ends and screaming silences, yet it is an epistemological struggle within the insurgent cosmopolitanism platforms (Sousa Santos, 2008) both inside and beyond the Western dominant cartography (Paraskeva, 2011a).

As Sousa Santos (2005) argues, his project, which aims to reinvent social emancipation, "did not have a structured theoretical framework" (p. xxv). Instead, he argues,

> it is imperative to open up the theoretical, analytical, and methodological cannons as a combination for renovation and transformation. Instead of a theoretical framework, the project had a set of broad analytical orientations that constituted a horizon within which various theoretical frameworks could fall. Such analytical horizons were was strictly necessary to motivate social scientists to join forces in the pursuit of objectives that are sufficiently important to be actively shared. These violations of the methodological cannon were not committed lightly. The risk of chaos and cacophony was there. (p. xxv)

An itinerant curriculum theory (ICT), is a "deliberate disrespect of the canon, a struggle against epistemological orthodoxy" (p. xxv), and it attempts "to bring scientific knowledge face-to-face with non-scientific, explicitly local knowledges, knowledges grounded in the experience of the leaders and activists of the social movements studied by social scientists" (p. xxv). This is the very core of its nutritive faculty, to use Agamben's (1999) Aristotelic approach. An itinerant curriculum theory (ICT) is an exercise of "citizenship and solidarity" (p. xxv) and, above all, an act of social and cognitive justice. It is, as Žižek (2006) would put it, the very best way to understand how reality can explode in and change the real.

Locke's claims "that at the beginning the entire world was America are *quasi* over" (Sousa Santos, 2009, p. 28) . This new itinerant curriculum theory (ICT) challenges modern/post modern western thinking, which is an abyssal thinking in which the knowledge of the Other is produced as non-existent. Sousa Santos (2009, p. 23) deserves to be quoted in length here.

> Modern Western thinking is an abyssal thinking. It is a system of visible and invisible distinctions, and the invisible sustain the visible. The invisible distinctions are established through radical lines that divide social reality into two distinctive realms: the universe from this side of the line and the universe of the other side of the line. The division is such that the other side of the line vanishes as reality, becomes nonexistent and is simultaneously produced as nonexistent. Everything that is produced as nonexistent is radically excluded for it lies beyond the realm of what the accepted conception of inclusion.

The knowledge and modern law, Sousa Santos (2009, p. 8) adds, represents the most accomplished pillars of modern western abyssal thinking.

> In the field of knowledge, abyssal thinking concedes to modern science the monopoly of the universal distinction between true and false. Tensions between science, philosophy and theology are explicit although they occur just on this side of the line. Its visibility is based on the invisibility of forms of knowledge that do not fit into any of these ways of knowing. I refer to the popular, lay, plebeian, peasant and indigenous knowledge's across the line. Across the line there is no knowledge, there are beliefs, opinions, magic, idolatry, intuitive understandings, or subjective, which, at best, can become objects or raw material for scientific inquiry.

What we are claiming here, is a new emergent ideology, as Nkrumah (1964, p. 70), would put it, "which can solidify in a philosophical statement [...] and will be born out of the crises" of the field's historical consciousness. An itinerant curriculum theory (ICT) calls for a "philosophical consciencism" (Nkrumah (1964, p. 70), that will not oppress the "Ellisonian self" (Taliaferro-Baszile, 2008, p. 487; Paraskeva, 2011a).

It is interesting to notice how we can find some of the same symptoms in the curriculum projects that I was able to analyze in Brazil. I am not claiming any kind of prescription for the field. Not at all. It is just my understanding of how to overcome particular tensions and fractures that need not necessarily be seen as negative or malignant. Currently, the critical progressive curriculum river has shown us a myriad of different flows both in the United States and in many other countries (arguably difficult to accommodate in an encyclopaedia or handbook), and it is our task to encourage such a kaleidoscope of flows. It is likely that the more complex and unjust society becomes, the more flows will emerge. Interesting to note, however, is the fact that for a substantive percentage of such flows, curriculum relevance is still a powerful proposition.

Summing up several years ago, I had the privilege of being invited to the Grupo de Trabalho de Currículo (Curriculum Working Group) da Associação Nacional de Pós Graduação e Pesquisa em Educação (ANPEd, the National Association of Graduate and Research in Education) in Brazil to analyze samples of the curriculum research that was developed in a number of curriculum departments and education faculties at several top universities in Brazil. This analysis testifies to how this line of approach is emerging and consolidating in a very powerful way in some curriculum research projects I examined.[7] It shows us where the curriculum river is going, and that we have a lot to learn from such well-grounded and well-developed Southern theory—that it is actually much more than a curriculum theory and, in some aspects, it does not waste its time in engaging in "hopeless Western epistemological tensions," choosing instead to follow a different path. As odd as it might be, non-Western scholars know a lot more, in some cases in precise detail, about what has been called Western epistemology than those in the West know, or care to know, about non-Western epistemologies. This needs to stop. It seems that an itinerant curriculum theory (ICT) offers a respectable way to address such concerns.

These are real examples that the struggle against epistemicides is possible, that (an)other knowledge is possible, that the existence of a Southern theory (Connell, 2007) and of a multifarious platform of Southern epistemologies (Sousa Santos, 2009) is not an unattainable ideal. A Southern epistemology, Sousa Santos (2009) claims, respects three fundamental pillars: (1) learning that the South exists, (2) learning to go to the South, and (3) learning from and with the South. This implies not only non-Westernizing the West, but also avoiding any kind of Eurocentrism, something that some postmodern and postcolonial approaches ignored (Sousa Santos, 2009). Although, as Autio (2011) accurately claims, some postmodern, postcolonial, and postcultural theories did challenge a classed, gendered, and racialized Eurocentric tradition, the task is, as Goody (2006) stresses, to seek a "global history" that is only possible if both Eurocentrism and anti-Eurocentrism-Eurocentric, as well as Occidentalism and Orientalism, are overcome. As Goody (2006) states, some postmodern and post-colonial approaches end up being Eurocentric in their very claim against Eurocentrism. Thus, the re-narrativization of modernity and colonialism, to complexify Autio's (2006) claim, implies also the re-narrativization of postmodernity and postcolonialism.

As we have mentioned before, however, this is not an *indige-noustude*. The struggle against the mystification and monopoly of Western forms of knowledge cannot fall into the same trap of mysticism. The task is to try to understand and analyze not only how counterhegemonic knowledge is a particular form of indigenous knowledge, but also how the two forms compare—what are their similarities and where do they differ. We need to ask crucial questions: whose indigenous knowledge? who benefits? how racialized is that knowledge? how classed is that knowledge? how gendered is that knowledge? how democratic are such indigenous knowledge forms? In doing so, we will avoid romanticizing indigenous knowledge, for it would be intellectually inaccurate to claim that indigenous cultural formations are free of any form of class, gender, and racial segregation.

As Smith (2009) argues, educational scholars need to engage in indigenous theory. However, the itinerant theoretical posture that we recommend challenges the attempt to favor counterhegemonic indigenous knowledge from the North over indigenous knowledge from the South. This type of engagement can be a struggle that is deeply related to identity and does not dichotomize the ontological and the epistemological. It is not a struggle against science, but a political commitment to advancing a new understanding of science that implies an effort to decolonize the universities, in particular the teacher-education programs. Why, Barnhardt (2009) asks, does one way of life have to die so another can live? One cannot ignore the fact that at the same time the curriculum field is claiming its internationalization, countries including the United States refuses to sign the United Nations Declaration on the Rights of Indigenous Peoples (2007). With knowledge being the very core of the curriculum field, this is not a minor issue. The task is to fight for a pedagogy of indigenous knowledge that is seen as a struggle for a global onto-episteme one that understands the interplay between the ontological and the epistemological, and that sees indigenous knowledge forms as local knowledge that is significant within the global scenario. This is not a utopian aim. As Wa Thiong'o (1986) argues, "The peasantry saw no contradiction between speaking their own mother-tongues and belonging to a larger national or continental geography...[They] saw no necessary antagonistic contradiction between belonging to their immediate nationality, to their multinational state along the Berlin-drawn boundaries, and to Africa as a whole" (p. 23).

The new itinerant curriculum theory (ICT) will challenge one of the fundamental characteristic of abyssal thinking: the impossibility of co-presence of the two sides of the line; it will challenge the cultural politics of denial, that produces a radical absence, the absence of humanity, the modern sub-humanity (Sousa Santos, 2009, p., 30). Such new theoretical task understands that modern humanity is not conceivable without a modern sub-humanity, an that the denial of a part of humanity is sacrificial, in that it is the condition for the other part of humanity, which considers itself as universal.

(An)other science is really possible. It is possible for an itinerant curriculum theory (ICT)—which we argue is the best path for critical progressive curriculum scholars—not only to grasp precious concepts and dynamics such as hegemony, ideology, power, social emancipation, class, race, and gender in the complex age of globalization (Sousa Santos, 2008) or globalisms, but also to better (re)address the towering questions of curriculum, starting with the one asked by Counts in the last century: *Dare the schools build a new social order?* Addressing this question implies a new thinking, a new theory. A post-abyssal thinking (cf. Sousa Santos, 2009); a post-abyssal theory; an itinerant curriculum theory.

Notes

1 The Nature of Conflict

1. As we examined in detail elsewhere, Apple's work and thought needs to be understood and mapped in what I coined while ago three trilogies that are anchored in particular backgrounds, namely, curriculum sphere, analytical philosophy, political science, and the new sociology of education (cf. Paraskeva, 2004).

3 A Simplistic Tool for a Lethal Phenomenon

1. Kliebard, in "The Struggle for the American Curriculum, 1893–1958", demarcates 1896 as the year the National Association of Manufacturers emerged. However, in a book published in 1999, "Schooled to Work: Vocationalism and the American Curriculum, 1876–1946", Kliebard dates the emergence of the National Association of Manufacturers to 1895. We opted for the date mentioned in the more recent work because its main focus is vocational education; in other words, the whole investigation is directed to this topic, whereas the previous work (1995) deals with vocational education only secondarily.

6 The Struggle for Curriculum Relevance

1. In this regard cf. Williams (1960), "Can Negroes Afford to be Pacifists?" and Dellinger (1960) "Are Pacifists Willing to Be Negroes?"
2. In fact, the Robeson case is today a public document, made available by the Federal Bureau of Investigation, of about 3,000 pages. The alleged "FBI HQ File 100–12304 Section: 1, Paul Robeson, Sr.," despite having many censured paragraphs, offers unshakeable evidence of the far-reaching effects of McCarthyism in the United States of America.
3. Haubrich, "Freedom, Bureaucracy and Schooling". However, it is important to stress that the conference of 1969 and of 1970 of the ASCD had already caused some controversy. The former, "in Chicago[,] experienced confrontation tactics by militant white and black proponents of

black concerns"; the latter, "in San Francisco[,] saw the emergence of a radical caucus that met at conferences until its demise a few years later". With this regard, cf: Til (1986).

4. In this regard cf "Curriculum Inquiry", 6 (4), pp., 331–40, e pp., 358–69.

5. Op. cit., p., 335. If we take into consideration that, in 1971, Apple published "The Hidden Curriculum and the Nature of Conflict", and in 1976 Bowles and Gintis published "Schooling in Capitalist America", and when faced by the established debate, one easily determines at whom the criticism of Jackson was directed.

6. Some of them were drawing from Williams and Gramsci, among others, making the neo-Marxist approach more accurate; others were trying to go beyond such perspectives; and others were reacting vividly against such platforms.

7. I am not claiming here that Pinar's earlier material is not important and valuable, but precisely the opposite.

7   THE EMERGENCE AND VITALITY OF A SPECIFIC CRITICAL CURRICULUM RIVER

1. Around that time, Johnson (1929) was already questioning the problematic of sex in the world of education (pp. 220–243).

2. In 1944, this name was changed to the American Education Fellowship. In 1953 the association would be renamed Progressive Education Association (cf. Graham, 1967).

3. As I was able to claim elsewhere (Paraskeva, 2004), Gerth played a key role in Dwayne Huebner's thought. Profoundly frustrated with the mainstream reductive understand of the nature of human(ity), and stimulated by Gerth, Huebner increasingly detached himself from the empiricist dimension of research and established contact with the works of Marx (*Das Kapital* was "the best book I have ever read, the best written book I have ever read" Tape # 1), Langer, Parson and Shils, Russell, and Cassirer, among others, deepening and widening his intellectual dimension, understanding thus that "part of the difficulty in the curriculum field was its narrow range of concepts and its heavy dependency upon behavioural sciences" (Tape #2). The constant search for a more complex intellectual tool took him to the domain of Existentialism, largely influenced by the work of Marcel, Merleau-Ponty, and Sartre, and of theology, where the thought of Tillich—"the first German professor to be dismissed from his position [in Frankfurt] by Adolf Hitler—must be highlighted as well (cf. Greffrath, 1982l; also, for an acccurate analysis regarding the 'vulgarization' of the nature of human(ity) cf. Arendt, 1951).

8 CHALLENGING EPISTEMICIDES: TOWARD AN ITINERANT CURRICULUM THEORY

1. The critique of the reductionism of the neo/Marxist tradition is not that linearly peaceful. As Eagleton (2003, pp. 31–33) claims, to say that Marxism did not have not much to say about gender, sexuality, race colonialism, nation, ethnicity is not accurate:

    "Marxism ha certainly sidelined gender and sexuality. But it had by no means ignored these topics, even tough much of what it had to say about was painfully insufficient (…) Marxism had been largely silent on the environment, but so at the time had almost everyone else. There were, evens so, some pregnant reflections on Nature in the early Marx and later socialist thinkers (…) The charge that Marxism has had nothing to say about race, nation, colonialism and ethnicity is equally false. Indeed, the Communist movement was the only place in the early twentieth century where the issues of nationalism and colonialism - along with the question of gender – were systematically raised and debated. (…) But Marxism is not some Philosophy of Life or Secret of the Universe, which feels duty bound to pronounce on everything from how to break your way into a boiled egg to the quickest way to delouse cocker spaniels. It is an account, roughly speaking, of how one historical mode of production changes into another. It is not a deficiency of Marxism that it has nothing very interesting to say about whether physical exercise or wiring your jaws together is the best way of dieting. Nor it is a defect of feminism that it has so far remained silent about the Bermuda Triangle. Some of those who upbraid Marxism with not saying enough are also allergic to grand narratives which try to say too much"

2. Anton Wilhelm Amo (1703–1765).

3. Origen (AD 354–430), Tertullian (ca. AD 155–240), Plotonius (AD 354–430), and Hypatia (ca. AD 370–415).

4. For a better understanding of the tensions between an 'activist [welfare] state' and the rise of an assertive predatory politically powerful neoliberal neoconservatism which vehemently opposes the role of an activist government please cf. Piersen & Skocpol (2002).

5. Cf. the work of Malangatana Valente, the great Mozambican painter.

6. Cf. the work of Jackson Pollock, an icon of U.S. expressionism.

7. In this regard, please cf. also Pinar (2011) "Curriculum Studies in Brazil: Intellectual Histories, Present Circumstances (International and Development Education)". New York: Palgrave. Unfortunately when Pinar's volume came out this manuscript was already well ahead in production preventing me from giving it due attention.

BIBLIOGRAPHY

Abu-Lughod, I. (2001) "Territorially-based Nationalism and the Politics of Negation," in E. Said and C. Hitchens (eds.) *Blaming the Victims: Spurious Scholarship and the Palestinian Question*. New York: W. W. Norton & Co Inc, pp., 193–206.

Abu-Lughod, J. (1989) *Before European Hegemony*. New York: Oxford University Press.

Achebe, Ch. (1977) *Conversations with Chinua Achebe*. Bernth Lindfors (ed). Jackson: University Press of Mississippi.

——— (2000) *Home and Exile*. Oxford: Oxford University Press.

Adams, C. (1879) *The New Departure in the Common Schools of Quincy and other Papers on Educational Topics*. Boston: Estes & Lauriat.

Adams, F. & Horton, M. (1975) *Unearthing Seeds of Fire: The Idea of Highlander*. North Carolina: John F. Blair Publisher.

Agamben, G. (1999) "Absolute Immanence," in J. Khalfa (ed) *An Introduction to the Philosophy of Gillen Deleuze*. London: Continuum, pp., 151–69.

——— (2005) *State of Exception*. Chicago: University of Chicago Press, p., 76.

Agbebi, M. (1903) *Inaugural Sermon Delivered at the Celebration of the First Anniversary of the "African Church."* New York: Edgar Howorth. In this regard bide also T. Falola (2003) *The Power of African Cultures*. New York: University of Rochester Press, pp., 20–48.

Aidoo, A. (1997) *Our Sister Killjoy*. Reading, Massachusetts: Addison Wesley.

Akiwowo, A. (1980) "Sociology in Africa Today," *Current Sociology*, 28 (2), pp., 1–73, p., 67.

——— (1986*)* "Contributions to the Sociology of Knowledge from African Oral Poetry". *International Sociology*, 1 (4), pp., 343–58.

Alexander, H. (2003) "Education as Spiritual Critique: Dwayne Huebner's Lure of the Transcendent," *Journal of Curriculum Studies*, 35 (2), pp., 231–45., pp., 234–5.

Alves, N. Sgarbi, Passos, M. e Caputo, S. (2007) "Nos e Nossas Historias em Imagens e Sons Uma Historia em Imagens," *Associação Nacional de Pós-Graduação e Pesquisa em Educação. Grupo de Trabalho Curriculo. Trabalho Encomendado.* Caxambu: Brazil.

Altbach, Ph. (2008) Literary Colonialism. Books in the Third World. In M. Villegas, S. Neugebauer and K. Venegas (eds) *Indigenous Knowledge and Education. Sites of Struggle, Strength and Survivance*, Cambridge: Harvard Education Review, pp., 55 – 64.

American Youth Commission (1940) *What the High Schools Ought to Teach: The Report of a Special Committee on the Secondary School Curriculum.* Washington: American Council on Education.

Amin, S. (1989) *Eurocentrism.* London: Zed Books.

Amorim, A. C. (2007) "*Escritas*curriculo, Representacao e Diferenças." *Associação Nacional de Pós-Graduação e Pesquisa em Educação. Grupo de Trabalho Curriculo. Trabalho Encomendado.* Caxambu: Brazil.

Andrew, D. (2009) *Leaner and Meaner? The Perils of McDonaldizing the Academy and Kinesiology* Alan G. Ingham Memorial Lecture, McGuffey Hall Auditorium, Oxford: Miami University.

Appiah, K. (1992) *In My Father's House. Africa in the Philosophy of Culture.* Oxford: Oxford University Press.

——— (1998) "Old Gods, New Worlds," in P. H. Coetzee and A. J. Rox (eds) *The African Philosophy Reader.* London: Routledge, pp., 245–74, p., 245.

——— ([1979],1990) *Ideology and Curriculum.* New York: Routledge.

Apple, M. (1971) "The Hidden Curriculum and the Nature of Conflict." *Interchange*, 2, (4), pp., 27–40.

——— (1975) "Commonsense Categories and Curriculum Thought," in J. Macdonald & E. Zaret (1975) *Schools in Search of Meaning.* Washington: ASCD, pp., 116–48.

——— (1977a) "Discussion, Jackson, P. Beyond Good and Evil. Observations on the Recent Criticism of Schooling," *Curriculum Inquiry*, 6 (4), pp., 331–40.

——— (1977b) "Discussion, Apple, Michael & King, Nancy. What do Schools Teach?" *Curriculum Inquiry,* Volume 6 (4), pp., 361–9.

——— (1986) *Teachers and Texts: A Political Economy of Class and Gender Relations in Education.* New York: Routledge.

——— (1995) *Education and Power.* New York: Routledge.

——— (1999) *Power, Meaning and Identity. Essays in Critical Educational Studies.* New York: Peter Lang.

——— (2000a) "Michael W. Apple: Revisiting and Revising a Curriculum Tradition," in J. Marshall, J. Sears & W. Schubert (eds.) *Turning Points in Curriculum. A Contemporary American Memoir.* Ohio: Prentice Hall, pp., 81–6.

——— (2000b) "On the Shoulders of Giants: Apple," in J. Marshall, J. Sears & W. Schubert (eds). *Turning Points in Curriculum. A Contemporary American Memoir.* Merrill: Prentice Hall., pp. 103–242.

——— (2001) *Standards, Subject Matter and a Romantic Past: Left Back: A Century of Failed School Reforms, by Diane Ravitch.* New York: Simon and Schuster. Draft presented at the Friday Group, Mimeographed.

——— (2010) Putting Critical Back into Educational Research. *Educational Researcher*, 39 (2) pp., 152 – 155.

Apple, M. & King, N. (1977) What do Schools Teach? *Curriculum Inquiry,* Volume 6 (4), pp., 341–358.

Apple, M. and Weis, L. (1983) (eds) *Ideology and the Practice of Schooling.* Philadelphia: Temple University Press.

Applebee, A. (1996) *Curriculum as Conversation: Transforming Traditions of Teaching and Learning.* Chicago: University of Chicago Press.

Archambault, R. (1966) *John Dewey Lectures in the Philosophy of Education, 1899.*New York: Random House.

Arendt, H. (1951) *The Origins of Totalitarianism.* New York: Harcourt Brace.

Aristotle (1945) *Politics.* New York: Oxford University Press.

Armstrong, O. (1940) "Treason in the Textbooks," *The America Legion Magazine.*

Aronowitz, S. (1981) "Preface," in H. Giroux. *Ideology, Culture and the Practice of Schooling.* Philadelphia: Temple University Press, pp. 1–4.

———(2001) *The Last Good Job in America. Work and Education in the New Global Technoculture.* Lanham: Rowman & Littlefield Publishers.

Atkin, J. (1983) "American Graduate Schools of Education: A View from Abroad," *Oxford Review of Education,* 9(1), pp., 62–9.

Auge, M. (1994) (2003). *Não-Lugares: introdução a uma antropologia da supermodernidade.* Campinas: Papirus Editora.

Autio, T. (2007) "Towards European Curriculum Studies: Reconsidering Some Basic Tenets of Building and Didaktik," *Journal of the American Association for the Advancement of Curriculum Studies,* Volume 3, February.

——— (2011–forthcoming) "Um Caso Educacional de Ocidentalismo. Um Pre-historia Colonialista dos Estudos do Curriculo e da Didactica," in J. Paraskeva, T. Autio e H. Sunker (eds) *Nova Teoria e Investigacao Curricular.* Mangualde: Edicoes Pedago.

Ayers, W. (1992) "The Shifting Ground of Curriculum Thought and Everyday Practice," *Theory Into Practice,* XXXI (3), pp., 259–63.

———(2001) *Fugitive Days: A Memoir.* New York: Penguin.

Ayres, L. (1909) *Laggards in our Schools: A Study of Retardation and Elimination in City Schools Systems.* New York: Charities Publication Committee.

Baber, Z. (1995) *The Science of Empire: Scientific Knowledge, Civilization, and Colonial Rule in India.* Albany: State University of New York Press.

Bagley, W. (1905) *The Educative Process.* New York: MacMillan.

——— (1914) "Fundamental Distinctions Between Liberal and Vocational Education" *National Education Association, Addresses and Proceedings,* 52nd Annual Meeting, pp., 161–70.

——— (1921) "Projects and Purposes in Teaching and Learning," *Teachers College Record,* 22, pp., 288–97.

——— (1945) "The Harvard University Report on General Education in a Free Society," *School and Society,* 62, pp., 69–70.

Baker, B. (2009) *New Curriculum History.* Rotterdam: Sense Publishers.

Barnhardt, R. (2009) *Indigenous Knowledge.* American Educational Research Association, S. Diego.

Basler, R.(1947) "Life Adjustment Education for Youth: Commission to Develop a Program for Universal Secondary Education," *School Life*, 30 (2), pp., 3–6.

Bataille, G. (1986) *Eroticism, Death and Sensuality*. San Francisco: City Lights Books, p., 63.

Bauman, Z. (2004) *Globalization. The Human Consequences*. London: Blackwell Publishers.

Beauchamp, G. (1964) *The Curriculum of Elementary School*. Boston: Allyn & Bacon, INC.

Beck, U. (2009) *What is Globalization?* London: Polity.

Bell, B. (1949) *Crisis in Education: A Challenge to American Complacency*. New York: Whittlesey House.

Bell, B., Gaventa, J. & Peters, J. (1990) *Myles Horton and Paulo Freire, We Make the Road by Walking. Conversations on Education and Social Change*. Philadelphia: Temple University Press, p. 99.

Bellack, A. (1973) "What Knowledge Is of Most Worth?" in R. Hyman (ed.) *Approaches in Curriculum*. New Jersey: Prentice-Hall, INC, pp., 101–20.

Bellack, A., Kliebard, H., Hyman, R., Smyth, Jr., F. (1966) *The Language of the Classroom*. New York: Teachers College Press, Columbia University.

Bellini, M. e Anastácio, M. (2007) *Em tempos Pos-Modernos.Associação Nacional de Pós-Graduação e Pesquisa em Educação. Grupo de Trabalho Curriculo. Trabalho Encomendado*. Caxambu: Brazil.

Bennett, H. (1917) *School Efficiency, A Manual of Modern School Management*. Boston: Ginn and Company, p., 215.

Bennett, K. (2007) "Epistemicide! The Tale of a Predatory Discourse." *The Translator. Studies in Intercultural Communication*, 13 (2), pp. 151–69.

Bernal, M. (1987) *Black Athena: The Afroasiatic Roots of Classical Civilization*. New Brunswick: Rutgers University.

——— (2001) *Black Athena Writes Back: Martin Bernal Responds to His Critics*: Duke University Press.

Bernstein, B. (1971) "On the Classification and Framing of Educational Knowledge," in Michael F. D. Young (ed) *Knowledge and Control. New Directions for the Sociology of Education*. London: Open University Set Book, pp., 47–69.

——— (1977) *Class, Codes and Control, vol. 3*. London: Routledge and Kegan Paul.

Berube, M. (2000) "John Dewey: American Genius," in M. Berube. *Eminent Educators. Studies in Intellectual Influence*. London: Greenwood Press, pp. 33–45, p. 33.

Bestor, A. (1952) "Life Adjustment Education: A Critique," *Bulletin of the American Association of University Professors*, 38, pp., 413–41.

———(1953) "Anti-Intellectualism in the Schools," *New Republic*, 128, pp., 11–13.

Beyer, L. & Liston, D. (1996) *Curriculum in Conflict: Social Visions, Educational Agendas and Progressive School Reform*. New York: Teachers College.

Bhabha, H. (1995) "Signs Taken for Wonders," in B. Ashcroft, G. Griffiths, and H. Tiffin (eds) *The Post Colonial Reader.* London: Routledge, pp., 38–43, pp., 38–39.

Blauner, R. and Wellman, D. (1973) "Toward the Decolonization of Research," in J. Ladner (ed) *The Death of White Sociology.* New York: Random house, pp., 310–30, p., 324.

Blaustein, A. & Ferguson Jr., C. (1957) *Desegregation and the Law: The Meaning and Effect of the School Segregation Cases.* New York: Rutgers University Press.

Bobbitt, J. (1912) "The Elimination of Waste in Education," *Elementary School Teacher*, 12, pp., 259–71.

——— (1913) "Some General Principles of Management Applied to the Problems of City School Systems," in S. Parker (ed.) *Twelfth Yearbook of the National Society for the Study of Education*, Part 1. Chicago: University of Chicago Press, pp., 7–96.

——— (1918) *The Curriculum.* Boston: Houghton Mifflin, Co.

——— (1922) *How to Make a Curriculum.* Boston: Houghton Mifflin.

——— (1924) "The New Technique of Curriculum Making," *The Elementary School Journal*, 25, (1), pp., 45–54.

——— (1925) "Education as a Social Process," *School and Society*, XXI, n° 538, pp., 453–59.

——— (1926) "The Orientation of the Curriculum Maker," in G. Whipple (ed) The Foundations and Technique of Curriculum Construction. *Twenty-Sixth Yearbook of the National Society for the Study of Education*, Part II, Bloomington: Public School Publishing Co, pp., 41–55.

——— (1934) "A Summary Theory of the Curriculum," *Society for Curriculum Study News Bulletin*, 5 (12), pp., 2–4.

——— (1946) "Harvard Reaffirms the Academic Tradition," *The School Review*, 54 pp., 326–33.

Bode, B. (1924) "Why Educational Objectives?" *School and Society*, 19, pp., 533–9.

——— (1927) *Modern Educational Theories.* New York: MacMillan.

——— (1929) *Conflicting Psychologies of Learning.* Boston: D. C. Heath and Company.

——— (1938) *Progressive Education at the Crossroads.* New York: Newson & Company.

——— (1940) *How We Learn.* Boston: D. C. Heath and Company.

Boroujerdi, M. (2001) "The Paradoxes of Politics in Postrevolutionary Iran," in J. Esposito and R. Ramaazani (eds) *Iran at the Crossroads.* New York: Palgrave, pp., 13–27, p., 13.

Bourdieu, P. (1971) "Systems of Education and Systems of Thought," in M. F. D. Young (ed) *Knowledge and Control: New Directions for the Sociology of Knowledge.* London: Collier Macmillan, pp., 189–208.

——— (2001) *Language and Symbolic Power.* Cambridge: Harvard University Press.

Bowles, S. & Gintis, H. (1976) *Schooling in Capitalist America. Educational Reform and the Contradictions of Economic Life.* New York: Basic Books.

Boydstom, J & Poulos, K. (1978) *Checklist of Writings about John Dewey, 1887–1977.* Carbondale: Southern Illinois University Press.

Bradley, J. (1894) "The Report of the Committee of Ten. From the Point of View of the Smaller Colleges," *Educational Review*, Vol. VII, pp., 370–3.

Brameld, Th. (1950a) *Philosophies of Education in Cultural Perspective.* New York: The Dryden Press.

——— (1951) *The Battle for Free Schools.* Boston: The Beacon Press.

——— (1957) *Cultural Foundations of Education. An Interdisciplinary Exploration.* New York: Harper & Brothers Publishers.

——— (1961) *Education for an Emerging Age.* New York: Harper & Row.

——— (1965) *The Use of Explosive Ideas in Education. Culture, Class and Revolution.* Pittsburgh: University of Pittsburgh Press.

——— (1970) *The Climactic Decades. Mandate to Education.* New York: Praeger Publishers.

——— (1956) *Toward a Reconstructed Philosophy of Education.* New York: The Dryden Press Publishers.

——— (1950b) *Ends and Means in Education: A Mid-Century Appraisal.* New York: Harper & Brothers.

Bruner, J. (1960) *The Process of Education. A Searching Discussion of School Education Opening New Paths to Learning and Teaching.* New York: Vintage Books.

Bullock, H. (1970) *A History of Negro Education in the South From 1619 to the Present.* New York: Praeger.

Burnham, W. (1897) "Suggestions From the Psychology of Adolescence," *School Review*, 5, pp., 652–65.

Burns, R. & Brooks, G. (1970) "The Need for Curriculum Reform," in R. Burns & G. Brooks (eds.) *Curriculum Design in a Changing Society.* New Jersey: Educational Technology Publications, pp., 3–18.

Butler, N. (1888) *The Argument for Manual Training.* New York: E. L. Kellog.

Button, H. & Provenzo, Jr., E. (1983) *History of Education and Culture in America.* Englewood Cliffs: Prentice-Hall, INC.

Cabral, A. (1969) "The Weapon of Theory," in A. Cabral *Revolution in Guine Bissau.* New York: Monthly Review, pp., 90–111. p., 95.

——— (1974) *Return to the Source.* New York: Monthly Review Press.

——— (1980) *Unity and Struggle. Speeches and Writings.* London: Heinmann.

Campbell, J. (1996) *Understanding John Dewey.* Chicago: Open Court.

Carlson, D. (2005) "The Question Concerning Curriculum Theory," *Journal of the American Association for the Advancement of Curriculum Studies*, 1.

Carlson, D., and Apple, M. (1998) *Power, Knowledge, Pedagogy.* Boulder: Westview Press, p., 6.

Carnoy, M. (1972) (ed) *Schooling in a Corporate Society. The Political Economy of Education in America.* New York: McKay; Vide also Carnoy, M. (1974) *Education as Cultural Imperialism.* New York: McKay.

Caswell, H. (1950) "Sources of Confusion in Curriculum Theory," in V. Herrick & R. Tyler (comp. & ed.) "Toward Improved Curriculum Theory." *Papers Presented at the Conference on Curriculum Theory.* Chicago: University of Chicago Press, pp., 110–17.

—— (1952–53) "The Great Reappraisal of Public Education," *Teachers College Record*, LIV, pp., 12–22.

Chambliss, J. (1963) *Boyd H. Bode's Philosophy of Education.* Ohio: Ohio State University Press.

Charters, W. (1901) *Methods of Teaching: Developed from a Functional Standpoint.* Chicago: Row, Peterson and Co.

—— (1922) "Regulating the Project," *Journal of Educational Research*, 5, pp. 245–6.

Charters, W. (1923) *Curriculum and Construction.* New York : MacMillan.

—— (1926a) "Curriculum for Women," *Bulletin of the University of Illinois*, 23 (27), pp., 327–30.

—— (1926b) "Statement," in G. Whipple (ed) "The Foundations and Technique of Curriculum Construction, Part II. The Foundations of Curriculum Making." *The Twenty-Sixth Yearbook of the National Society for the Study of Education.* Bloomington: Public School Publishing.

Chomsky, N. (1992) *Chronicles of Dissent: Interviews with David Barsamian— Noam Chomsky.* Monroe: Common Courage Press.

Clark, K. (1952) "The Effects of Prejudice and Discrimination," in Helen Witmer & Ruth Kotinsky (eds.) *Personality in the Making: The Fact-finding Report of the Mid-century White House Conference on Children and Youth.* New York: Harper and Brothers.

Clark, J. (1894) "Art in Secondary Education—An Omission by the Committee of Ten," *Educational Review*, Vol. VII, pp., 374–81.

Cobb, S. (1928) *The New Leaven. Progressive Education and its Effect Upon the Child and Society.* New York: The John Day Company.

Coleman, J. *et al.* (1966) *Equality of Educational Opportunity.* Washington: Office of Education, United States Department of Health, Education and Welfare.

Collier, P. (1950) What Is Education for Life Adjustment? *Bulletin of the National Association of Secondary-School Principals*, 34 (169), pp., 122–8.

Commission on the Reorganization of Secondary Education, *Cardinal Principles of Secondary Education* (1918), Bulletin, n° 35. Washington: U.S. Government Printing Office, pp., 11–15.

Committee on the Objectives of General Education in a Free Society (1945) *General Education in a Free Society.* Report of the Harvard Committee. Cambridge: Harvard University Press.

Committee on the Objectives of General Education in a Free Society (1945) *General Education in a Free Society.* Report of the Harvard Committee. Cambridge: Harvard University Press.

Connel, R. (1980) *A History of Education in the Twentieth Century World.* Canberra: Curriculum Development Program.

Connell, R. (2007) *Southern Theory. The Global Dynamics of Knowledge in Social Science*. Cambridge: Polity.

Connelly, F, M., Fang He, M., Phillion, J. and Schlein, C. (2008) Introduction. In F. M. Connelly (ed) *The Sage Handbook of Curriculum and Instruction*. Los Angeles: SAGE, pp., ix–xv.

Coomaraswamy, A. (1947) *The Bugbear of Literacy*. London: Dennis Dobson.

Copley, F. (1923) *Frederick W. Taylor: Father of Scientific Management*. Vol. 1. New York: The American Society of Mechanical Engineers.

Corey, S. (1953) *Action Research to Improve School Practices*. New York: Teachers College, Columbia University.

Counts, G. (1922) *The Selective Character of American Secondary Education*. Chicago: The University of Chicago Press.

——— (1926) *The Senior High School Curriculum*. Chicago; The University of Chicago Press.

——— (1928) *School and Society in Chicago*. New York: Harcourt, Brace & Company.

——— (1929) *Secondary Education and Industrialism*. Cambridge: Harvard University Press.

——— (1930) *The American Road to Culture. A Social Interpretation of Education in the United States*. New York: John Day.

——— (1931) *The Soviet Challenge to America*. New York: The John Day Company.

——— (1932) *Dare Schools Build a New Social Order?* Carbondale, Il.: Southern Illinois University Press.

——— (1934) (Editorial) "Orientation," *The Social Frontier*, 1, pp., 3–10, p., 3.

——— (1945) *Education and the Promise of America*. New York: The Macmillan Company.

——— (1959) *Khrushchev and the Central Committee Speak on Education*. Thesis of the Central Committee of the Communist Party and the Council of Ministers of the USSR. Dr. George S. Counts' commentary and analysis. Pittsburgh: The University of Pittsburgh Press.

——— (1962) *Education and the Foundations of Human Education*. Pittsburgh: University of Pittsburgh Press.

Counts, G., Kimmel, W., Kelley, T. (1934) *The Social Foundations of Education. Part IX: Report of the Commission on the Social Studies— American Historical Association*. (A. Krey—Chairman Director of the Investigation). New York: Charles Scribner's Sons.

Couto. M. (2005) *Pensatempos*. Lisboa: Caminho, p., 10.

Cox, R. (2002) *The Political Economy of a Plural World. Critical Reflections on Power, Morals and Civilization*. London: Routledge, p., 76.

Crary, R. (1969) *Humanizing the School. Curriculum Development and Theory*. New York: Alfred A. Knopf.

Cremin, L (1964) *The Transformation of the School. Progressivism in American Education, 1876–1957*. New York: Vintage Books.

Crosby, M. (1964) *Curriculum Development of Elementary Schools in a Changing Society*. Boston: D. C. Heath and Company.

Cruikshank, K. (2000) "Integrated Curriculum and the Academic Disciplines: The NCTE Correlated Curriculum of 1936," in B. Franklin (ed) *Curriculum and Consequence. Herbert Kliebard and the Promise of Schooling*. New York: Teachers College Press, pp., 178–96.

Dahrendorf, R. (1959) *Class and Class Conflict in an Industrial Society*. Stanford: Stanford University Press.

——— (1993) *Ensaios sobre o Liberalismo*. Lisboa: Editorial Fragmentos.

Dale, R. (1977). "Implications of the Rediscovery of the Hidden Curriculum for the Sociology of Teaching," in D. Gleeson (ed.).*Identity and Structure: Issues in the Sociology of Education*. Driffield: Nafferton Books, pp., 44–54.

Dale, R., Esland, and MacDonald, M. (1982) *Schooling and Capitalism*. London: Routledge and Kegan Paul.

Darder, A., Baltodano, M., and Torres, R. (2002) "Introduction," in A. Darder, R. Torres and M. Baltodano (eds) *The Critical Pedagogy Reader*. New York: Routledge, pp. 24–6.

Davenport, E. (1909) *Education for Efficiency*. New York: D. C. Heath & Co., Publishers.

Davidson, Th. (1901) *The History of Education*. New York: Scribner

De Garmo, C. (1894) "Report of the Committee of Ten. From the Point of View of Educational Theory," *Educational Review*, Vol. VII, pp., 275–80.

——— (1895) "Discussion on Report of Dr. Harris," *Journal of Education*, Vol. XLI (21), pp., 165–7.

Deleuze, G. (1990a) *The Logic of Sense*. New York: Columbia University Press.

——— (1990b) *Pourparlers*. Paris: Les Editions de Minuit.

——— (1994) *What is Philosophy*. New York: Columbia University Press

Deleuze, G. e Guattari, F. (1987) *A Thousand Plateaus. Capitalism and Schizophrenia*. Minneapolis: University of Minnesota Press.

Dellinger, D. (1960) "Are Pacifists Willing to be Negroes?" *New Left Review*, 1/1, pp., 46–7.

Dennison, G. (1969a) *The Lives of Children*. New York: Random House.

——— (1969b) "The First Street School," in R. Gross & B. Gross (eds.) *Radical School Reform*. New York: Simon and Schuster, pp. 227–46.

Dewey, J. (1887) "Process of Knowledge," In J. Boydston (Ed) *John Dewey, The Early Works, 1882–1898*, Carbonale: Southern Illinois University Press, 2, pp., 75–136.

——— (1895) In J. Boydston (Ed) *John Dewey, The Early Works, 1882–1898*, Carbonale: Southern Illinois University Press, Vol. 5.

——— (1897) "Criticisms Wise and Otherwise on Modern Child Study," *Journal of Proceedings and Addresses of the Thirty-Sixth Annual Meeting of the National Education Association*, pp., 867–868.

——— (1899) *The School and Society*. Chicago: University of Chicago Press.

Dewey, J. (1900) *The School and Society.* Chicago: University of Chicago Press.

———— (1902) *The Child and the Curriculum.* Chicago. University of Chicago Press.

————(1909) *The Moral Principles in Education.* Boston: Houghton Mifflin Company.

————(1910) *How we Think.* Boston: D. C. Heath & Co. Publishers.

————(1913) *Interest and Effort in Education.* Boston: Houghton Mifflin Company.

———— (1915). Education *vs.* Trade-Training—Dr. Dewey's reply, *The New Republic,* 5, pp., 40–2.

———— (1916) *Democracy and Education.* New York: MacMillan.

———— (1929a) "My Pedagogical Creed," *The Journal of the National Education Association,* 18 (9), pp., 291–5.

———— (1929b) *Impressions of Soviet Russia and the Revolutionary World.* New York: New Republic, INC.

————(1929c) *The Sources of a Science of Education.* New York: Liveright.

———— (1930) *Democracy and Education.* New York: The Macmillan Company.

————(1934a) "Why I am Not a Communist," in B. Russel, J. Dewey, M. Cohen, S., Hook e S. Eddy. *The Meaning of Marx.* New York: Farrar & Rinehart Incorporated Publishers, pp., 86–90.

————(1934b) "Can Education Share in Social Reconstruction?" *The Social Frontier,* 1, pp. 11–12.

———— (1935–1937) "Authority and Social Change," In J. Boydston (Ed) John Dewey, *The Later Works, 1925–1953.* Carbonale: Southern Illinois University Press, Volume 11 (2), pp., 130–45.

————(1935) *Liberalism and Social Action.* New York: G. P. Putnam's Sons.

————(1937) "First Session," *The Case of Leon Trotsky: Report of Hearings on the Charges Made against him in the Moscow Trials.* New York: Harper & Brothers Publishers.

————(1939) *Freedom and Culture.* New York: Capricorn Books.

————(1946) *The Problems of Men.* New York: Philosophical Library.

———— (1966) Means and Ends. In L. Trotsky, J. Dewey & G. Novak, *Their Morals and Ours. Marxist Versus Liberal Views on Morality.* New York: Merit Publishers, pp. 55–60.

Dewey, J. & Dewey, E. (1943) *Schools of To-Morrow.* New York: E. P. Dutton & Co INC.

Diamonti, M. (1977a) "Yes, We Have No Curriculum Theory: Response to Herbert Kliebard," *Curriculum Inquiry,* 6 (4), pp., 269–76.

———— (1977b) "Discussion. Kliebard, H. Curriculum Theory: Give Me a for Instance," *Curriculum Inquiry,* 6 (4), pp., 277–282.

Doll, W. (1993) *A Post-Modern Perspective on Curriculum.* New York: Teachers College Press.

Douglas, H. (1949) "Education of All Youth for Life Adjustment," *The Annals of the American Academy of Political and Social Science,* 265, pp., 108–14.

Doyle, W. (1986). "Classroom Organization and Management," in M. Wittrock (ed.). *Handbook of Research on Teaching*. New York: MacMillan Publishing, pp., 392–431.

Dreeben, R. (1968). *On What is Learned in School*. Massachusetts: Addison-Wesley.

—— (1970) "Schooling and Authority: Comments on the Unstudied Curriculum," in N. Overly (ed.) *The Unstudied Curriculum*. Washington: ASCD, pp., 85–103.

Drost, W. (1967) *David Snedden and Education for Social Efficiency*. Madison: The University of Wisconsin Press.

DuBois, W., & Dill, A. (1912) *The Negro American Artisan*. Atlanta: Atlanta University Press.

DuBois, W. E. B. (1932) "Education and Work," *Journal of Negro Education*, 1 (1), pp., 60 – 74.

Eagleton, T. (1994) "Ideology and its Vicissitudes in Western Marxism," in S. Zizek (ed.) *Mapping Ideology*. London: Verso, pp., 179–226.

—— (2003) *After Theory*. New York: Basic Books.

Eco, U. (1984) *Proscript to the Name of the Rose*. New York: Harcourt, Brace and Jovanovich.

Educational Policies Commission (1944) *Education for ALL American Youth*. Washington: Educational Policies Commission, National Education Association, American Association of School Administrators.

Eggleston, J. (1977) *The Sociology of School Curriculum*. London: Routledge & Kegan Paul.

Eisinger, P. (1970) *Protest Behavior and the Integration of Urban Political Systems*. Unpublished paper. Institute for Research on Poverty. Madison: University of Wisconsin–Madison.

Eliot, C. (1892) *Shortening and Enriching the Grammar School Course*. National Education Association.

—— (1894) "The Report of the Committee of Ten," *Educational Review*, Volume VII, pp., 105–10.

—— (1905a) (ed.) *Educational Reform, Essays and Addresses*. New York: The Century Company.

—— (1905b) "The Fundamental Assumptions in the Report of the Committee of Ten (1893)," *Educational Review*, Vol. 30 (4), pp., 325–43.

—— (1908) "Industrial Education as an Essential Factor in our National Prosperity," *National Society for the Promotion of Industrial Education*. Bulletin 5. New York: The Society, pp., 9–14.

Ellison, R. (1952) *Invisible Man*. New York: Random House.

Ellsworth. E. (1989) "Why Doesn't This Feel Empowering? Working Through the Repressive Myths of Critical Pedagogy," *Harvard Educational Review*, 59, (3), pp., 297–324.

Ellul, J. (1964) *The Technological Society*. New York: Vintage Books.

Ellwood, C. (1914) "Our Compulsory Education Laws, and Retardation and Elimination in our Public Schools," *Education*, XXXIV, pp., 572–6.

Emerson, H. (1917) *The Twelve Principles of Efficiency*. New York: The Engineering Magazine Co.

Espinosa-Dulanto, M. (2004) "Silent Screams: Deconstructing (Academia) the Insider/Outsider Indigenous Researcher Positionalities," in K. Mutua and B. Swadener (eds) *Decolonizing Research in Cross-Cultural Contexts. Critical Personal Narratives*. New York: New York University Press, pp., 45–51.

Ethridge, S. (1974) "Brown *vs*. Topeka: Twenty Years Later. Two Perspectives. Perspective 2," in D. Della-Dora & J. House (eds.) *Education for an Open Society*. Washington. ASCD, pp. 1–27.

Eyng, A. and Chiquito, R. (2007) *Politicas Curriculares: As Respresentacoes dos Profissionais da Educacao a Luz da Teorizacao Pos-Critica do Currículo. Associação Nacional de Pós-Graduação e Pesquisa em Educação. Grupo de Trabalho Curriculo. Trabalho Encomendado*. Caxambu: Brazil.

Falola, T. (2003) *The Power of African Cultures*. New York: University of Rochester Press.

Fantini, M. & Weinstein, G. (1969) *Toward a Contact Curriculum*. New York: Anti-Defamation League of B'nai B'irth.

Feinberg, W. (1975) *Reason & Rhetoric. The Intellectual Foundations of 20th Century Liberal Educational Policy*. New York: John Wiley & Sons, INC.

Ferraco, C. (2007) *Currículo e Pesquisa com o Cotidiano: Sobre Usos, Traducoes, Negociacoes e Hibridismos da Cultura como Enunciacao. Associação Nacional de Pós-Graduação e Pesquisa em Educação. Grupo de Trabalho Curriculo. Trabalho Encomendado*. Caxambu: Brazil.

Finney, R. (1917) "Social Studies in Junior High School," *Journal of Education*, 86, pp., 633–4.

Flagg Young, E. (1915) "Industrial Training," *National Education Association. Addresses and Proceedings*, 53rd Annual Meeting.

Fones-Wolf, E. (1983) "The Politics of Vocationalism: Coalitions and Industrial Education in the Progressive Era," *The Historian* , 46, pp., 39–55.

Ford, N. (1973) *Black Studies: Threat or Change*. New York: Kennikat Press.

Foucault, M.(1994) *História da Sexualidade I – A Vontade de Saber*. Lisboa. Relógio D'Água.

Fraser, N. (1997) *Justice Interrupts. Critical Reflections on the 'Postcolonialist' Condition*. New York: Routledge.

Freire, P. (1974) *Education: The Practice of Freedom*. London: Writers Readers Publishing Cooperative.

———(1990) *Pedagogy of the Oppressed*. New York: Continuum.

———(1998) *Teachers as Cultural Workers. Letters to Those Who Dare Teach*. Boulder: Westview Press, pp., 17–26.

———(2009) "Amilcar Cabral. Pedagogue of the Revolution," in S. Macrine, (ed). (2009). *Critical Pedagogy in Uncertain Times: Hope & Possibilities*. New York, NY: Palgrave Macmillan.

Friedenberg, E. (1962) *The Vanishing Adolescent*. New York: Dell Publishing.

Frymier, J. & Hawn, H. (1970) *Curriculum Improvement for Better Schools*. Ohio: Charles Jones Publishing Company.

Fuller, H. (1951) "The Emperor's New Clothes, or Prius Demendat," *The Scientific Monthly*, p. 72, pp., 32–41.

Garcia, A. e Cinelli, M. (2007) "Os estudos do cotidiano ajudam a des-invisibilizar as práticas educativas emancipatórias?" *Associação Nacional de Pós-Graduação e Pesquisa em Educação. Grupo de Trabalho Curriculo. Trabalho Encomendado*. Caxambu: Brazil.

Gardner, B. (1975) "The Educational Contributions of Booker T. Washington," *Journal of Negro Education*, 44 (4), pp., 502–18.

Generals, D. (2000) "Booker T. Washington and Progressive Education: An Experimentalist Approach to Curriculum Development and Reform," *Journal of Negro Education*, 69 (3), pp., 215–34.

Giroux, H. (1980) "Beyond the Correspondence Theory: Notes on the Dynamics of Educational Reproduction and Transformation." *Curriculum Inquiry*, 10 (3), pp., 225–47.

——— (1981a) *Ideology, Culture & the Process of Schooling*. Philadelphia: Temple University Press.

——— (1981b) "Toward a New Sociology of Curriculum," in H. Giroux, A. Penna and W. Pinar (eds) *Curriculum and Instruction*. Berkeley: McCutchan Publishing Corporation, pp., 98–108.

——— (1983) *Theory and Resistance in Education. Towards a Pedagogy for the Opposition*. New York: Bergin and Garvey.

——— (1988) *Teachers as Intellectuals. Toward a Critical Pedagogy of Learning*. Westport: Bergin and Garvey.

———(1994) *Doing Cultural Studies: Youth and the Challenge of Pedagogy*. Retrieved August 2008 http://www.gseis.ucla.edu/courses/ed253a /giroux/giroux1.html

——— (1996) "Towards a Postmodern Pedagogy," in L. Cahoone (ed) *From Modernism to Postmodernism. An Anthology*. Oxford: Blackwell Publishers, pp., 687–97, p., 691.

Glen, J. (1988) *Highlander, No Ordinary School, 1932–1962*. Lexington: The University Press of Kentucky.

Goldman, E. (1956) *The Crucial Decade: America, 1945–1955*. New York: Alfred A. Knopf.

Gonzalez, G. (1982) *Progressive Education: A Marxist Interpretation*. Minneapolis: Marxist Educational Press.

Good, H. (1956) *A History of American Education*. New York: The MacMillan Company.

Goodlad, J. & Kein, M. and Associates (1970) *Behind Classroom Doors*. Ohio: Charles A. Jones.

Goodlad, J. (1976) "Introduction," in R. Tyler. *Perspectives on American Education. Reflections on the Past…Challenges for the Future*. Chicago: Science Research Associates, INC, pp., 3–11.

Goodlad, J., Von Stoephasius, R., Klein, M. (1966) *The Changing School Curriculum*. A Report From the Fund for the Advancement of Education. New York: The Fund for the Advancement of Education, pp., 105–06.

Goodman, P. (1969) "No Processing Whatever," in R. Gross & B. Gross (eds.) *Radical School Reform*. New York: Simon and Schuster, pp., 98–106.

Goody, J. (1996) *The East in the West*. Cambridge: Cambridge University Press.

────── (2006) *The Theft of History*. Cambridge: Cambridge University Press.

────── (2010) *Renaissance. The One or the Many?* Cambridge: Cambridge University Press.

Gore, J. (1993) *The Struggle for Pedagogies. Critical and Feminist Discourses as Regimes of Truth*. New York: Routledge.

Gough, N. (2000) "Locating Curriculum Studies in the Global Village," *Journal of Curriculum Studies*, 32 (2), pp., 329–42.

────── (2011 – forthcoming) "Planos de Mudanca: Jogo Rizosemiotico na Investigacao do Curriculo Internacional," in J. Paraskeva, T. Autio e H. Sunker (eds) *Nova Teoria e Investigacao Curricular*. Mangualde: Edicoes Pedago.

Gouldner, A. (1970) *The Coming Crisis of Western Sociology*. New York: Basic Books.

Graham, P. (1967) *Progressive Education: From Arcady to Academe*. New York: Teachers College Press.

Gramsci, A. (1957) *The Open Marxism of Antonio Gramsci*. Translated and Annotated by Manzani, C. New York: Cameron Associates, INC.

────── (1971) *Antonio Gramsci: Selections from the Prison Notebooks*. Edited by Q. Hoare and G. Smith. New York: International Publishers.

Graubard, A. (1972) *Free the Children*. New York: Random House.

Greene, M. (1973) *Teacher as a Stranger*. California: Wadsworth Publishing Company, INC.

────── (1977) "The Artistic-Aesthetic and Curriculum," *Curriculum Inquiry*, 6 (4), pp., 283–96.

────── (1979) "Letters to the Editor," *Educational Researcher*, 8 (9), p. 25.

Greenwood, J. (1894) "The Report of the Committee of Ten. Its Use for the Improvement of Teachers Now at Work in Schools," *National Education Association Proceedings*.

Greffrath, M. (1982) "As in the Book of Fairy Tales: All Alone…a Conversation with Hans Gerth," in J. Bensman, L. Vidich & N. Gerth (1982) *Politics, Character and Culture*. Westport: Greenwood Press, pp., 14–47.

Grumet, M. (1981) "Autobiography and Reconceptualization," in H. Giroux, A. Penna and W. Pinar (eds) *Curriculum and Instruction*. Berkeley: McCutchan Publishing Corporation, pp., 139–44.

Guha, R. (1983) "The Prose of Counter Insurgency," in R. Guha (ed.) *Subaltern Studies II*. Oxford: Oxford University Press, pp., 1–42.

Gutek, G. (1991). *An Historical Introduction to American Education.* Illinois: Waveland Press, INC.

Gyekye, G. (1987) *An Essay on African Philosophical Thought. The Akan Conceptual Scheme.* Cambridge: Cambridge University Press.

Hagstrom, W. (1965). *The Scientific Community.* New York: Basic Books.

Hall, S. (1883) "The Contents of Children's Minds," *Princeton Review* (11), pp., 249–72.

——— (1892) "Editorial," in S. Hall (ed.). *The Pedagogical Seminary.* Vol. II. Worcester: J. H. Orpha.

——— (1894) "Child Study," *Journal of Proceedings and Addresses of the National Education Association.* National Education Association, pp., 173–9.

——— (1901a). "How Far Is the Present High-School and Early College Training Adapted to the Nature and Needs of Adolescents?" *School Review*, 9, pp., 649–51.

——— (1901b). *The Ideal School as Based on Child Study.* National Education Association, pp., 474–88.

——— (1904a) *Adolescence: Its Psychology and its Relations to Physiology, Anthropology, Sociology, Sex, Crime, Religion and Education.* Vol. 2. New York: D. Appleton.

——— (1904b) "The Natural Activities of Children as Determining the Industries in Early Education," *Journal of Proceedings and Addresses of the Forty-Third Annual Meeting of the National Education Association.*

Hallen, B. (2002) *A Short History of African Philosophy.* Bloomington: Indiana University Press.

Hamminga, B. (2005) Knowledge Cultures. Comparative Western African Epistemology. Amsterdam: Rodpi.

Hardt, M., and Negri, T. (2000). *Empire.* Cambridge: Harvard University Press.

Harrington, M. (1962) *The Other America: Poverty in the United States.* New York: Macmillan.

Harris, W. (1880) "Equivalents in a Liberal Course of Study," *Journal of Proceedings and Addresses.* National Education Association, pp., 167–75.

——— (1889a) "The Intellectual Value of Tool-Work," *Journal of Proceedings and Addresses.* National Education Association, pp., 92–8.

——— (1889b) "Report of the Committee on Pedagogics," National Education Association. *Addresses and Proceedings.*

——— (1895) "Discussion on Report of Dr. Harris," *Journal of Education*, Vol. XLI (21), pp., 165–7.

——— (1896) "How the Will Combines With the Intellect in the Higher Orders of Knowing," *Journal of Proceedings and Addresses.* National Education Association, pp., 440–6.

——— (1900) "The Study of Arrested Development in Children as Produced by Injudicious School Methods," *Education*, XX, pp., 453–66.

Hartley, D. (1977) *Re-schooling Society*. Washington: Falmer Press.

——— (1998) "What's Green and Makes the Environment Go Round?" in F. Jameson and M. Miyoshi (eds) *The Cultures of Globalization*. Durham: Duke University Press, pp., 327–55.

Harvey, D. (1998) What's Green and Makes the Environment go Round? In F. Jameson and M. Miyoshi (eds) *The Cultures of Globalization. Post-Contemporary Interventions*. Duke University Press, pp., 327–355.

Haubrich, V. (ed.) *Freedom, Bureaucracy and Schooling*. Washington. ASCD.

Haubrich, V. & Apple, M. (1975) *Schooling and the Rights of Children*. California: McCutchan Publishing Corporation.

Henderson, C. (1902) *Education and the Larger Life*. Boston: Houghton, Mifflin and Company, p., 69.

Henry, J. (1963) *Culture Against Man*. New York: Random House.

——— (1969) "In Suburban Classrooms," in R. Gross & B. Gross (eds.) *Radical School Reform*. New York: Simon and Schuster, pp., 77–92.

Herrick, V. (1950) "What Should be the Organizing Elements of the Curriculum," in V. Herrick & R. Tyler (comp. & ed.) "Toward Improved Curriculum Theory." *Papers Presented at the Conference on Curriculum Theory*. Chicago: University of Chicago Press, pp., 37–50.

Herrick, V. & Tyler, R. (1950) (comp) & (ed) "Toward Improved Curriculum Theory." *Papers Presented at the Conference on Curriculum Theory*. Chicago: University of Chicago Press.

Hessong, R. & Weeks, Th. (1991) *Introduction to the Foundations of Education*. New York: MacMillan Press.

Holt, J. (1969) "How Children Fail," in R. Gross & B. Gross (eds.) *Radical School Reform*. New York: Simon and Schuster, pp., 59–77.

Holt, J. (1970) *What Do I Do on Monday?* New York: Dutton.

hooks, b. (1994) *Teaching to Transgress. Education as a Practice of Freedom*. New York: Routledge.

Hopkins, L (1954) *The Emerging Self in School and Home*. New York: Harper & Brothers.

Hountondji, P. (1976) *African Philosophy. Myth and Reality*. London: Hutchinson.

Hountondji, P. (1983) *African Philosophy*. Bloomington. Indiana University Press.

http://www.uwstout.edu/soe/jaaacs/vol1/carlson.htm

http://www.uwstout.edu/soe/jaaacs/vol3/autio.htm

Huebner, D. (1959) *From Classroom Action to Educational Outcomes*. An *Exploration in Educational Theory*. Madison: University of Wisconsin-Madison, pp., 35–78.

——— (1961) *Creativity in Teaching*. Unpublished paper.

——— (1962a) "Politics and Curriculum," in H. Passow, (ed.). *Curriculum Crossroads*. New York: Teachers College Press, pp., 87–95.

——— (1962b) *The Complexities in Teaching*. Unpublished paper.

—— (1964) "Curriculum as a Guidance Strategy." *Paper delivered at Elementary Guidance Workshop*. Mimeographed, pp., 1–15.

—— (1966) "Curricular Language and Classroom Meanings," in J. Macdonald & R, Leeper. (eds.). *Language and Meaning*. Washington: ASCD.

—— (1967) "Curriculum as Concern of Man's Temporality," *Theory into Practice*, 6 (4), pp., 172–9.

—— (1968) *Teaching as Art and Politics*. Mimeographed.

—— (1968) "The Tasks of the Curricular Theorist." *Paper presented at ASCD*. Mimeographed.

—— (1974a) "The Remaking of Curriculum Language," in W. Pinar (ed) *Heightened Consciousness, Cultural Revolution and Curriculum Theory*. Berkeley: McCutchan Publishing Corporation, pp., 36–53.

—— (1974b) "Curriculum...With Liberty and Justice for All." Unpublished paper.

—— (1975a) "The Recreative and the Established," in Macdonald, J. & Zaret, E. (1975) *Schools in Search of Meaning*. Washington: ASCD, pp., 27–37.

—— (1975b) "Poetry and Power: The Politics of Curricular Development,: in W. Pinar (ed) *Curriculum Theorizing, The Reconceptualists*. Berkeley: McCutchan Publishing Company, pp., 271–80.

—— (1976) "The Moribund Curriculum Field: It's Wake and Our Work," *Curriculum Inquiry*, 6 (2) pp., 153–67.

—— (1977a) "Response to Maxine Greene. The Artistic-Aesthetic and Curriculum," *Curriculum Inquiry*, 6 (4), pp., 296–301.

—— (1977b) "Discussion. Jackson, P. Beyond Good and Evil. Observations on the Recent Criticism of Schooling," *Curriculum Inquiry*, 6 (4), pp., 331–40, p., 332.

—— (1977c) *Dialectical Materialism as a Method of Doing Education*. Mimeographed.

—— (1979) "Perspectives for Viewing Curriculum," *Curriculum Symposium. British Columbia Teachers Federation*. Unpublished paper.

—— (2002) Tape # 1, recorded at 3718 Seminary Rd, Alexandria, VA 22304. Washington. USA.

—— (2002) Tape # 2, recorded at 3718 Seminary Rd, Alexandria, VA 22304. Washington. USA.

Hullfish, G. (1924) "Looking Backward with David Snedden," *Educational Review*, LXVII, pp., 61–9.

Hypolito, A. (2001) "Class, Race and Gender in Education. Towards a Spiral Non-Parallelist Non-Synchronous Position," *Paper presented at the Friday Seminar*. Madison. University of Wisconsin–Madison.

Ignas, E. & Corsini, R. (1979) *Alternative Educational Systems*. Illinois: F.E. Peacock Publishers, INC.

Illich, I. (1971) *Deschooling Society*. New York: Harper & Row.

Inlow, G. (1966) *The Emergent in Curriculum*. New York: John Wiley & Sons INC.

Jackson, P. (1977a) "Beyond Good and Evil. Observations on the Recent Criticism of Schooling," *Curriculum Inquiry*, 6 (4), pp., 311–29.

——— (1977b) "Discussion" Jackson, P. (1977) "Beyond Good and Evil. Observations on the Recent Criticism of Schooling," *Curriculum Inquiry*, 6 (4), pp., 331–40.

Jackson, Ph. (1977c) Discussion, Apple, Michael & King, Nancy. "What Do Schools Teach?" *Curriculum Inquiry*, Volume 6 (4), pp., 361–9.

——— (1980) "Curriculum and Its Discontents," *Curriculum Inquiry*, 1, pp., 28–43.

——— (1992) Conceptions of Curriculum and Curriculum Specialists. In P. Jackson (ed) *Handbook of Research on Curriculum*. New York: McMillan, pp., 3–40.

Jackson, Ph (1968) *Life in Classrooms*. New York: Holt, Rinehart, and Winston.

Jahanbegloo, R. (2007) *Elogio da Diversidade*. Barcelona: Arcadia.

Jarvis, P. (1987) *Twentieth Century Thinkers in Adult Education*. London: Croom Helm, p. 246.

Jencks, C., Smith, M., Acland, H., Bane, M., Cohen, D., Gintis, H., Heyns, B., & Michelson, S. (1972) *Inequality. A Reassessment of the Effect of Family and Schooling in America*. New York: Basic Books.

Jencks, Ch. (1971) *Inequality: A Reassessment of the Effect of Family and Schooling in America*. New York: Basic.

Jin, H. (2008) *The Writer as Migrant*. Chicago: The University of Chicago Press.

Johnson, M. (1929) *Youth in a World of Me, the Child, the Parent and the Teacher*. New York: The John Day Company.

Johnson, M. (1968) "The Translation of Curriculum Into Instruction." *Paper prepared for an invitational presession on curriculum theory at AERA*, in February.

Johnson, M. (1974) *Thirty Years With an Idea*. Alabama: The University of Alabama Press.

Journal of Negro Education (1932) 1(1). Editorial Comment. Why A Journal of Negro Education? pp., 1–4.

Judd, C. (1909) "Editorial Notes," *School Review*, 17, pp., 570–571.

——— (1923) "How Modern Business May Aid in Reconstructing the Curriculum," *School and Society*, XVIII, pp., 281–287.

Kaestle, C. (1983) *Pillars of the Republic, Common Schools and American Society, 1780–1860*, New York: Hill and Wang.

Kaomea, J. (2004) "Dilemmas of an Indigenous Academic: A Native Hawaiian Story," in K. Mutua and B. Swadener (eds). *Decolonizing Research in Cross-Cultural Contexts. Critical Personal Narratives*. New York: New York University Press, pp., 27–44.

Kaphagawani, D. (1998) "Themes in a Chewa Epistemology," in P. H. Coetzee and A. J. Roux (eds) *The African Philosophical Reader*. London: Routledge, pp., 240–244, p., 241.

Kassir, S. (2006) *Being Arab*. London: Verso.

Kasson, F. (1893–1894) "Editorial." *Education*, XIII-XIV, pp., 432–433.

Kawagely, O. (2009) *Indigenous Knowledge*. American Education Research Association, San Diego.

Kebede, M. (2004) *Africa's Quest for a Philosophy of Decolonization*. Amsterdam: Rodopi.

Keenan, B. (1977) *The Dewey Experiment in China. Educational Reform and Political Power in the Early Republic*. London: Council on East Asian Studies, Harvard University Press.

Kelly, A. (1989) *The Curriculum, Theory and Practice*. London: Paul Chapman Publishing, p., 50.

Kemmis, S. (1988) *El Curriculum: Más Allá de la Teoría de la Reproducción*. Madrid: Ediciones Morata.

——— (1992) "Practica de la teoria critica ensenanza: Experiencias." *Lectures given at International Symposium, March, University of Valladodid*, Spain.

Kennedy, W. (1981) "Highlander Praxis: Learning with Myles Horton," *Teachers College Record*, 83 (1), pp., 105–19.

Kenyatta, J. (1960) "The Kenya Africa Union Is Not the *Mau Mau*," in F. D. Cornfield, *The Origins and Growth of Mau Mau*, Sessional Paper, N. 5 of 1959–1960. Nairobi, pp. 301–8.

Khalfa, J. (1999) "Introduction," in J. Khalfa (ed) *An Introduction to the Philosophy of Gillen Deleuze*. London: Continuum, pp., 1–6.

Khoza, R. (1994) *Ubuntu as African Humanism. Conference Paper Read at Ekhaya Promotions Diepkloof Extension*. Unpublished Paper.

Kilpatrick, W. (1918) "The Project Method," *Teachers College Record*, 19, pp. 319–35.

——— (1922) "Subject Matter and the Educative Process," 1. *The Journal of Educational Method*, 2, pp. 95–101.

——— (1926) *Foundations of Education*. New York: MacMillan.

——— (1933) *The Educational Frontier*. New York: The Century Co.

——— (1951) *Philosophy of Education*. New York: The MacMillan Company.

——— (1971) *Foundations of Method, Informal Talks on Teaching*. New York: Arno Press & The New York Times.

Kincheloe, J. (1991) *Teachers as Researchers. Qualitative Inquiry as a Path to Empowerment*. London: Falmer.

——— (1993) *Toward a Critical Politics of Teacher Thinking. Mapping the Postmodern*. Westport: Bergin & Garvey.

King, I. (1913) *Education for Social Efficiency*. New York: D. Appleton and Company.

Kliebard, H. (1968) "The Curriculum Field in Retrospect," in P. Witt (ed). *Technology and Curriculum*. New York: Teachers College Press, pp., 69–84.

——— (1971) "Bureaucracy and Curriculum Theory," in V. Haubrich (ed.) *Freedom, Bureaucracy and Schooling*. Washington. ASCD, pp., 74–93.

Kliebard, H. (1975a) "Persistent Issues in Historical Perspective," in W. Pinar (ed) *Curriculum Theorizing. The Reconceptualists.* Berkeley: McCutchan, pp., 39–50.

—— (1975b) "The Rise of Scientific Curriculum Making and its Aftermath." *Curriculum Theory Network,* 5 (1), pp., 27–38.

—— (1977a) "Curriculum Theory: Give Me a for Instance." *Curriculum Inquiry,* 6 (4), pp., 257–76.

—— (1977b) "Discussion. Kliebard, H. Curriculum Theory: Give Me a for Instance." *Curriculum Inquiry,* 6 (4), pp., 277–82.

—— (1982) "Education at the Turn of the Century: A Crucible for Curriculum Change." *Educational Researcher,* 11, pp., 16–24.

—— (1988) "The Effort to Reconstruct the Modern American Curriculum," in Landon Beyer &M. Apple (eds.). *The Curriculum, Problems, Politics and Possibilities.* New York: State University of New York Press, pp., 21–33.

—— (1992) "Dewey and the Herbartians: The Genesis of a Theory of Curriculum," in H. Kliebard, *Forging the American Curriculum. Essays in Curriculum History and Theory.* New York: Routledge, pp. 68–82.

—— (1995) *The Struggle for the American Curriculum: 1893–1958.* New York: Routledge.

—— (1999a) *Schooled to Work. Vocationalism and the American Curriculum, 1876–1946.* New York: Teachers College.

—— (1999b) "The Liberal Arts Curriculum and Its Enemies: The Effort to Redefine General Education," in M. Early & K. Rehage (eds). Issues in Curriculum: A Selection of Chapters from Past NSSE Yearbooks. *Ninety-eighth Yearbook of the National Society for the Study of Education,* Part II. Chicago: The University of Chicago Press, pp., 3–25.

—— (1999c) "Dewey and the Herbartians: The Genesis of a Theory of Curriculum," in W. Pinar (Ed.). *Contemporary Curriculum Discourses, Twenty Years of Journal of Curriculum Studies.* New York: Peter Lang, pp., 68–81.

Kohl, H. (1988) *36 children.* New York: Plume.

Kohlberg, L. (1970) "The Moral Atmosphere of the School," in N. Overly (ed.). *The Unstudied Curriculum.* Washington: ASCD, pp., 104–27.

Kolesnik, W. (1979) *Mental Discipline in Modern Education.* Madison: University of Wisconsin Press.

Kozol, J. (1967) *Death at an Early Age: The Destruction of the Hearts and Minds of Negro Children in the Boston Public Schools.* Boston: Houghton Mifflin.

—— (1972) *Free Schools.* Boston: Houghton Mifflin.

—— (1992). *Savage Inequalities.* New York: Harper Collins.

Krug, E. (1969) *The Shaping of the American High School, 1880–1920.* Madison: The University of Wisconsin Press.

Krutch, J. (1970) "A Humanistic Approach." *Phi Delta Kappan,* LI (7), pp., 376–8.

Lancaster, E. (1905) *President's Address*. National Education Association.

Latour, B. (2006) *O Poder da Crítica*. Discursos. Cadernos de Políticas Educativas e Curriculares. Viseu: Livraria Pretexto Editora.

Lawson, M. & Peterson, R. (1972) *Progressive Education: An Introduction*. London: Angus and Robertson.

Levine, A. (1917) "Better Schools Through Scientific Management," *Educational Foundations*, XXVIII, 10, pp., 593–6.

Levine, D. and Ornstein, A. (1981) *An Introduction to the Foundations of Education*. Dallas: Houghton Mifflin Company.

Lipscomb, A. (1903) (ed.) *The Writings of Thomas Jefferson*, Vol 2., Charlottesville: Thomas Jefferson Memorial Association.

Liston, D. (1988) *Capitalist Schools. Explanation and Ethics in Radical Studies of Schooling*. New York: Routledge.

Liston, D. and Zeichner, K. (1987) "Critical Pedagogy and Teacher Education," *Journal of Education*, 169, pp., 117–37.

Lopes, A. (2007) "Currículo no debate modernidade, pós-modernidade," *Associação Nacional de Pós-Graduação e Pesquisa em Educação. Grupo de Trabalho Curriculo. Trabalho Encomendado*. Caxambu: Brazil.

Lovejoy, A. (1936) *The Great Chain of Being*. Cambridge: Harvard University Press.

Lumumba, P. (1963) Lumumba Speaks. In J. Van Lierde (ed) *The Speeches and Writings of Patrice Lumumba, 1958–1961*. Boston: Little, Brown and Company.

Luke, A. (2010) Curriculum in Context. In F. M. Connelly (ed) *The Sage Handbook of Curriculum and Instruction*. Los Angeles: SAGE, pp., 145–150.

Lundgren, U. (1983). *Between Hope and Happening: Text and Context in Curriculum*. Vic. Deakin University.

Maccia, E. (1963) *An Educational Theory Model: Information Theory*. Occasional paper. Center for the Construction of a Theory in Education.

—— (1962) *An Educational Theory Model: General Systems Theory*. Occasional paper. Center for the Construction of a Theory in Education.

Macdonald, J. (1966a) "Language, Meaning and Motivation: An Introduction," in J. Macdonald & R. Leeper (eds.). *Language and Meaning*. Washington: ASCD, pp., 1–7.

—— (1966b) "The Person in the Curriculum," in H. Robinson (ed) *Precedents and Promise in the Curriculum Field*. New York: Teachers College, Columbia University, pp., 38–52.

—— (1967) "An Example of Disciplined Curriculum Thinking." *Theory Into Practice*, 6 (4), pp., 166–71.

——(1969–70) "The School Environment as Learner Reality." *Curriculum Theory Network*, 4, pp., 45–52.

—— (1971a) "Curriculum Theory." *Journal of Educational Research*, 64 (5), p. 195–200.

—— (1971b) "The Nature of Instruction: Needed Theory and Research," in R. Leeper (ed) *Curriculum Decision Concerns in a Revolutionary Era*. Washington: ASCD, pp., 105–7.

Macdonald, J. (1975) "The Quality of Everyday Life in School," in J. Macdonald & E. Zaret (1975) *Schools in Search of Meaning*. Washington: ASCD, pp., 78–94.

——(1977) "Values Bases and Issues for Curriculum," in A. Molnar & A. Zahorik (eds.) *Curriculum Theory*. Washington: ASCD, pp., 10–21.

——(1982) "How Literal is Curriculum Theory," *Theory Into Practice*, 21 (1), pp., 55–61.

Macdonald, J. & Zaret, E. (1975) *Schools in Search of Meaning*. Washington: ASCD.

Macdonald, J., Wolfson, B. & Zaret, E. (1973) *Reschooling Society: A Conceptual Model*. Washington: ASCD.

Macedo, D. (2000) "The Colonialism of the English Only Movement," *Educational Researcher*, 29 (3), pp., 15–24.

——(2003). *The Hegemony of the English Language*. Boulder: Paradigm.

——(2006) *Literacies of Power*. Boulder; Westview Press.

Macedo, E. and Frangella, R. (2007) "Currículo e Cultura: deslizamentos e hibridizações," *Associação Nacional de Pós-Graduação e Pesquisa em Educação. Grupo de Trabalho Curriculo. Trabalho Encomendado*. Caxambu: Brazil.

Machel, S. (1985) "Samora Machel," In B. Munslow (ed) *Samora Machel. An African Revolutionary*. London: Zed Books.

——(1979) *Fazer da Escola uma Base para o Povo Tomar o Poder*. Maputo: FRELIMO.

MacLean, K. (1966) "Myles Horton and the Highlander Folk School," *Phi Delta Kappan*, XLVII, pp. 487–97.

Mahoney, J. (2000) "Path Dependence in Historical Sociology." *Theory and Society*. Vol. 29, No. 4, pp. 507–48, p., 512.

Malewski, E. (2010) Introduction. Proliferating Curriculum. In E. Malewski (ed) *Curriculum Studies Handbook. The Next Momentum*. New York: Routledge, pp., 1–39.

Manacorda, M. (1970). *O Princípio Educativo em Gramsci*. Porto Alegre: ArtesMédicas.

Manchester, W. (1974) *The Glory and the Dream: A Narrative History of America, 1932–1972*. Boston: Little Brown.

Mann, J. (1968) *Toward a Discipline of Curriculum Theory*. Baltimore: The John Hopkins University, The Center for the Study of Social Organization of Schools. (Mimeographed).

——(1975) "On Contradictions in Schools," in J. Macdonald & E. Zaret (1975) *Schools in Search of Meaning*. Washington: ASCD, pp., 95–115.

Maphisa, S. (1994) "Man in Constant Search of Ubuntu—A Dramatist's Obsession," Conference Paper Read at Ubuntu Conference (AIDSA) Pietmaritzzburg. University of Natal, Unpublished.

Marble, A. (1894) "City School Administration," *Educational Review*, 8, pp., 154–68.

——(1895) "Dr. Harris and His Critics," *Journal of Education*, Volume XLI (15), pp., 247–8.

Marshall, J. Sears & W. Schubert (2000) (eds). *Turning Points in Curriculum. A Contemporary American Memoir.* Merrill: Prentice Hall.

Masolo, D. (2004) "African Philosophers in the Greco-Roman Era," in K. Wiredu (ed) *A Companion to African Philosophy.* Oxford: Blackwell Publishing, pp., 50–65.

Maxwell, W. (1895) "Introduction," in *Report of the Committee of the Fifteen on Elementary Education.* National Education Association. New York: The American Book Company, pp., 7–18.

Mbiti, J. (1969) *African Religion and Philosophy.* London: Heinemann.

McCarthy, C, and Apple, M. (1988). "Race, Class, and Gender in American Education. Towards a Nonsynchronous Parallelist Position," in L. Weis (ed) *Class, Race, and Gender in American Education.* Albany: State University of New York Press, pp., 3–39.

McCarthy, C. (1998) *The Uses of Culture.* New York: Routledge.

McCarthy and Crichlow, W. (1993) (eds) *Race, Identity and Representation in Education.* New York: Routledge.

McGuffey, W. (1839) *New Fifth Eclectic Reader—Selected and Original Exercises for Schools.* New York: Cincinnati, Winthrop B. Smith and Co.

McLaren, P (1994) *Life in Schools: An Introduction to Critical Pedagogy in the Foundations of Education.* New York: Longman, p. 191.

——— (1986) *Schooling as a Ritual Performance.* New York: Routledge.

McLuhan, M. & Leonard, G. (1969) "Learning in the Global Village," in R. Gross & B. Gross (eds.) *Radical School Reform.* New York: Simon and Schuster, pp., 106–115.

McLure, H. & Fisher, G. (1969) *Ideology and Opinion Making, General Problems of Analysis.* Bureau of Applied Social Research: Columbia University.

——— (1969). *Ideology and Opinion Making. General Problems of Analysis.* Unpublished paper. Bureau of Applied Social Research. New York: Columbia University.

McMurry, C. (1895) "Discussion on Report of Dr. Harris." *Journal of Education,* Vol. XLI (21), pp., 165–7.

McMurry, F. (1895) "Discussion on Report of Dr. Harris." *Journal of Education,* Vol. XLI (21), pp., 165–7.

McNeil, J. (1977) *Curriculum. A Comprehensive Introduction.* Boston: Little, Brown and Company.

Merlau-Ponty, M. (1973) *The Prose of the World.* Evanston: Northwestern University Press.

Metcalf, L. & Hunt, M. (1970) "Relevance and Curriculum," *Phi Delta Kappan,* Volume LI (7) pp., 358–61.

Meyer, A. (1961) *The Development of Education in the Twentieth Century.* Englewood Cliffs, N.J.: Prentice-Hall.

Miel, A. (1964) *Changing Curriculum. A Social Process.* New York: D. Appleton-Century Company, INC.

Mills, C. (1951) *White Collar.* New York: Oxford University Press.

Mphahlele, E. (1965) "Negritude and Its Enemies. A Reply," in G. Moore (ed) *African Literature and the Universities*. The Congress for Cultural Freedom. Dakar: Ibadan University Press, pp., 22–6.

Mudimbe, V. (1988) *The Invention of Africa*. Bloomington: Indiana University Press.

Mudimbe, V., Y. (1994) *The Idea of Africa*. Bloomington: Indiana University Press.

Muelder, H. (1984) *Missionaries and Muckrakers: the First Hundred Years of Knox College*. Urbana. University of Illinois Press.

Mutua, K., and Swadener, B. (2004) "Introduction," in K. Mutua and B. Swadener (eds). *Decolonizing Research in Cross-Cultural Contexts. Critical Personal Narratives*. New York: New York University Press, pp., 1–23.

Myrdal, G. (1944) *An American Dilemma: The Negro Problem and Modern Democracy*. New York: Harper & Brothers.

National Defense Education Act (1958) Public Law 85–864, 85th Congress, September, 2.

National Education Association (1893) *Report of the Committee on Secondary School Studies*. Washington: U.S. Government Printing Office.

National Education Association (1894) *Proceedings*.

Neagley, R., & Evans, N. (1967) *Handbook for Effective Curriculum Development*. New Jersey. Prentice-Hall.

Nelson, D. (1975) *Managers and Workers: Origins of the New Factory System in the United States, 1880–1920*. Madison: University of Wisconsin Press.

NKrumah, K. (1964) *Consciencism. Philosophy and Ideology for De-Colonization and Development with Particular Reference to the African Revolution*. New York: Monthly Review Press.

Nkrumah, K. (2006) *Class Struggle in Africa*. London: PANAF.

Noble, S. (1938) *A History of American Education*. New York: Rinehart and Company INC.

Nussbaum, M. (1997) *Cultivating Humanity: a Classical Defense of Reform in Liberal Education*. Cambridge, Massachusetts: Harvard University Press.

Nyerere, J. (1998) "Good Governance for Africa." *Marxism and Anti-Imperialism in Africa* www.marxists.ort retrieved December 2006.

O'Brien, M. and Penna, S. (1999) *Theorizing Welfare*. London: Sage.

Oliver, A. (1963) *Curriculum Improvement. A Guide to Problems, Principles and Procedures*. New York: Dodd, Mead & Company.

Onyewuenyi, I. (1991) "Is There an African Philosophy?" in T. Serequeberhan (ed). *African Philosophy. Thee Essential Readings*. New York: Paragon House, pp., 29–46. p., 41.

Oppenheim, N. (1898) *The Development of the Child*. London. The MacMillan Company, p., 112.

Original Papers in Relation to a Course of Liberal Education. In B. Silliman (1829). *The American Journal of Science and Arts*, Vol. XV, pp., 297–351.

Oruka, H. (1990) *Trends in Contemporary African Philosophy*, Nairobi: Shirikon Publishers.

Oruka, O. (1975) "Fundamental Principles in the Question of African Philosophy," *Second Order*, 4 (2).

Oseghare, A. (1990). "Sage Philosophy. New Orientation in African Philosophy," in H. Odera Oruka (ed) Sage Philosophy, Leiden: E. J. Brill, pp., 249–58.

Packard, V. (1957) *The Hidden Persuaders*. New York: David McKay.

Pagano, J. (1999) "The Curriculum Field. Emergence of a Discipline," in W. Pinar (ed) *Contemporary Curriculum Discourses. Twenty Years of JCT*. New York: Peter Lang, pp., 82–101.

Page, R. (2003) *Division B Vice President Address—American Education Research Association*. Chicago.

Paraskeva, J. (2001) *As Dinâmicas dos Conflitos Ideológicos e Culturais na Fundamentação do Currículo*. Porto: ASA.

——— (2004) *Here I Stand. A Long (R)evolution. Michael Apple and Critical Progressive Tradition*. Minho. University of Braga.

——— (2005) *Dwayne Huebner. Mitografias da Abordagem Curricular*. Lisboa: Editora Platano.

——— (2006a) Desterritorializar a Teoria Curricular. *Papeles de Trabajo sobre Cultura, Educación y Desarrollo Humano*, 2 (1), http://www.doaj.org/doaj

——— (2006b) Desterritorializar a Teoria Curricular. In, J. Paraskeva (org) *Currículo e Multiculturalismo*. Lisboa: Edicoes Pedago, pp., 169–204:

——— (2007) Continuidades e Descontinuidades e Silêncios. Por uma Desterritorialização da Teoria Curricular. *Associação Nacional de Pós-Graduação e Pesquisa em Educação*, (ANPEd), Caxambu: Brazil.

——— (2008) "Por uma Teoria Curricular Itinerante," in J. Paraskeva (org) *Discursos Curriculares Contemporaneos*. Lisboa: Edicoes Pedago, pp., 7–21.

——— (2010a) "Hijacking Public Schooling: The Epicenter of Neo Radical Centrism," in S. Macrine, P. McLaren and D. Hill (eds) *Revolutionizing Pedagogy: Educating for Social Justice within and Beyond Neo-liberalism*. New York: Palgrave.

——— (2010b) Privatização dos Benefícios e Socialização dos Custos em Educação. In J. Paraskeva and Wayne Au (eds) O Direito a Escolha em Educação. Cheques Ensino, Projectos Charter e Ensino Domestico. Lisboa: Edições Pedago, pp., 17–53.

——— (2010c) Academic Capitalism in Portugakl. Westernzing the West. In J. Paraskeva (ed) *Unnacomplished Utopia. Neoconservative Dismantling of Public Higher Education in the European Union*. Rotterdam: Sense Publisher, pp., 15–40.

——— (2011a) Nova Teoria Curricular. Lisboa: Edicoes Pedago.

——— (2011b) Desafiando os Slogans Educacionais. *Itinerarios*. Edicoes Pedago.

——— (forthcoming) "Targeting Public Education," in S. Macrine, P. McLaren and D. Hill (eds) *Organizing Pedagogy: Educating for Social Justice within and Beyond Neo-liberalism*. New York: Palgrave.

Parker, F. (1894a) "The Report of the Committee of Ten. It's Use for the Improvement of Teachers Now at Work in the Schools," *Educational Review*, Vol. VII, pp., 479–91.

—— (1894b) *Talks on Pedagogics*. New York: E. L. Kellogg & Co.

—— (1895) "Discussion on Report of Dr. Harris," *Journal of Education*, Vol. XLI (21), pp., 165–7, p., 165.

Parker, F. & Parker, B. (s/d) *Myles Horton (1905–90) of Highlander; Adult Educator and Southern Activist*. School of Education and Psychology, Western Carolina University. Mimeographed.

Passow, A. (1962) *Curriculum Crosswords*. New York: Teachers College, Columbia University.

Pedroni, T. (2002) *Can Post Structuralism and Neo-Marxist Approaches be Joined? Building Compositive Approaches in Critical Educational Theory and Research*. Unpublished Paper, pp., 2 and 6.

Perkinson, H. (1968) *The Imperfect Panacea: America Faith in Education: 1865–1965*. New York: Random House.

Pessanha, E. e Silva, F. (2007) *Observatório da Cultura Escolar: Ênfases e Tratamentos Metodológicos de Pesquisa sobre Currículo*. Associação Nacional de Pós-Graduação e Pesquisa em Educação. Grupo de Trabalho Currículo. Trabalho Encomendado. Caxambu: Brazil.

Phenix, P. (1964) *Realms of Meaning. A Philosophy of the Curriculum for General Education*. New York: McGraw-Hill Book Company.

—— (1969) "The Moral Imperative in Contemporary Education," *Perspectives on Education*, Vol. II.

Philbrick, J. (1885) *City School Systems in the United States*. U.S. Bureau of Education, Circular of Information, nº 1. Washington: D.C.O.

Pierson, P. and Skocpol, T. (2002) *The Transformation of American Politics: Activist Government and the Rise of Conservatism*. University of Princeton Press.

Pinar, W. (1974) (ed.) *Heightened Consciousness, Cultural Revolution and Curriculum Theory. Proceedings of the Rochester Conference*. California: McCutchan Publishing Corporation.

—— (1975) *Curriculum Theorizing. The Reconceptualists*. Berkeley: McCutchan Publishing Corporation.

—— (1979) "What is Reconceptualization?" *Journal of Curriculum Theorizing*, 1 (1), pp., 93–104.

—— (1988) "The Reconceptualization of Curriculum Studies, 1987: A Personal Retrospective," *Journal of Curriculum and Supervision*, 3 (2), pp., 157–167.

—— (1994) *Autobiography, Politics and Sexuality*. New York: Peter Lang.

—— (2003) *International Handbook of Curriculum Research*. New Jersey: Lawrence Erlbaum Associates, Publishers.

—— (2004) *What is Curriculum Theory*. Mahwah: Lawrence Erlbaum Associates Publishers.

Pinar, W. (2011) "Curriculum Studies in Brazil: Intellectual Histories, Present Circumstances (International and Development Education)". New York: Palgrave.

Pinar, W. and Grumet, M. (1976) *Towards a Poor Curriculum.* Dubuque: Kendal/Hunt.

Pinar, W., Reynolds, W., Slattery, P. and Taubman, P (1995) "Understanding Curriculum," New York: Peter Lang.

Pinar, W., Reynolds, W., Slattery, P., and Taubman, P. (1995) *Understanding Curriculum: An Introduction to the Study of Historical and Contemporary Curriculum Discourses.* New York: Peter Lang.

Pinar. W. (1980) "Life History and Educational Experience." *Journal, of Curriculum Theorizing.* 2 (2), pp., 159–212.

——— (1981) "A Reply to my Critics," in H. Giroux, A. Penna and W. Pinar (Eds) *Curriculum and Instruction: Alternatives in Education.* Berkeley: McCutchaan, pp., 392–9.

Pokwewitz, Th. (1978) "Educational Research: Values and Visions of a Social Order," *Theory and Research in Social Education*, Vol. 4, (4), p., 28.

——— (1979a) *Teacher Education as Socialization. Ideology or Social Mission.* Paper presented at the American Educational research Association Annual Meeting, San Francisco.

——— (1979b) "Educational Research: Values and Visions of Social Order," *Theory and Research in Social Education*, 6 (4), pp., 19–39.

——— (2001) "A Changing Terrain of Knowledge and Power: A Social Epistemology of Educational Research," in R. G. McInnis (ed) *Discourse Synthesis. Studies in Historical and Contemporary Social Epistemology.* WestPort: Praeger, pp., 241–66.

——— (2005) "Inventing the Modern Self and John Dewey: Modernities and the Traveling of Pragmatism in Education—An Introduction," In Th. Popkewitz (ed.) *Inventing the Modern Self and John Dewey: Modernities and the Traveling of Pragmatism in Education.* New York: Palgrave MacMillan, pp. 3–37.

——— (2007) *Cosmopolitanism and the Age of School Reform. Science, Education, and Making Society, by Making the Child. New York*: Taylor and Francis.

Poulantzas, N. (1980) *Estado, poder y socialismo.* Madrid: Siglo XXI.

Popenoe, P. and Johnson, R. (1918) *Applied Eugenics.* New York: Macmillan.

President's Committee on Civil Rights (1947). *To Secure These Rights. The Report of the President's Committee on Civil Rights.* New York: Simon & Schuster.

Prinsloo, E. (1998) "Ubuntu Culture and Participatory Management," in P. H. Coetzee and A. J. Roux (eds) *The African Philosophy Reader.* London: Routledge, pp., 41–51.

Pritzkau, P. (1959) *Dynamics of Curriculum Improvement.* Englewood-Cliffs: Prentice-Hall.

Prosser, C. (1912) "Discussion," *National Education Association, Addresses and Proceedings*, 50th Annual Meeting, pp., 928–32.

────── (1912) "The Training of the Factory Worker Through Industrial Education," *National Society for the Promotion of Industrial Education*, N°. 15, Proceedings Fifth Annual Meeting, pp., 137–55.

Prosser, C. & Allen, C. (1925) *Have We Kept the Faith? America at the Cross-Roads in Education*. New York: The Century Co.

Pulliam, J. (1991) *History of Education in America*. New York: MacMillan Publishing Company.

Purpel, D., & Belanger, M. (1972) (eds.) *Curriculum and Cultural Revolution: A Book of Essays and Readings*. Berkeley: McCutchan.

Quantz, R. (in press) Introduction. In R. Quantz (ed) *Liderança, Cultura e Educação*. Lisboa: Edicoes Pedago.

Ratner, J. (1940) *Education Today by John Dewey*. New York. G. P. Putnam's Sons.

Reafferty, M. (1970) *Classroom Countdown. Education at the Crossroads*. New York: Hawthorn Books, INC.

Report of the Committee of Ten on Secondary School Studies (1894) National Education Association. New York. American Book Company.

Report of the Massachusetts Commission on Industrial and Technical Education. (1906). Boston: Massachusetts Commission on Industrial and Technical Education.

Report of the Sub-committee on the Correlation of Studies in Elementary Education (1895) In *The Report of the Committee of Fifteen on Elementary Report of the Committee of Fifteen on Elementary Education*. National Education Association. New York: The American Book Company.

Rice, J. (1912) (ed) *Scientific Management in Education*. New York: Hinds, Noble & Eldredge, pp., v–xx.

────── (1969) *The Public School Systems of the United States*. New York: Arno Press & New York Times.

Rickover, H. (1959) *Education and Freedom*. New York: E. P. Dutton.

────── (1963) *American Education—A National Failure. The Problem of our Schools and What We Can Learn From England*. New York: E. P. Dutton.

Ridings, J. (1989) "An Interview with Ralph Tyler," in G. Madaus & D. Stufflebeam (comps. & eds.) *Educational Evaluation: Classical Works of Ralph Tyler*. London: Kluwer Academic Publishers, pp., 243–74.

Rippa, A. (1988) *Education in a Free Society. An American History*. New York: Longman.

Robeson, P. (1971) *Here I Stand*. Boston: Beacon Press.

Rorty, R. (1979) *Philosophy and the Mirror of Nature*. Princeton: Princeton University Press.

Rosa, M. et el. (2007) *Narrar Currículos: Inventando Tessituras Metodológicas. Associação Nacional de Pós-Graduação e Pesquisa em Educação. Grupo de Trabalho Curriculo. Trabalho Encomendado*. Caxambu: Brazil.

Rosario, J. & Demarte, P. (1977a) Curriculum Theorizing Since 1947: Rhetoric or Progress? *Curriculum Inquiry*, 6 (4).

——— (1977b) "Foreword. Curriculum Theorizing Since 1947: Rhetoric or Progress?" *Curriculum Inquiry*, Volume 6 (4), pp., 249–50.

Ross, E. (1896) "Social Control." *American Journal of Sociology*, pp., 518–34.

Roszack, Th. (1969) *The Making of a Counter Culture: Reflections on the Technocratic Society and Its Youthful Opposition*. New York: Anchor Books.

Roy, K. (2003) *Teachers in Nomadic Spaces*. New York: Peter Lang.

Rugg, H. (1926a) "Curriculum Making, Points of Emphasis," in G. Whipple (ed) *The Twenty-Sixth Yearbook of the National Society for the Study of Education, The Foundations and Technique of Curriculum-Construction*, Part I, Curriculum-Making, Past and Present, pp. 67–116.

——— (1926b) "Curriculum Making, Points of Emphasis," in G. Whipple (ed) *The Twenty-Sixth Yearbook of the National Society for the Study of Education, The Foundations and Technique of Curriculum-Construction*, Part II, The Foundations of Curriculum-Making, pp. 147–62, pp. 147–61.

——— (1930) "The School and the Drama of American Life," in Whipple, G. (ed) (1930) Curriculum Making: Past and Present. *Twenty-Sixth Yearbook of the National Society for the Study of Education, Part I*, Bloomington: Public School Publishing, pp., 3–16.

——— (1931) *Culture and Education in America*. New York: Harcourt, Brace and Company.

——— (1932) *Changing Governments and Changing Cultures*. Boston: Ginn and Company.

——— (1933) *The Great Technology*. New York: The John Day Company.

——— (1936) *American Life and the School Curriculum. Next Steps Toward Schools of Living*. Boston: Ginn and Company.

——— (1939) *Democracy and the Curriculum*. New York: D. Appleton-Century Company.

——— (1943) *Foundations for America Education*. New York: World Book Company.

——— (1952) *The Teacher of Teachers. Frontiers of Theory and Practice in Teacher Education*. New York: Harper & Brothers Publishers.

Rugg, H. & Brooks, D. (1950) *The Teacher in School and Society*. New York: World Book Company.

Rugg, H. & Shumaker, A. (1969) *The Child-Centered School*. New York: Arno Press & N. Y. Times.

Rugg, H. & Withers, W. (1955) *Social Foundations of Education*. New York: Prentice Hall, INC.

Rukare, E. (1971) "Aspirations for Education in the 'New' and Free Nations of África," in R. Leeper (ed.) *Curricular Concerns in a Revolutionary Era*. Washington: ASCD, pp., 283–6.

Rush, B. (1965) A Plan For the Establishment of Public Schools and the Diffusion of Knowledge in Pennsylvania. In F. Rudolph (ed.). *Essays on Education in the Early Republic.* Cambridge: Mass, pp., 1–40.

Sachs, J. (1894) "The Report of the Committee of Ten. From the Point of View of the College Preparatory School," *Educational Review,* Vol. VII, pp., 75–83.

Said, E. (1978). *Orientalism.* New York: Pantheon Books.

Said. E. (2005) "Reconsiderando a Teoria Itinerante," in Manuela Sanches (orga) *Deslocalizar a Europa. Antroplogia, Arte, Literatura e História na Pós-Colonialidade.* Lisboa: Cotovia, pp., 25–42.

Sassen, S. (2004) "Space and Power," in Nicholas Gane (ed) *The Future of Social Theory.* London: Continuum, pp., 125–42.

Sassoon, A. (1982) *Approaches to Gramsci.* London: Writers and Readers.

Schneider, H. (1893) "Dr. Rice and American Public Schools." *Education,* V. XIII, pp., 357–359.

Schubert, W. (1986) *Curriculum. Perspective, Paradigm and Possibility.* New York: MacMillan Publishing Company.

Schubert, W. (2008) Curriculum Inquiry. In F. M. Connelly (ed) *The Sage Handbook of Curriculum and Instruction.* Los Angeles: SAGE, pp., 391–419.

Schurman, J. (1894) "The Report of Secondary School Studies." *School Review,* 2, pp., 83–97.

Schwab, J. (1969) *College Curriculum and Student Protest.* Chicago: The University of Chicago Press.

—— (1970) *The Practical: A Language for Curriculum.* Center for the Study of Instruction. Washington: National Education Association.

—— (1978) "The Practical: A Language for Curriculum," in I. Westbury and N. Wilkof (eds) *Joseph Schwab, Science, Curriculum and Liberal Education, Selected Essays.* Chicago: The University of Chicago Press, pp., 287–320.

Sears, J., and Marshal, D. (2000) "General Influences on Contemporary Curriculum Thought." *Journal of Curriculum Studies,* 32 (2), pp., 199–214.

Seguel, M. (1966) *The Curriculum Field: Its Formative Years.* New York: Teachers College Press.

Selden, S. (2000) "Eugenics and the Social Construction of Merit, Race and Disability." *Journal of Curriculum Studies,* 32 (2), pp., 235–52.

Sen, A. (1999) "Democracy as a Universal Value." *Journal of Democracy,* 10 (3), pp., 3–17.

Senghor, L. (1998) *The Collected Poetry. Caribbean and African Literature.* Charlottesville. University Press of Virginia.

Shane, H. (1968) "The Curriculum in Confrontation with Tomorrow," in R. Beck, P. Meadows, H. Shane & J. Saylor (eds.) *Curriculum Imperative: Surviving of the Self.* Department of secondary education: University of Nebraska, pp., 33–46.

Sharp, G. (1951) *Curriculum Development as the Re-education of the Teacher.* New York: Teachers College Press.

Shiva, V. (1993a) "Reductionism and Regeneration. A Crisis in Science," in M. Mies and V. Shiva (eds) *Ecofeminism*. London: Zed Books, pp., 21–35.

—— (1993b) "Decolonizing the North," in M. Mies and V. Shiva (eds) Ecofeminism. London: Zed books, pp., 264–76.

Shivji, I. (2003) "The Struggle for Democracy," *Marxism and Anti-Imperialism in Africa* www.marxists.ort retrieved December 2006.

Shorey, P. (1909) "Hippias Paidagogos," *School Review*, XVII (1), pp., 1–9.

Siegel, R. (1970) *Learning about Politics*. New York: Random House.

Silberman, C. (1970) *Crisis in the Classroom: The Remaking of American Education*. New York: Random House.

Silliman (1829) "Original Papers in Relation to a Course of Liberal Education," *The American Journal of Science and Arts*, Vol. XV, pp., 297–351.

Sisson, E. (1910) "An Educational Emergency," *Atlantic Monthly*, 106.

Sizer, T. (1964) *Secondary Schools at the Turn of the Century*. New Haven: Yale University Press.

Small, A. (1896) "Demands of Sociology upon Pedagogy." *Journal of Proceedings and Addresses of the Thirty-Fifth Annual Meeting of the National Education Association*, 3 (10), pp., 174–84.

Smith, & Tyler, R. (1942) *Appraising and Recording Student Progress*. New York: Harper & Brothers, p., 11.

Smith, B. (1942) "The War and Educational Program." *Curriculum Journal*, 13, pp., 113–16.

Smith, G. (2009) *Indigenous Knowledge*. American Educational research Association, S. Diego.

Smith, L. (1999) *Decolonizing Methodologies: Research and Indigenous Peoples*. London: Zed Books.

Smith, M. (1949) *And Madly Teach: A Layman Looks at Public School Education*. Chicago: Henry Regnery.

Snedden, D. (1905) "Conditions of Developing Special Teachers of Drawing and Manual Training in Every School," West. J. *Education*, X.

—— (1910) *The Problem of Vocational Education*. New York: Houghton Mifflin Company.

—— (1912) "Report of Committee on National Legislation," *National Society for the Promotion of Industrial Education* (15), pp., 126–34.

—— (1919) "The Cardinal Principles of Secondary Education," *School and Society*, 3, pp., 520–7.

—— (1920) *A Digest of Educational Sociology*. New York: Teachers College, Columbia University.

—— (1921) *Sociological Determination of Objectives in Education*. Philadelphia: J. B. Lippincott Company.

—— (1925) "Planning Curriculum Research," *School and Society*, XXII, pp., 259–65.

—— (1927) "What's Wrong with American Knowledge of Education?" in D. Snedden. *What's Wrong with American Education*. Philadelphia: J. B. Lippincott Company, pp., 36–63.

Snedden, D. (1934) "Education and Social Change," *School and Society*, XL, pp., 311–314.

——— (1935) "Social Reconstruction: A Challenge to Secondary School," *Pennsylvania Schoolmen's Week*, pp., 48–54.

Sousa Santos, B. (1997) *Um Discurso sobre as Ciencias*. Porto: Afrontamento.

——— (1998) *Reinventar a democracia*. Lisboa: Gradiva.

——— (2004) *A Gramatica do Tempo*. Porto: Afrontamento.

——— (2005) *Democratizing Democracy. Beyond the Liberal Democratic Cannon*. London: Verso.

——— (2007) *Another Knowledge is Possible*. London: Verso.

——— (2008) "Globalizations." *Theory, Culture and Society*.23, pp., 393–9.

——— (2009) *Epistemologias do Sul*. Coimbra: Almedina.

Sousa Santos, B., Nunes, J. and Meneses, M. (2007) "Open Up the Cannon of Knowledge and Recognition of Difference," in B. Sousa Santos (ed) *Another Knowledge is Possible*. London: Verso, pp., ix–lxii.

Soyinka, W. (1988) *Art, Dialogue and Outrage: Essays on Literature and Culture*. Ibadan: New Horn press.

Spears, H. (1951) *The Teacher and Curriculum Planning*. New York: Prentice-Hall.

Spencer, H. (1860) *Education: Intellectual, Moral and Physical*. New York: D. Appleton and Company.

——— (1902) *Education: Intellectual, Moral and Physical*. London: Williams and Norgate.

——— (1969) *Social Statics*. New York: Augustus M. Kelley.

Spikav, G. (1990) "Question of Multiculturalism," in S. Harasayam (ed.) *The Post-Colonial Critic: Interviews, Strategies, Dialogues*. New York: Routledge, pp., 59–60.

——— (1995) "Can the Subaltern Speak?" in B. Ashcroft, G. Griffiths, and H. Tiffin (eds) *The Post Colonial Reader*. London: Routledge, pp., 28–36, p., 28.

Spring, J. (1976) *The Sorting Machine*. New York: Longman.

——— (1986) *The American School, 1942–1985*. New York: Longman.

Storer, N. (1966) *The Social System of Science*. New York: Holt, Reinhart & Winston.

Strike, K. (1982) *Educational Policy and the Just Society*. Chicago: University of Illinois Press, p., 19.

Taliaferro-Baszile, D. (2010) In Ellisonian Eyes, What is Curriculum Theory? In E. Malewski (ed) *Curriculum Studies Handbook. The Nest Momentum*. New York: Routledge, pp., 483–495.

Tanner, D. & Tanner, L. (1995) *Curriculum Development Theory into Practice*. Columbus: Prentice Hall.

——— (1979) "Emancipation From Research. The Reconceptualists' Prescription," *Educational Researcher*. 8 (6), pp., 8–12.

Taylor, F. (1903) "Shop Management." *Transitions of the American Society of Mechanical Engineers*, 24.

―――― (1911) *Scientific Management Comprising Shop Management. The Principles of Scientific Management; Testimony before the Special House Committee*. New York: Harper and Brothers.

Tempels. P. (1945) *Bantu Philosophy*: Paris: Presence Africaine.

The Problem of Poverty in America (1964) *The Annual Report of the Council of Economic Advisers*. Washington: Government Printing Office.

The Social Frontier (1934) A Journal of Educational Criticism and Reconstruction, 1 (1).

The United States Commission on Civil Rights (1962) *Civil Rights U.S.A.; Public Schools Southern States*. Washington: U.S. Government Printing Office.

Torres Santomé, J. (1990) "La Práctica Refléxiva y la Comprensión de lo que Acontece en las Aulas," in Ph. Jackson (1990) *La Vida en las Aulas*. Madrid: Morata.

―――― (1998) *El Curriculum Oculto*. Madrid. Morata.

―――― (2011 – forthcoming) "O Cavalo de Tróia da Cultura Escolar," in J. Paraskeva, T. Autio and H. Sunker (eds) *Nova Teoria e Investigação Curricular*. Magualde: Edições Pedago.

Townsend, A. (1948), "Implications Contained in the Life Adjustment Program Concerning the Tools of Learning." *Bulletin of the National Catholic Educational Association*, 45 (1), pp., 363–75.

Troen, S. (1976) "The Discovery of the Adolescent by American Educational Reformers, 1900–1920: An Economic Perspective," in L. Stone (ed.). *Schooling and Society: Studies in the History of Education*. Baltimore: Johns Hopkins University Press, pp., 239–51.

Trueit, D., Doll, W., Wang, H., & Pinar, W. (eds) "The Internationalization of Curriculum Studies." *Selected Proceedings from the LSU Conference 2000*. New York: Peter Lang.

Tuskegee Catalogue (1904) *Unpublished Raw Data. BTW Papers*. Library of Congress.

Tyack, D. (1974). *The One Best System. A History of American Urban Education*. Cambridge: Harvard University Press.

Tyler, R. (1931) "More Valid Measurements of College Work," *The Journal of the National Education Association*, 20, pp., 327–328.

―――― (1949) *Basic Principles of Curriculum and Instruction*. Chicago: University of Chicago Press.

―――― (1950) "The Organization of Learning Experiences," in V. Herrick & R. Tyler (comp. & ed.) Toward Improved Curriculum Theory. *Papers Presented at the Conference on Curriculum Theory*. Chicago: University of Chicago Press, pp., 59–67.

―――― (1968) "The Virgil E. Herrick Memorial Lecture Series," in R. Tyler *The Challenge of National Assessment*. Ohio: Charles E. Merrill Publishing Company.

―――― (1974a) "Introduction. A Perspective on the Issues," in R. Tyler & R. Wolf (eds) *Crucial Issues in Testing*. Berkeley: McCutchan Publishing Corporation, pp., 1–10.

Tyler, R. (1974b) "The Use of Tests in Measuring the Effectiveness of Educational Programs, Methods, and Instrumental Materials." in R. Tyler & R. Wolf (eds) *Crucial Issues in Testing*. Berkeley: McCutchan Publishing Corporation, pp., 143–155, p., 145.

——— (1976a) (ed) *Perspectives on American Education. Reflections on the Past…Challenges for the Future*. Chicago: Science Research Associates, INC.

——— (1976b) (ed) *Prospects for Research and Development in Education*. Berkeley: McCutchan Publishing Company.

——— (1977a) "Toward Improved Curriculum Theory: The Inside Story," *Curriculum Inquiry*, 6 (4), pp., 251–6.

——— (1977b) "Discussion. Kliebard, H. Curriculum Theory: Give Me a for Instance," *Curriculum Inquiry*, 6 (4), pp., 277–82.

——— (1977c) "Discussion. Greene, M. The Artistic-Aesthetic and Curriculum," *Curriculum Inquiry*, 6 (4), pp., 301–9.

——— (1978) "Conserving Human Resources. The School Dropout," in R. Tyler (ed) *From Youth to Constructive Adult Life: The Role of the Public School*. Berkeley: McCuthan Publishing Company, pp., 122–6.

———(1987) *Education: Curriculum Development and Evaluation. An Oral History Conducted 1985–1987*, by Malca Chall. Regional Oral History Office, Berkeley: The Brancroft Library, University of California.

——— (1989a) "New Dimensions in Curriculum Development," in G. Madaus & D. Stufflebeam (comp. & eds) *Educational Evaluation. Classical Works of Ralph Tyler*. London: Kluwer Academic Publishers, pp., 201–221.

———(1989b) J. Ridings "An Interview with Ralph Tyler," in G. Madaus & D. Stufflebeam (comps. & eds.) *Educational Evaluation: Classical Works of Ralph Tyler*. London: Kluwer Academic Publishers, pp., 243–74.

United Nations Declaration on the Rights of Indigenous Peoples (2007). United Nations.

United Sates Office Education (1948) *Life Adjustment Education for Every Youth*. Washington: United States Government Printing Office.

——— (1945) *Vocational Education in the Years Ahead. A Report of a Committee to Study Postwar Problems in Vocational Education*. Washington: Government Printing Office.

United States Office of Education (1951) *Vitalizing Secondary Education. Education for Life Adjustment*. Washington: Government Printing Office.

Urban, W. & Wagoner Jr, J. (1996) *American Education, a History*. New York: The McGraw-Hill Companies, INC.

———(2000) *American Education. A History*. Boston: McGraw-Hill.

Van Til, W. (1970) "Editorial. Curriculum for the 1970's." *Phi Delta Kappan*, LI (7), pp., 345 and 356–7.

———(1986) "ASCD and Social Forces," in W.Van Til (ed.) *ASCD in retrospect*. Alexandria: ASCD, pp., 43–51.

Vavi, Z (2004) "Democracy Has By-passed the Poor," *Marxism and Anti-Imperialism in Africa* www.marxists.ort retrieved December 2006.

Veiga Neto, A. e tal (2007) *Grupo de Estudos e Pesquisas em Curriculo e Pos-Modernidade.* Universidade Luterana do Brazil (ULBRA) e à Universidade Federal do Rio Grande do Sul (UFRGS).*Associação Nacional de Pós-Graduação e Pesquisa em Educação. Grupo de Trabalho Curriculo. Trabalho Encomendado.* Caxambu: Brazil.

Verplank, G. (1836) *The Advantages and the Dangers of the American Scholar. A Discourse Delivered on the Day Preceding the Annual Commencement of Union College.* New York: Wiley and Long.

Vieira, J.: Hypolito, A.; Klein, M.; Garcia, M. (2007) *Percurso Teorico Metodologico das Pesquisas sobre Currículo. Associação Nacional de Pós-Graduação e Pesquisa em Educação. Grupo de Trabalho Curriculo. Trabalho Encomendado.* Caxambu: Brazil.

Visvanathan, S. (2009) "Encontros Culturais e o Oriente. Um Estudo das Políticas de Conhecimento," in B. Sousa Santos (ed.) Epistemologias do Sul. Coimbra. Almedina, pp., 487–505.

Wa Thiong'o, N. (1986) *Decolonizing the Mind.* Nairobi: East African educational Publishers.

Ward, L. (1883). *Dynamics Sociology, or Applied Social Science as Based upon Statistical Sociology and the less Complete Sciences,* Vol. 2. New York: D. Appleton.

Ward, L. (1893) *The Psychic Factors of Civilization.* Boston: Guin and Company.

Washington, B, T. (1905) *Tuskegee and Its People.* New York: D. Appleton and Company.

———. (1904a) *Working with the Hands.* New York: Doubleday, Page and Company.

——— (1904b) *Newspaper Editorial. Unpublished Raw Material, BTW Papers,* Manuscript Division, Library of Congress.

Watkins, W. (2001) *The White Architects of Black Education.* New York: Teachers College Press.

———(2010) Response to Ann G. Winfield. The Visceral and the Intellectual in Curriculum Past and Present. In E. Malewski (ed*) Curriculum Studies Handbook. The Next Momentum. New York: Routledge,* pp., 158–167.

Wexler, Ph. (1976) *The Sociology of Education: Beyond Inequality.* Indianapolis: The Bobbs-Merrill Company, INC.

——— (1987) *Social Analysis of Culture. After the New Sociology.* Boston: Routledge & Kegan and Paul, p. 127. Liston, D. (1988) *Capitalist Schools. Explanation and ethics in Radical Studies of Schooling.* New York: Routledge.

Whipple, G. (ed) (1930) "Curriculum Making: Past and Present." *Twenty-Sixth Yearbook of the National Society for the Study of Education, Part I,* Bloomington: Public School Publishing; and Whipple, G. (ed) (1930) "The Foundations of Curriculum Making." *Twenty-Sixth Yearbook of the National Society for the Study of Education, Part II,* Bloomington: Public School Publishing.

Whitty, G. (1985) *Sociology and School Knowledge.* London: Methuen & Co. Ltd.

Whyte, W. (1956) *The Organization Man.* New York: Simon and Schuster.

Wilentz, S. (1997) "Speedy Fred's Revolution," *New York Review of Books,* 20, pp., 32–37.

Willis, P. (1977) *Learning to Labour.* Farnborough: Saxon House.

Williams, Ro. (1960) "Can Negrões Afford to be Pacifists?" *New Left review,* 1/1, pp., 44–6.

Williams, Ra. (1976) Base and Superstructure in Marxist Cultural Theory. In R. Dale, G. Esland and Madeleine MacDonald (eds) *Schooling and Capitalism. A Sociological Reader.* London and Kegan Paul, pp., 202–210, p., 210.

Winfield, A. (2010) Eugenic Ideology and Historic Osmosis. E. Malewski (ed) *Curriculum Studies Handbook. The Next Momentum. New York: Routledge,* pp., 142–157.

Winship, A. (1895) "Dr. Harris Masterpiece." *Journal of Education,* Vol. XLI (8), pp., 128–9.

Wiredu, K. (1991) *African Philosophy. The Essential Readings.* New York: Paragon House, pp., 87–110.

Wood, G. (1988) "Democracy and Curriculum," in Landon Beyer & Apple (eds.) *The Curriculum, Problems, Politics and Possibilities.* New York: State University of New York Press., pp., 166–87.

Woodward, C. (1885) "Manual Training in General Education," *Education* (5), pp., 614–26.

――― (1890) *Manual Training in Education.* New York: Scribner & Welford.

Worthen, B. & Sanders, J. (1987) *Educational Evaluation: Alternative Approaches and Practical Guidelines.* New York: Pitman Publishing.

Wraga, W. (1999) "The Continuing Arrogation of the Curriculum Field: A Rejoiner to Pinar," *Educational Researcher,* 28 (1), p. 16.

――― (2002) "Recovering Curriculum Practice: Continuing the Conversation," *Educational Researcher,* 31 (6), pp., 17–19, p., 17.

Wraga, W. and Hlebowitsh, P. (2003a) "Commentary. Conversation, Collaboration, and Community in the US Curriculum Field," *Journal of Curriculum Studies,* 35 (4), pp., 453–7.

――― (2003b) "Toward a Renaissance in Curriculum Theory and Development in the USA," *Journal of Curriculum Studies,* 35 (4), pp., 425–37.

Wright, E. (1994) *Interrogating Inequality. Essays on Class Analysis, Socialism, and Marxism.* London: Verso.

Young, M. and Whitty, G. (1977) *Society, State and Schooling.* London: The Falmer Press.

Young, M. F. (1971) (ed) *Knowledge and Control. New Directions for the Sociology of Education.* London: Collier-MacMillan.

Zaret, E. (1975) "Women/Schooling/Society," in J. Macdonald & E. Zaret (1975) *Schools in Search of Meaning.* Washington: ASCD, pp., 38–50.

Zerby, C. (1975) "John Dewey and the Polish Question: A Response to the Revisionist Historians," *History of Education Quarterly*, XV (1), pp., 17–30.

Zinn, H. (2005) *Howard Zinn on Democratic Education*, Boulder, Colorado: Paradigm Publishers.

Žižek, S. (1996) Introduction. The Spectre of Ideology. In S. Žižek (ed) *Mapping Ideology*. London: Verso, pp., 1–33.

———(2006) *Bem-Vindo ao Deserto do Real*. Lisboa: Relogio D'Agua.

Author Index

SUBJECT INDEX

Henry Fielding, Jane Austen, and the Establishment of the Novel

Jo Alyson Parker

The Author's Inheritance

The Author's Inheritance is the first extended study to focus on Henry Fielding's influence on the works of Jane Austen. Parker explores how Fielding and Austen rely upon a common comedic vision, employ similar themes and plot structures, and follow a similar trajectory in their careers. Each author reinforces the social and cultural status quo while simultaneously revealing its deficiencies, creating a comforting social vision that ensures their place in the literary canon.

Parker alternates readings of Fielding's novels with comparable works by Austen in order to examine the ways both authors draw upon and test variations of the inheritance plot. For Parker, the inheritance plot serves as both a thematic link and a metaphor for literary and moral authority in the